1990

The Myths of Love

The Myths of Love

Classical Lovers in Medieval Literature

Katherine Heinrichs

The Pennsylvania State University Press
University Park and London

Library of Congress Cataloging-in-Publication Data

Heinrichs, Katherine.
The myths of love : classical lovers in medieval literature /
Katherine Heinrichs.
p. cm.
Includes bibliographical references.
ISBN 0-271-00689-7
1. Chaucer, Geoffrey, d. 1400—Sources. 2. Chaucer, Geoffrey, d. 1400—Criticism and interpretation. 3. Poetry, Medieval—Classical influences. 4. Mythology, Classical, in literature. 5. Love poetry—History and criticism. 6. Classicism. I. Title.
PR1912.A3H45 1990
809.1′9354′0902—dc20 89–43498

Printed in the United States of America

It is the policy of The Pennsylvania State University Press to use acid-free paper for the first printing of all clothbound books. Publications on uncoated stock satisfy the minimum requirements of American National Standard for Information Sciences—Permanence of Paper for Printed Library Materials, ANSI Z39.48–1984.

For

Thomas Alan Heinrichs
Shirley Darwin Heinrichs

Contents

Acknowledgments

I am grateful to V. Irene Norvelle and Margaret M. O'Bryant, formerly Interlibrary Loans Assistant and Librarian at the Alderman Library of the University of Virginia, for their years of accurate and courteous attention to my many requests. My gratitude goes also to Robert Cook, who read and commented usefully upon a draft of this book.

My debt to Hoyt N. Duggan is too fundamental to reckon. This study really began with his suggestion, some twelve years ago, that an investigation into medieval responses to the *Heroides* of Ovid might illuminate Chaucer's *Legend of Good Women*. That investigation led first to a thesis on mythological allusions in Chaucer's *Troilus and Criseyde*, written under his direction, and then to this book and several related articles. Throughout the successive incarnations of the project, he has been an unfailing source of encouragement, instruction, advice, and rare books. His contributions are reflected in whatever there may be here of merit; my deficiencies are my own.

1

Mythological Allusion and Literary Interpretation

Most specialized studies of the classical *Nachleben* seek mainly to document the appearances of particular classical figures in the vernacular literatures. This is not such a study. For me, the medieval appearances of the Ovidian and Virgilian lovers are of interest mainly for the light they shed upon the works in which they appear and upon certain difficult issues in medieval studies in general: the issues of narrative voice, "courtly love," "historical" criticism, and thematic unity in the poetry of Chaucer and his sources. The process of demonstration required to establish the connections between the literary history of the classical lovers and these larger issues will be gradual and cumulative, and cannot well be undertaken in an introduction. It may be well, however, to begin with some preliminary indication of where those connections lie. To do so will require me to suggest conclusions I have not yet proved, and will require the reader to suspend judgment until proof can be undertaken.

The most important critical questions about the poems I will address in this study—the *Roman de la Rose,* certain works of

Boccaccio, Machaut, and Froissart, and the early poetry of Chaucer—concern, at bottom, the issue of narrative voice. Too often, those questions have been answered by scholars on the basis of the assumption that the lover/narrators of the medieval love poems are simply identical with the poets themselves. When Alan Gunn claims that, to Jean de Meun, "the generative passion of man and woman was the chief manifestation of the goodness . . . of God,"[1] he is in effect claiming that the Lover in the *Roman de la Rose* (whose opinion this is) speaks for Jean. When F. S. Shears, discussing Froissart's *Joli Buisson de Jonece,* speaks of "our nonchalant and pleasure-loving poet,"[2] he is identifying Froissart himself with the lover/narrator of the poem, a heedless fellow who says he would rather have a flower chaplet than all the wisdom of the University of Paris. And when Paulin Paris describes Machaut's *Voir Dit* as autobiographical, "voir" in the literal sense,[3] he implies that the narrator of the poem—lovestruck, gullible, and ultimately deceived—speaks for Machaut. Even certain very recent critics of the medieval French and Italian poetry of love have assumed, without much investigation, that poet and narrator must be identical; indeed Henry Ansgar Kelly explicitly defends that assumption, saying that, "When discussing the first-person narratives of these [Chaucer and Boccaccio] and other authors, I have found it cumbersome and not very helpful to distinguish between the author and an assumed persona."[4]

This tendency to confuse speaker and poet is not unnatural, for—as some recent scholars have noted—it is a convention of much fourteenth-century poetry for the poet to give to his narrator certain

1. Gunn, *The Mirror of Love* (Lubbock, Tex., 1952), 495.
2. Shears, *Froissart: Chronicler and Poet* (London, 1930), 196.
3. Paris, Le Livre du Voir-Dit *de Guillaume de Machaut* (Paris, 1875), xiii–xx.
4. Kelly, *Love and Marriage in the Age of Chaucer* (Ithaca, N.Y., 1975), 27; others are Anthime Fourrier, who in the introductions to his editions of the works of Froissart—*L'Espinette Amoureuse* (Paris, 1972), *La Prison Amoureuse* (Paris, 1974), and *Le Joli Buisson de Jonece* (Geneva, 1975)—consistently refers to the narrators of those poems as "Froissart"; Daniel Poirion, who identifies Machaut explicitly with his narrator in the *Voir Dit,* and Froissart implicitly with his in the *Buisson* (*Le Poète et le Prince* [Paris, 1965], 199 and 208); Audrey Graham, who concludes that "Froissart" was "no doubt sincere" in saying he would prefer a flower chaplet to all the learning of the universities ("Froissart's Use of Classical Allusion in his Poems," *MAE* 32 [1963]: 24–33, p. 25; and Michelle Freeman, who regards the *Buisson* as Froissart's "personal farewell to poetry" ("Froissart's *Le Joli Buisson de Jonece:* A Farewell to Poetry," in *Machaut's World: Science and Art in the Fourteenth Century,* ed. Madeleine Pelner Cosman and Bruce Chandler [New York, 1978]: 235–47, p. 235).

recognizable characteristics of his own, even including his own name. Boccaccio, Machaut, Froissart, and Chaucer all follow this practice often, and on occasion we may indeed be justified in concluding that there is very little distinction to be made between the point of view of the narrator and that of the poet himself. In most cases, however, that is a dangerous conclusion. Chaucerians generally recognize this, as do some students of Machaut and Boccaccio, and one (at least) of Froissart.[5] Robert Hollander and Janet Smarr (for Boccaccio) and Jacqueline Cerquiglini, William Calin, Kevin Brownlee, Douglas Kelly, R. Barton Palmer, and G. B. Gybbon-Monypenny (for Machaut) attempt in various ways to characterize the speakers in the fourteenth-century love-narratives that influenced Chaucer. They agree that the narrators of Boccaccio and Machaut, despite surface resemblances to the poets themselves, are often figures of fun. Those of Boccaccio—in the *Amorosa Visione, Ameto, Elegia di Madonna Fiammetta,* and in portions of other works—are foolish lovers, blindly sensual and self-deluding; those of Machaut, "comic, naive, maladroit" characters who incongruously combine the mental habits of clerks with the ambitions of lovers *par amours*.[6] They blunder through the love affairs that (ostensibly, at least) constitute the principal *matière* of the *dits amoureux,* constantly missing opportunities, insulting ladies and misinterpreting their motives, comically and incompetently aping the conduct of their betters in the aristocratic avocation of *fin'amors*. They do not represent Machaut himself, but "pseudoautobiographical" characters created for the amusement of his noble audience. J. A. Burrow, in an analysis of Gower's portrayal of his Lover in the *Confessio Amantis,* has put it best: Gower's Amans, and the lovers of Machaut and Froissart from whom he is derived, is not an individual, but a conventional type, the "Portrait of the Author as Lover." To quote the Latin sidenote to verse I, 59 in a manuscript of the *Confessio:* "Hic quasi in persona aliorum, quos amor alligat, fingens se auctor esse Aman-

5. That one is William Kibler, who in his article "Self-Delusion in Froissart's *Espinette amoureuse," Romania* 97 (1976): 77–98, concludes correctly that "if we . . . look . . . to the *Espinette amoureuse* as literature (and not as autobiography), we may better be able to understand the relationship between the lover and his lady and to read the warnings which the poet has scattered throughout the *dit* to avoid this kind of love situation, which can lead only to self-delusion and suffering" (82–83).

6. The quotation is from Calin, "Le 'moi' chez Guillaume de Machaut," in *Guillaume de Machaut: Poète et Compositeur,* Colloque organisé par l'Université de Reims (Paris, 1982): 241–52, p. 241 (my translation).

tem, varias eorum passiones variis huius libri distinccionibus per singula scribere proponit."[7]

These are valuable insights, but they do not explain just *why* Machaut (or Gower) would have wished to create such narrators, or exactly what role they play in the medieval poems of love. Critics of Chaucer and Boccaccio, dealing with somewhat different, although closely related, types of fictional narrators, have addressed those questions in detail; critics of Machaut and Froissart, by and large, have not. The belief of the majority seems to be that Machaut (I do not include Froissart, whose *dits* are still most often considered simply autobiographical) presents us with lover/narrators incompetent at love *par amours* in order to glorify the correct practice of "noble love" by poking fun at the incorrect practice of it. Speaking of the narrator of Machaut's *Voir Dit,* an aging clerk infatuated with a coquettish young woman, Calin characterizes him as a bad lover, "totally unequipped to enter into a meaningful relationship with his beautiful young admirer"; Machaut, he says, laughs at his lover/narrator because he is old (a lover should be young), timid and passive (a lover should show initiative), and a clerk (a lover should be a knight).[8] Douglas Kelly agrees both that Machaut's narrator is—at least initially—a foolish character and that Machaut himself entertained a higher conception of *fin'amors* than his pseudoautobiographical cleric.[9] The consensus seems to be that, as Shirley Lukitsch writes in her discussion of Machaut's "Prologue," the poet's true *matière* is "the celebration of the joy to be found in the imaginative experience of love—in reverie, in the pleasure it entails and in the hope which results."[10]

A few scholars have seemed momentarily to doubt this: Brownlee notes that Machaut's "comic undercutting" of his narrator in the *Voir Dit* seems, to some extent, to undercut the ideals of *fin'amors* as well, Cerquiglini believes that the narrator's error is to abandon the love of God for "un amour humain, failli," and Palmer, speaking of the *Jugement dou Roy de Behaingne,* notes that "the Narrator's

7. "The Portrayal of Amans in *Confessio Amantis,*" in *Gower's* Confessio Amantis: *Responses and Reassessments,* ed. A. J. Minnis (Cambridge, 1983): 5–24, pp. 11 and 13.

8. *A Poet at the Fountain* (Lexington, Ky., 1974), 186.

9. *Medieval Imagination: Rhetoric and the Poetry of Courtly Love* (Madison, Wis., 1978), 137–47.

10. "The Poetics of the Prologue: Machaut's Conception of the Purpose of His Art," *MAE* 52 (1983): 258–71, p. 262.

uncritical acceptance of love . . . contrasts with the poet's sympathetic portrait of Reason (who advocates emotional temperance). . . ."[11] In general, however, scholars continue the old practice of identifying Machaut with his narrators at least to the extent of assuming that he is as enthusiastic a champion of *fin'amors* as they are. Aside from this conviction, though, they have not much faith that his views can be known through his works. Calin claims that, in the *Voir Dit,* the poet Machaut plays such complex tricks with narrative perspective that he becomes invisible; we see that the narrator is a failure as a lover and that his lady hides behind a mask, but we cannot penetrate her mask—or the poet's—in order to determine Machaut's opinion of the persons or the action he describes. Calin makes the same claim with respect to Jean de Meun's portion of the *Roman de la Rose,* in which there are so many speakers developing so many different arguments that it is impossible "to determine Jean's position on any given question."[12] For some questions raised in the *Rose,* that may be true; for the most important ones, however, John Fleming, Charles Dahlberg, and others have demonstrated exhaustively that it is not. They have done so by examining the teachings of Jean's sources (and of commentaries on his sources) on the questions he raises in the poem, then examining the poem's structure in the light of that information. It is a part of my purpose in this study to conduct a similar, if more limited, examination of certain sources of mythological material in Machaut and Froissart, with the object of demonstrating that their opinions, too, can be known.

Wide differences of opinion about the autobiographical, "pseudoautobiographical," or wholly fictional character of the narrators in the love-narratives of Boccaccio, Machaut, and Froissart have created considerable confusion in the criticism of Chaucer's French and Italian sources. There has been somewhat less confusion about the works of Chaucer himself, principally on account of the enormous amount of intelligent research that has been concentrated upon them over several generations. As a way of indicating certain directions that Romance scholarship might profitably pursue, it

11. Kevin Brownlee, *Poetic Identity in Guillaume de Machaut* (Madison, Wis., 1984), 106–7; Jacqueline Cerquiglini, *Un Engin si Soutil: Guillaume de Machaut et l'Écriture au Quatorzième Siècle* (Paris, 1985), 87–88; R. Barton Palmer, ed. and trans., *Guillaume de Machaut:* The Judgment of the King of Bohemia (New York, 1984), xxviii.

12. "Le 'moi' " 250 and 245 (my translation).

may be well to review the very extensive, ongoing discussion of Chaucer's narrative *personae*. In 1915, Kittredge expressed the view that the narrator in the *Book of the Duchess* is not Chaucer but a fictional creation of the poet, a childlike character who can report what he sees and hears but has no access to its meaning. By creating such a *persona,* he argued, Chaucer intensified both the humorous and the pathetic effects of the poem, as the reader was forced to meditate upon the significance of the acts and speeches reported, but not interpreted, by the naive Dreamer.[13] This argument stimulated later scholars to attempt analysis of the relationship between Chaucer the poet and his literary *personae*. In a well-known essay published in 1954, E. T. Donaldson maintained that the pilgrim-narrator of the General Prologue to the *Canterbury Tales* is the same sort of fictional creation described by Kittredge, a literal-minded reporter "acutely unaware of the significance of what he sees."[14] This uncritical fellow really agrees with the Monk that Austyn ought to have his swink to him reserved, and he really marvels at the Prioress's elegant singing (and her elegant French). Indeed, he is all admiration of the vanity, selfishness, acquisitiveness and chicanery of his fellow pilgrims; his only interest is in material success, or the appearance of it. Similar analyses by John Lowes, Kemp Malone, Dorothy Bethurum, and Bernard Huppé reinforced this notion of Chaucer's narrator as a comical character created by the poet.[15] Pointing up the difficulty of specifying the relationship between poet and narrator, Huppé writes that Chaucer "includes himself" as a pilgrim to Canterbury, but also warns that "the pilgrim-narrator is not to be confused with the author; he is in fact the comic projection of most of what the poet hopes he is not."[16]

Other critics objected strenuously to this divorce between poet and *persona*. Bertrand Bronson sensibly pointed out that at least some of the poems of Chaucer were written to be delivered orally by the poet to an audience who knew him personally, so that Chaucer the speaker could not possibly dissociate himself completely from the "I" of the poems. Rather than a separate, fictional narrator,

13. *Chaucer and His Poetry* (Cambridge, Mass., 1915), 45–54.

14. "Chaucer the Pilgrim," *PMLA* 69 (1954): 928–36, p. 929.

15. See Donaldson, "Chaucer the Pilgrim," and summaries of the debate by William R. Crawford, *Bibliography of Chaucer 1954–63* (Seattle, 1967), xxiv–xxviii, and Thomas Garbáty, "The Degradation of Chaucer's 'Geffrey,'" *PMLA* 89 (1974): 97–104.

16. *A Reading of the* Canterbury Tales (Albany, N.Y., 1964), 28.

there is a constant, ironic tension between the "wryly comic" self-presentation of the poet and the auditors' knowledge of the real characteristics of Chaucer the man.[17] The opinion of Bronson is also, in essence, that of Wolfgang Clemen, James R. Kreuzer, R. M. Lumiansky, and John Major, all of whom interpret the narrator's devastating remarks on his fellow pilgrims as the conscious irony of "a *persona* whose outlook is almost indistinguishable from Chaucer's own."[18] Donald Howard has well noted that this difference of critical opinion is, in fact, more apparent than real; Donaldson and Bronson do not really disagree, they only describe the same perceived phenomenon in different ways.[19] That phenomenon, simply stated, is the disjunction between the foolish things that Chaucer's narrators sometimes say and our perception of Chaucer's own opinions. Thomas Garbáty describes the lack of consistency in the pose of the narrator in Chaucer's poems; sometimes he appears naive, sometimes omniscient.[20] How, then, do we perceive Chaucer's opinions, and how do we know they are Chaucer's? What, precisely, is normative in the poems? With their constant alternations in tone, what prevents them from being completely inaccessible?

It is, I will suggest (and I am far from the first to suggest) Chaucer's constant appeals to the knowledge, and the values, that he shares with his audience. Let us return for a moment to Howard's very interesting observation that two apparently warring camps of scholars do not really disagree. What is it, exactly, that they do not disagree upon? When we examine their writings, we see that, by and large, they disagree remarkably little upon the interpretation that Chaucer would have wished his audience to make of the statements of his narrators. Whether we regard them as consciously ironical or comically obtuse, they often say things that neither Chaucer nor any reasonable man could approve. Donaldson, Bronson, and practically everyone who has ever read the *Canterbury Tales* know, for instance, that Chaucer did not seriously believe that Austyn ought to have his swink to him reserved. Clearly monks, and everybody else, ought to contribute to society by working rather

17. *In Search of Chaucer* (Toronto, 1960), 25–30.

18. The quotation is from Major, "The Personality of Chaucer the Pilgrim," *PMLA* 75 (1960): 160–62, p. 162. For a summary of the views of others mentioned, see Garbáty, "Degradation" 104n3.

19. "Chaucer the Man," in *Chaucer's Mind and Art,* ed. A. C. Cawley (London, 1969), 31–45, p. 32.

20. "Degradation" 98.

than spending their time in vain pursuits. Once we have granted this, it is still possible either that Chaucer's narrator, who makes this statement, is to be perceived as the sort of person who really believed it or is to be interpreted as speaking ironically. Critical debate centers around these questions, and not around the proper interpretation of what the narrator actually says. It is narrowed down to these questions by the fundamental agreement of practically all of us upon the social value of work, and more specifically upon the authority of Augustine who prescribed the rule of work for the members of his order.

This is neither a difficult nor a controversial point. Our intuition that work was valued by Chaucer's fourteenth-century audience, as it is by us today, may be easily shown to be sound. It has been more difficult for modern scholars to achieve agreement on matters upon which *a priori* assumptions—shared values and shared knowledge—have changed since the Middle Ages. As the above (very simple) example illustrates, our ability to understand the perspective, and assess the roles, of narrators in medieval poetry depends greatly upon our ability to interpret what they say in the light of the knowledge and the values that poets of the time shared with their audiences. The characteristics ascribed by critics to Chaucer's narrator are based upon attempts to understand the things he says as Chaucer's original audience would have understood them. This task is most often a great deal more difficult than in the instance of Austyn's swink. It has taken us a very long time, for example, to agree that the Wife of Bath is a corrupt and unreliable narrator (if, indeed, we do agree; Larry Benson, in the notes to the *Riverside Chaucer,* claims that we do, at least generally, but proceeds to document a number of instances of disagreement).[21] It has taken so long because great labor has been required to reconstruct the knowledge and values probably shared by Chaucer and his original audience upon the matters discussed in the Wife's prologue. To take just one example, common esteem of the Christian ideal of virginity has declined enough in modern times so that it has required a number of scholarly discussions to establish that we should perceive the Wife's attack upon it as undermining her credibility. It is easy, too, to miss the implications of others of her arguments, which may indeed be superficially ingratiating to a modern audience; her modest claim to be a "vessel of tree," and her notion of the conjugal

21. Benson, ed., *The Riverside Chaucer* (New York, 1987), 865.

debt, seem reasonable enough until they are examined in the light of medieval interpretations of their sources.[22]

To repeat, then; we assess the roles, and the reliability, of narrators in medieval poetry at least in part by trying to reconstruct the probable attitude of the poets toward the arguments their narrators develop. We do not, however, assess these things in this way alone; in each work, there are also complex requirements of internal consistency. In *The Aims of Interpretation,* E. D. Hirsch describes the method of D. W. Robertson (and, by extension, of others of the "historical" school of critics) as "the fallacy of the homogeneous past."[23] What Hirsch objects to in their method is overdependence upon precisely the sort of research I have been describing, that which attempts to define a "fourteenth-century consensus" upon, say, work, virginity or the conjugal debt that will serve as a guide to Chaucer's intention in putting certain kinds of speeches on these matters into the mouth of his narrator or the Wife of Bath. Hirsch describes this method of research in a syllogism: "Medieval Man believed in alchemy. Chaucer was a Medieval Man. Chaucer believed in alchemy." This syllogism, however, is seriously inadequate as a description of good "historical" criticism, because it fails to take into account requirements of internal consistency that take priority in the consideration of every thorough student of medieval poetry. In exposing the Wife's errors concerning virginity and the conjugal debt, Robertson—and Howard—make sense of details within the Wife's prologue and tale that would appear incongruous if she were doctrinally correct on these matters.[24] A sympathetic reading of the Wife's arguments makes nonsense of her character and her personal history; if she is really so learned about marriage, why have her own marriages been so inharmonious, and why is her experience so ludicrously circular? In this case, at least, assembling medieval lore on doctrinal matters raised by Chaucer tends to resolve potential internal contradictions in the text. We are thus able to characterize the Wife with some confidence as a particular kind of unreliable narrator.

Notice that we have not said simply that "Medieval Man revered virginity and placed an invidious interpretation upon wooden ves-

22. For a discussion of the Wife's misguided exegesis in these matters, see D. W. Robertson, *A Preface to Chaucer* (Princeton, 1962), 317–31.

23. Hirsch, *The Aims of Interpretation* (Chicago, 1976), 40.

24. For comment on the work of Howard see Benson, *Riverside Chaucer* 866n67.

sels; Chaucer was a medieval man; therefore Chaucer revered virginity and disdained wooden vessels." We have said that, in order for "historical" criticism to be of aid in assessing the reliability of a particular medieval narrative voice, we must ascertain two things: the poet's probable opinion on the matters raised by (or concerning) the narrator, and the relationship of that opinion to the principles of internal consistency that appear to operate within the poem as a whole, which is to say its relationship to an infinite number of details within the poem. There is probably no medieval poem that can be read with equal consistency both *in bono* and *in malo*. When we misinterpret arguments or details within a poem, we are invariably confronted, sooner or later, with what appear to be structural inconsistencies. We can ignore these, of course, or try to explain them away, but we will not really gain access to the structural principles of a medieval composition until we have evaluated—usually through a process of historical investigation—the arguments offered by the various speakers within that composition, in an effort to understand their characters and roles. On the whole, the history of scholarly approaches to the French and Italian sources of Chaucer has been one of attempts to ignore, or explain away, apparent structural inconsistencies arising from inadequate historical research into the knowledge and values that the poets shared with their audiences. C. S. Lewis's analysis of the *Roman de la Rose* as a "story of real life" marred by "digressions"—the speeches of Raison ("First Digression"), Ami ("Second Digression"), Faussemblant ("Third Digression"), La Vieille ("Fourth Digression"), and on through the Eighth, Ninth, and Tenth Digressions—is well known, and has been thoroughly refuted.[25] It provided the model, however, for modern analyses of Chaucer's other Romance sources (among them the most distinguished literary progeny of the *Rose*) that have never been questioned, and that continue to form our notions of Chaucer's relationship to those sources.

The Romance sources of Chaucer which I have chosen to discuss in this study—certain long narrative works of Machaut, Froissart, and Boccaccio—are composed of two sorts of material, "courtly love" material and mythological digressions. If we are to understand the roles of the narrators in these works (which is to say, if we are to understand the works at all), we must discern the purpose of their

25. Lewis, *The Allegory of Love: A Study in Medieval Tradition* (London, 1936), 137–40.

authors in making use of these two sorts of material. By "courtly love" material, I mean the love-narrative itself, lyrical praise of love and the lady, love-casuistry, and the ritual naming and deployment of the allegorical personifications of love. The debate concerning "courtly love" has extended over several generations, and while it would be unfair to say that we are never the nearer (at least, Alfred Karnein's recent work on medieval reception of Andreas' *De Amore* has finally knocked out that prop to arguments for a "code of courtly love"),[26] the fact is that the medieval narrative poems of love do not offer many clues to the meaning of the literary conventions they develop. The one great exception—the *Roman de la Rose,* whose extensive development of philosophical and religious topics has provided us with valuable clues to its interpretation—appears different enough from its progeny so that scholars have not felt justified in regarding it as a reliable guide to treatments of love by Machaut and Froissart. Those treatments generally present us with a suffering lover/narrator, a disdainful or deceitful lady, and elaborate development of certain conventional love-themes: complaint, praise of love, approach and rebuff, separation and reconciliation. This repetitious and (to moderns) largely impenetrable *matière* is varied mainly by mythological digressions and allusions borrowed from Ovid and Virgil.

Clearly, the "courtly love" material helps to characterize the narrators of these poems. It indicates that they are lovers. To the many modern scholars who regard the highly conventionalized behavior of medieval literary lovers as foolish, it has indicated that they are foolish; to another large group of modern scholars disposed to take "courtly love" seriously, it has indicated that they are—as Ferrante and Economou would have it—"in pursuit of perfection." Neither group has really succeeded in establishing their claims. In fact, no claims about the meaning of the poems can be finally established until we gain some understanding of the principles that unite their two disparate elements, love and learning. I will suggest that, in Chaucer's sources and in his own early poetry, certain often-repeated (and, in the fourteenth century, well-understood) Ovidian and Virgilian myths operate as a conventional device for characterization. As told and retold, interpreted and reinterpreted well or ill

26. De Amore *in Volkssprachlicher Literatur* (Heidelberg, 1985). For an assessment of Karnein's achievement, see Martin Wierschin's review in *Speculum* 62 (1987): 960–63.

by the narrator and the characters surrounding him, those myths give us a portrait of those characters as exegetes—much the sort of portrait that Chaucer gives us of the Wife of Bath, as she repeatedly quotes and interprets Holy Writ. Mythology, in other words, constitutes in these poems that essential key to interpretation to which I have referred, a body of knowledge shared by the poets and their audiences whose meaning we can reconstruct through research. In reconstructing it, however, we must attend carefully to requirements of internal consistency; and we will find, happily, that a reconstruction of the understanding of these common myths that was shared by fourteenth-century poets and their audiences will actually reveal the underlying principles of unity in poems hitherto described as shapeless and digressive. In order to prevent my discussion from becoming too abstract, I should perhaps review the present state of our understanding of a few of these poems, with the preliminary assurance that I shall soon provide fuller demonstration of what appear here as unsubstantiated claims. For the sake of brevity, I take one example from each of the poets I will consider in this study: Machaut, Froissart, and Boccaccio.

In the *Voir Dit,* the longest and most celebrated love-narrative of Machaut, a timid, aging poet is pursued by a clever and attractive young woman, who proposes to become both his apprentice and his *amie*. This *True Story,* which occupies some 370 pages in Paris's edition, purports to be the record of their love affair and their correspondence, although in fact it was almost certainly written entirely by Machaut. It includes a prose narrative of the events of the affair, elaborate descriptions of the poet's love-longing and love-sickness, letters and lyrics in praise of Love, and lengthy retellings of Ovidian tales. The lovers actually meet only a few times, with "Toute-Belle," as the poet calls her, making all the advances; on one occasion, they apparently consummate their love. Eventually, the poet conceives doubts of Toute-Belle's fidelity based upon the reports of friends; although she defends herself vehemently, apparently persuading her lover of her innocence, they do not again meet. The narrator protests that he calls his book the *True Story* because his lady bade him tell everything about their affair, omitting nothing; and this, he asserts proudly, he has done.

Most scholars of the poem have regarded it as simply autobiographical; Paris, James Wimsatt, and Daniel Poirion all state specifically that the lover/narrator is to be identified with Machaut himself.[27] Douglas Kelly calls the *Voir Dit* "pseudoautobiographical," acknowledging that the narrator, although he shares the name and some of the characteristics of Machaut, is essentially a fictional character.[28] There have been valuable new insights into the poem: Brownlee usefully distinguishes three speakers—Machaut himself, the lover/narrator in the present, and the lover/narrator at the time of the affair—and both he and Calin have seen that the principal character (the last) is portrayed as a "timid, inept, bumbling" fellow, a failure as a lover.[29] It remains uncertain, however, why Machaut would have wished to create such a narrator, or precisely what his function is with regard to the *Voir Dit's* very lengthy and elaborate development of the *topoi* of "courtly love": longing for the lady, fear and shame in her presence, idealistic love-talk, Ovidian love-symptoms, jealousy, alternating estrangement and reconciliation. The most recent critics of the poem imply that these *topoi* serve to establish love as a worthy goal and to emphasize the distance between the narrator's aspirations in love and his achievement; in this way, the *Voir Dit* may be seen as offering instruction in *fin'amors* by means of an amusing negative *exemplum,* the inept narrator.

This view of the poem, however, does not account for Machaut's numerous and extensive mythological digressions, or their relationship to the main narrative *persona* and to the love-narrative itself. The tales of Semiramis, Circe, Proteus, Polyphemus and Galatea, Phoebus and Coronis, and many Ovidian love-heroines and metamorphoses find their way into the *Voir Dit* in various contexts: in the lover's praise of his lady, in appeals by each of the lovers for the pity or trust of the other, in speeches of admonition addressed to the narrator by other characters. Taken together, they constitute about one-fifth of the work. Paris regards the poem's mythological episodes and allusions as a parade of learning and an excrescence upon the text; more recent scholars, although critical of the characters' interpretations of other matters, tend simply to accept their statements about the meaning of the mythological *exempla* they use.[30] In any

27. Paris, *Voir-Dit* i–xiii; Wimsatt, *Chaucer and the French Love Poets* (Chapel Hill, 1968), 83; Poirion, *Le Moyen Age* II (Paris, 1971), 193–94.

28. *Imagination* 243.

29. Brownlee, *Identity* 94–156; Calin, *Poet* 175, 186, 188–89.

30. For instance, Brownlee merely repeats—and apparently accepts—the narrator Guillaume's explanation of the meaning of his *exempla* of Semiramis and Iolaus, as well as the explanation given by the dream-king of his allusions to the metamorpho-

case, scholars interest themselves principally in the love-narrative, and treat the mythological material as of secondary importance. Brownlee, for instance, devotes fewer than three pages of his 62-page discussion of the *Voir Dit* to the mythological episodes, and most of that is summary. In fact, although he would certainly not agree with Paris that the mythological material is merely digressive, he describes it in similar terms as "display[s] of artful clerkliness," "an elaborate and playful deployment of clerkliness."[31] Calin, who explicitly protests against the older theory of mythological allusion as "filler" for the slender plots of the *dits,* nevertheless finds little to say about its meaning. He does, however, suggest—as does Cerquiglini—that the tales from mythology serve as a form of commentary upon the narrator and the love-narrative.[32] I shall presently try to show that that is precisely their function, and that it has far-reaching implications for the meaning of the *Voir Dit.*

In Froissart's long narrative poem *Le Joli Buisson de Jonece,* the speaker identifies himself as a poet and attibutes to himself precisely the works of Froissart to that date (1373), as well as his historically real patrons. The action of the poem begins when he is

---

ses of Ovid (*Identity* 130–33), while Douglas Kelly (*Imagination* 56) seems not to acknowledge the distinction between the author's understanding of the myths and that expressed by his characters; he writes, "Mythological figures as well as the Bible provided *poetries,* a rich source of Images made significant according to the author's intention, and effective by the quality of his artistry. . . . Indeed, the portrait of Peronne commissioned by her countrymen permitted Machaut to understand Semiramis as representing her qualities, just as Richart de Fournival used traditional bestiary illuminations to represent his love. Semiramis, Eurydice, Polixène, Pygmalion's statue and lady—these figures and others like them emerge from an idea that each serves to express. The poet's lady is in turn raised and abstracted onto that plane by Imagination." (I will argue, of course, that the traditionally assigned significances of certain very commonplace images should color our reading of fictional characters' attempts at exegetical innovation.) Calin makes the promising suggestions that the emphasis on metamorphosis points to the metamorphoses in the narrator's own life, that the tale of Coronis in fact weighs against the argument of the *ymage,* who tells it, and that the *exempla* of Polyphemus and Coronis "teach . . . that love brings in its wake suffering and death" (*Poet* 194, 199); although Calin gives little attention to the mythological material, my own study bears out the basic soundness of these insights. Cerquiglini (*Engin* 77, 87, 109, 151, 167, 207, and passim) gives the best account of the function of mythological *exempla* in the *Voir Dit.*

31. *Identity* 143, 146.

32. Cerquiglini (*Engin* 167) adds to the conclusions of Calin an analysis of the resemblances between the narrator and Polyphemus—and between the narrator and Ulysses, who appears in the *Ovide Moralisé* as a symbol of trickery.

reproached by the lady Philozophie, who demands that he make use of his talents to compose more poetry. He protests that he is middle-aged and his inspiration is exhausted. Philozophie then urges him to seek out a portrait of his former love, which he had stored in a chest; when he sees it again, he feels on fire with passion, just as Achilles did for Polyxena. Lost in memories, he dreams that Venus conducts him to the Buisson de Jonece, where the young man Jonece attempts to explain to him the philosophical significance of the bush: its leaves are like the stars, and its seven branches represent the seven planets. The infatuated poet, however, refuses to listen to this lecture, saying he wishes only to enjoy himself, not to "parler de grant astronomie." Jonece therefore brings him to a park, where he sees his lady as she was in youth and engages in lengthy and elaborate amorous fencing with her and her allegorized attributes, reciting a number of love lyrics. There is a long excursus on mythological love-heroes and heroines. Just as the poet is about to meet the God of Love himself, he awakens from his dream. Fully conscious, he renounces love; the flesh, after all, is nothing but "cendre et poureture." He ends this poem of over 5,500 lines with a 335-line lay to the Virgin, the holy *buisson* that burns but is not consumed.

Because of certain preconceived notions about the identity and characteristics of narrators in medieval love poems, most students of Froissart have imposed order upon this poem by branding significant portions of it as digressive or excrescent. It is generally assumed that the narrators represent Froissart himself, in gay youth and sour age. Since scholars detect that most of the poem's energy is concentrated in the long central section dealing with the love-adventure, they give short shrift both to the Ovidian material and to the concluding devotional lay. B. J. Whiting and F. S. Shears refer to Froissart's mythological *excurses* as digressive, a "proud display of learning"; Anthime Fourrier, the most recent editor of the *Buisson,* chastises the poet severely for abusing the convention of classical allusion in the *dits* by indulging in pointless and interminable embroidery on the familiar tales; and Audrey Graham deplores the "lengthy and usually irrelevant narration of classical legends" that mars all of Froissart's *dits.*[33] Jean-Louis Picherit, in his article on the role of mythology in the *Buisson,* defends the

33. Whiting, "Froissart as Poet," *MS* 8 (1946): 189–216, p. 204; Shears, *Froissart* 207; Fourrier, *Buisson* 27–28; Graham, "Classical Allusion" 32.

relevance of the classical tales of love; in his words, they serve to "illustrate, recall, or announce the events of the central story." As tales of unhappy love, they foreshadow the failure of the narrator's own love affair. The only conclusion he draws from this insight, however, is that the poet/protagonist had bad luck: having failed to win his lady back again, and having awakened inopportunely from his dream, he had no recourse but the comforts of religion.[34]

Other students of the poem have little more to say of its conclusion. Douglas Kelly says of the lay only that it is suited to the poet's advancing age, as the love-lyrics were suited to his youth; Whiting claims that Froissart "now begins to think about the inevitable end of his life, feels the need of precautions, and so concludes a poem not hitherto characterized by piety with a three hundred and thirty-five line lay to the Virgin."[35] Whether or not the poem as a whole is "characterized by piety" depends, of course, upon how we interpret the attitude of the poet Froissart toward the antics of his dream-lover, and we will presently see that the poem contains certain indications of what that attitude might be. It is notable that the entire work is built around the image of the burning bush, which is, however, never specifically evoked until the concluding lay; the bush whose center is everywhere, its circumference nowhere, is not a convention of medieval love poetry, but a variation of the familiar Biblical image. Whatever the implications of that, surely we must begin with the assumption that any interpretation of the poem that requires us to leave large portions of it completely out of account may legitimately be questioned.

In the *Amorosa Visione* of Boccaccio, the lover/narrator is visited in a dream by a celestial lady of marvelous beauty, who promises him eternal happiness if he will follow her. She shows him a wall in which are gateways to two paths: one wide and brightly lit, with sounds of merriment issuing from it, and the other dark, steep, and forbidding. She recommends the strait path, saying that only the cloud of worldly desires that obscures the narrator's vision prevents him from perceiving its superior beauty. The narrator, however, insists upon taking the wide path, and his guide graciously accom-

34. "Le Rôle des Éléments Mythologiques dans le *Joli Buisson de Jonece* de Jean Froissart," *Neophil.* 63 (1979): 498–508, pp. 498, 507 (my translation).

35. Kelly, "Les Inventions Ovidiennes de Froissart: Réflexions Intertextuelles comme Imagination," *Lit* 41 (1981): 82–92, p. 91; Whiting, "Froissart" 204.

panies him. This path leads them through four Triumphs—of Wisdom, Glory, Wealth, and Love—and finally to a vision of the house of Fortune. Each of the triumphs is elaborately depicted and decorated with numerous classical figures disposed in attitudes suggesting their adventures. Despite the admonitions of his guide, the narrator responds to each of these visions with enthusiasm and frank concupiscence, admiring everything he sees. Even after he has seen the terrible house of Fortune, ruthless queen over worldly goods, he remains vulnerable to temptation; ignoring his guide's recommendation that they now seek the strait path, he is drawn into a lovely garden where he meets a gracious lady and falls in love. Returning to his guide, he protests that he loves the lady purely, and that love for her will lead his desire upward. When lady and guide meet, they greet each other affectionately as sisters, and the guide, recognizing the lady's virtue, gives the lover into her keeping. The lover, however, imagining that he and the lady both desire it, attempts carnal possession of her, whereupon his dream is broken. But all is not lost, for the celestial guide reappears to the waking lover to offer him another opportunity to make a proper pilgrimage. Although he gratefully accepts, it is difficult to estimate his chances of success this second time.

Although the *Visione* is transparently allegorical, Boccaccio's emphasis upon the love-adventure has led most scholars to regard it as a love poem. Viewed in that way, of course, its proportions are distinctly odd, and it has been severely criticized for shapelessness and for pointless, interminable exhibitions of classical learning. Natalino Sapegno deplores its "enorme e caotico apparato erudito e mitologico," Salvatore Battaglia calls it "la piú inerte respetto ai sensi artistici" of all Boccaccio's works, and even Vittore Branca implies that Boccaccio did not plan the work very carefully.[36] All those scholars identify the lover/narrator with the poet himself, accepting Boccaccio's self-identification in the introductory acrostic sonnet as indicating an historically real love affair with the lady "Maria" (despite the fact that no other feature of the poem could possibly have any basis in reality). In addition, no student of the poem (except Robert Hollander, who discusses the role of Orpheus

36. Sapegno, *Storia Letteraria del Trecento* (Milan, 1963), 305 n. 1; Battaglia, *La Letteratura Italiana,* Vol. I: *Medioevo e Umanesimo* (Milan, 1971), 246; Branca, "Introduction," in *Giovanni Boccaccio* Amorosa Visione, trans. Robert Hollander et al. (Hanover, N.H., 1986), xviii.

in the triumph of Love)[37] has investigated the role of the long mythological "digressions" within the scheme of the *Visione* as a whole. To most critics, who attempt to read it as a "courtly" poem in praise of Love—but composed mainly of essentially irrelevant erudite *excurses*—it appears as a bundle of misplaced emphases and unresolved contradictions.

As these examples suggest, many scholars have so far been content to regard a large portion of the work of Machaut, Froissart, and Boccaccio—three of Chaucer's favorite source-authors—as tedious and ill-proportioned.[38] It is commonly believed that Chaucer, in borrowing from those authors, utterly transformed the material he took, making something vital and somehow even "modern" out of the flat, encyclopedic, essentially "medieval" originals. It would be foolish to dispute that Chaucer's style is both different from theirs and better, by any critical standard we can imagine or reconstruct. Nevertheless this notion, even if it did not do an injustice to those sources, would still misrepresent the extent of Chaucer's debt to them, which is enormous. In the case of Machaut, especially, it is far greater than scholars generally acknowledge, and probably even now has not been fully investigated; as recently as 1976, James Wimsatt found new evidence of borrowings from Machaut in the *Troilus*.[39] The nature of these borrowings—as well as of others reported by Lowes, Muscatine, and Wimsatt in *Chaucer and the French Love Poets*—suggests that Chaucer had committed to memory many of Machaut's verses. Evidently, he valued his work highly—as highly, I believe, as he is generally acknowledged to have valued that of Boccaccio. That we no longer value it so highly is due in large part to the fact that we no longer fully understand it. If we are to understand it, we must stop branding it as tedious and digressive and begin to investigate carefully the relationship between its two main elements, love and learning. In *The Allegory*

37. In *Boccaccio's Two Venuses* (New York, 1977), 83–86.

38. Hence the suggestion that Chaucer, in order to produce "a new kind of poetry," had to reject the "limited" and "conventional" terms of the contemporary French poetry of love; see Barbara Nolan, "The Art of Expropriation: Chaucer's Narrator in *The Book of the Duchess*," in *New Perspectives in Chaucer Criticism*, ed. Donald M. Rose (Norman, Okla., 1981): 203–22, and R. Barton Palmer, "The *Book of the Duchess* and the *Fonteinne Amoureuse*: Chaucer and Machaut Reconsidered," *CRCL* 7 (1980): 380–93.

39. See "Guillaume de Machaut and Chaucer's *Troilus and Criseyde*," *MAE* 45 (1976): 277–93.

of Love, C. S. Lewis delivers a ringing defense of artistic unity in medieval works:

> Unity of interest is not 'classical'; it is not foreign to any art that has ever existed or ever can exist in the world. Unity in diversity if possible—failing that, mere unity, as a second best—these are the norms for all human work, given, not by the ancients, but by the nature of consciousness itself. When schools of criticism or poetry break this rule, this rule breaks them. If medieval works often lack unity, they lack it not because they are medieval, but because they are, so far, bad.[40]

Lewis is right about this; the fact that he is wrong about the *Roman de la Rose,* to whose lamentable lack of unity he here refers, ought to constitute a warning.

I have said that, in the works of Chaucer and in his French and Italian sources, classical mythology constitutes a key to meaning, a part of the body of knowledge and values shared by the poets and their audiences. I have said, further, that we can make use of this key by evaluating the interpretations of mythological tales offered by the characters in the love poems in the light of the interpretations of those tales that were generally accepted by court poets and their educated audiences in the fourteenth century. Such claims must be diffidently made and carefully limited. Again, because little work has been done on the meaning of mythological allusions in Chaucer's sources, I shall illustrate that point by reference to Chaucer himself. In an important article published in 1959, Richard Green noted that ". . . the frequency, and indeed the conventionality, of classical allusion in Middle English poetry point to its importance as a part of the language of representation, common to the poet and his experienced contemporary audience, which we ought to try to recover."[41] A common—if not uniformly successful—approach to the recovery of that language has been simply to apply the interpretations of the encyclopedic mythographers to the classical allusions of the poets. Green himself, in the same article, suggests that the emblem of the Minotaur that appears on Theseus's banner in the

40. *Allegory of Love* 141.

41. "Classical Fable and English Poetry in the Fourteenth Century," in *Critical Approaches to Medieval Literature,* ed. Dorothy Bethurum (New York, 1959): 110–33, p. 112.

"Knight's Tale" evokes the conquest of lust by rationality, with consequent implications for the irrational behavior of the young lovers Palamon and Arcite.[42] His authorities for the conventional identification of the Minotaur with lust (specifically, the bestial lust of Pasiphae, its mother) are the mythographers Bersuire, Boccaccio, and Salutati, among others. The convention is indeed a well-established one, in poetry as well as in commentary, and it enriches our reading of the "Knight's Tale," difficult though it would be to demonstrate that Chaucer intended to convey such an association. Green suggests also that the reference of Satan in the "Friar's Tale" to the summoner's future descent into hell ("Thou shalt hereafterward, my brother deere, / Come there thee nedeth nat of me to leere. / For thou shalt, by thyn owene experience, / Konne in a chayer rede of this sentence / Bet than Virgile, while he was on lyve, / Or Dant also")[43] would have conveyed to Chaucer's audience the nature of the summoner's descent, based upon Salutati's classification of *descensus ad inferos* as natural, magical, vicious, and virtuous.[44] True it is that such a classification is found not only in Salutati, but also in other mythographers and in the commentaries on Dante; nevertheless, there are difficulties in establishing such a convention as part of Chaucer's meaning. The fundamental difficulty is that it is a convention of commentary, not of poetry; and Chaucer is writing poetry.

Whatever its occasional rewards, there are other difficulties in attempting to apply the conventions of mythographic commentary to the interpretation of mythological allusions in medieval poetry. Sometimes one finds a poet, even a very great one, not in possession of certain essential information included in the commentaries relevant to a particular allusion. Chaucer, for instance, was unsure of the gender of Marsyas, whose vainglorious behavior he included in the description of the castle on the glacier in the third book of the *Hous of Fame;* his allusion is to "Marcia that loste her skyn / Bothe in face, body, and chyn, / For that she wolde envien, loo, / To pipen bet than Appolloo" (III, 1229–32). The reference, of course, is ultimately to Ovid's story (*Met.* VI, 382–400) of the flaying of the satyr Marsyas for his presumption in challenging Apollo to a contest on

42. "Classical Fable" 132.

43. *CT* III, 1515–20. This and all references to the works of Chaucer are to the edition of Benson, cited above.

44. "Classical Fable" 127.

the reed-pipes. B. G. Koonce, in his book *Chaucer and the Tradition of Fame,* attempts to recover the meaning of Chaucer's allusion by referring to the Third Vatican Mythographer, Giovanni del Virgilio, and Pietro Alighieri's commentary on the *Divine Comedy:* "Whereas Apollo is moralized as divine wisdom *(sapientia),* Marsyas is interpreted as ignorance or folly *(insipientia),* and his contesting Apollo's wisdom is an example of vainglory".[45] In fact, Alfred David has demonstrated that Chaucer took his reference to Marsyas from a faulty manuscript of the *Roman de la Rose* which identifies the satyr as female and alludes to "her" flaying.[46] Chaucer may not have known, or may not have remembered, accounts of the same myth in Ovid, Dante, or the *Teseida* of Boccaccio.

Thus many scholars have become wary of applying the moralities of the commentaries directly to the interpretation of the poets. Some prefer to go back to the classical source itself, despite the fact that (as the above example illustrates) medieval poets often do not derive their mythological allusions directly from the classical source. Winthrop Wetherbee, discussing Chaucer's reference to Myrrha at the parting of the lovers in *Troilus* IV, 1138–41 ("So bittre teeris weep nought, as I fynde, / The woful Mirra thorugh the bark and rynde"), returns to the *Metamorphoses:*

> In one aspect Myrrha may be seen as the emblem of the victimization of the lovers: she came to grief through a passion for her father Cinyras which was brought to fulfillment through the contrivance of her nurse, and there are clear correspondences between the two situations. Troilus, longing for death and calling on the absent Criseyde, is discovered by Pandarus (I, 540–43), as Myrrha, saying her words of farewell to Cinyras, is overheard by her nurse, who rushes to prevent her suicide (*Met.* 10, 378–88). In each case a long interrogation ensues, followed by the confession of love, the confidant's promise to arrange the affair, and finally the moment when the virgin lover is unwillingly led to the darkened chamber where the love is consummated. Myrrha's ingenuous sense of shame and horror is comparable to the

45. Koonce, *Fame* (Princeton, 1966), 200.

46. David, "How Marcia Lost Her Skin: A Note on Chaucer's Mythology," in *The Lerned and the Lewed: Studies in Chaucer and Medieval Literature,* ed. Larry D. Benson (Cambridge, Mass., 1974): 19–29.

> moral-chivalric scruples and the powerful sense of *dangier,* dread, and vague guilt that encroach on Troilus' feelings as he approaches the moment of union with Criseyde.[47]

It is difficult to assess just how much of this detail from Ovid might be relevant to our understanding of Chaucer's allusion, especially since his reference is to Myrrha after her transformation. Again, the allusion is so brief that it is impossible to determine its immediate source; perhaps Chaucer only called upon his general recollection of the story, which he might have read in any one of many poems and commentaries. Leaving aside the fact that the correspondences between the love stories (the love-suffering, the presence of the *ami,* the dread and fear before the consummation) might be adduced between almost any two tales of love, it is surely just as difficult to believe that Chaucer bore in mind, and expected his reader to bear in mind, all this weight of narrative detail from the *Metamorphoses* as it is to believe that he bore in mind the allegorical identifications of half a dozen Christianizing commentaries. This approach has the additional disadvantage that it attempts to place neither Ovid's tale nor Chaucer's allusion within any sort of historical context; the tone of Wetherbee's summary implies that both are to be read with sentimental sympathy for the lovers, an attitude which may well do justice neither to Ovid's meaning nor to Chaucer's. It has been well established that Chaucer—and Boccaccio, and Machaut—did not read Ovid with the same assumptions that we do, nor in the same kinds of editions.[48] Sentimental readings

47. Wetherbee, *Chaucer and the Poets: An Essay on* Troilus and Criseyde (Ithaca, N.Y., 1984), 98–99.

48. For their assumptions, see Don C. Allen, *Mysteriously Meant: The Rediscovery of Pagan Symbolism and Allegorical Interpretation in the Renaissance* (Baltimore, 1970); Douglas Bush, *Mythology and the Renaissance Tradition in English Poetry* (Minneapolis, 1932); Jean Seznec, *The Survival of the Pagan Gods,* trans. Barbara Sessions (New York, 1953); J. B. Allen, *The Ethical Poetic of the Later Middle Ages* (Buffalo, 1971) and *The Friar as Critic: Literary Attitudes in the Later Middle Ages* (Nashville, 1971); the introductions of Earl Schreiber and Thomas E. Maresca, *The Commentary on the First Six Books of Virgil's* Aeneid *by Bernardus Silvestris* (Lincoln, Nebr., 1979), and J. Engels, *Petrus Berchorius* Reductorium Morale, Liber XV, Cap. II–XV: *Ovidius Moralizatus* (Utrecht, 1962), and numerous other works on the medieval Ovid cited in this study. On medieval manuscripts of the classics, encrusted with encyclopedic glosses and commentary, see Fausto Ghisalberti, "Medieval Biographies of Ovid," *JWCI* 9 (1946): 10–59, and the introductions to his editions of Arnulf of Orleans (*Mem. R. Ist. Lomb.,* 1932: 157–234) and Giovanni del Virgilio (*Il Giornale Dantesco* 34, n.s. 4, 1933: 3–110).

of classical allusions are rife in the modern criticism of medieval love poetry; Vittore Branca, for example, speaks warmly of the "passionate devotion and generosity"[49] of the classical heroines of love (Europa, Danae, Io, Daphne, Thisbe, Dido, and many others) who appear in the triumph of Love in the *Amorosa Visione* of Boccaccio, despite the fact that their actions are explicitly condemned within the poem itself. Faced with the difficulty of finding the right filter through which to view medieval references to the classical tales, some scholars are reluctant to find what Don Allen calls "undermeanings" in mythological allusions by Chaucer or any other medieval poet. Alastair Minnis believes that, far from constituting a symbolic subtext, Chaucer's allusions to the classics in poems set in pagan antiquity are often "literal-historical" in nature, a kind of local color.[50] Certainly they may sometimes serve that purpose, as well as others. I believe, however, that Green was right in maintaining that there are meaningful conventions associated with the classical myths most frequently cited in medieval poetry. Unfortunately, those conventions are not always to be found in the mythographic commentaries; the conventions of commentary are not necessarily those of poetry. How, then, are we to go about investigating the meaning of mythological allusions in medieval poetry?

I would like to begin with certain propositions, which I shall try to demonstrate. First of all, Douglas Bush, Jean Seznec, J. B. Allen and others have shown that the classical myths were understood by educated people throughout the Middle Ages not only as stories, but also as *exempla;* that is, they were understood by means of interpretation, or exegesis. Naturally the same myths might be interpreted in various ways by various persons and for various purposes—the multiple, and often conflicting, interpretations of the mythographers are well known—but it appears to have been universally granted that they required interpretation in order to be understood. This point is of some importance to my study as a whole, and so I shall presently illustrate it at length. Second, it seems to be the case that the Italian, French, and English vernacular poetry of love had its own mythographic conventions, firmly rooted in literary history but only partially congruent with those of the Latin mythographers. Third, these conventions involved repeated use of a very

49. In his introduction to Hollander's translation of the *Visione,* xxii.
50. Minnis, *Chaucer and Pagan Antiquity* (Totowa, N.J., 1982), 16.

limited number of myths, mainly those of certain lovers of Ovid's *Heroides* and *Metamorphoses,* but extending to a few non-amatory transformation-myths and certain figures from the classical underworld. Through historical investigation, it is possible to achieve reasonable certainty about the views of fourteenth-century court poets on the accepted meaning of this small number of related myths. Having achieved such a reasonable certainty, it is then possible to gain insight into the perspective of narrators—and of other characters—in medieval love-narratives by evaluating their interpretations of these myths in the light of the structural characteristics of the poems in which they appear. That is the modest goal of this study. It will, alas, leave unanswered many interesting questions about allusions to other classical tales in other sorts of poetry, but it may serve as an opening wedge in the exploration of mythographic conventions in the poetry of the Middle Ages.

Medieval love poetry, and especially Chaucer's French sources, makes very extensive use of mythographic exegesis. That has both surprised and dismayed many scholars, who do not see why, for instance, the lovers of Machaut's *Voir Dit* are always pausing *in medias res* to retell and comment upon apparently irrelevant mythological tales, or why Froissart's *Prison Amoureuse,* an exchange of letters between two men dedicated to love-service, should be largely taken up with Ovidian tales and the lovers' attempts to interpret them. We have already seen that mythological material in medieval love poetry is generally regarded by scholars as a pointless and intrusive display of learning. Evidently, however, the poets considered certain of the ancient tales relevant to the literary treatment of modern love-affairs. Why they did so will become clearer after a brief survey of the scope and importance of the activity of mythographic exegesis in medieval literature. Not only the French and Italian love poets, but every one of Chaucer's major sources—from the Christian Fathers to Macrobius, Martianus Capella, Boethius, Alanus, Walter Map, Jean de Meun, Dante, Petrarch, and even Gower—expressly defends the need to interpret classical mythology. Writers of the early Middle Ages simply moralize the myths, in ways that have been well described by Seznec, Bush, and others; later writers, at the same time that they continue the tradition of moralization, begin also to use the myths and their time-honored moralizations in subtle, humorous ways.

In preparation for our attempt to understand the use of a limited number of Ovidian and Virgilian myths by certain late medieval poets, it will therefore be useful to begin with a brief survey of the *literary* history—as distinct from the specifically mythographic history—of medieval exegesis of classical mythology. I have already suggested some of the difficulties of applying the glosses of the medieval mythographers to the interpretation of late medieval poetry. The most widely recognized difficulty, of course, is that the mythographers offer multiple interpretations—some *in bono,* some *in malo*—of many of the myths they address. In their view, all of the interpretations they offered—as well as others already promulgated or yet to be discovered—were "true" to the extent that they were in harmony with Christian moral teaching.[51] In modern critical practice, however, it is not entirely persuasive to argue that, because Chaucer knew Bersuire and Bersuire identifies the Minotaur with lust, the Minotaur signifies lust when he appears on the banner of Theseus in the "Knight's Tale." Bersuire tells us that the Minotaur may equally well signify "the devil, or hell, or death."[52] We need, in Hirsch's words, "narrowing data"[53]—some more specific indication of what meaning Chaucer intended to convey by alluding to the Minotaur in this particular context—if we are confidently to associate the Minotaur with any of these ideas, or indeed with any other. The same objection may be offered to all of the many attempts that have been made to gloss the poets in terms of the mythographers, except for those instances in which the mythographic text can be identified as a direct source of the allusion in question. The fact is that the poetry of Chaucer, and that of his French and Italian contemporaries, is not principally dependent upon the mythographers, but upon other sources. It has not been generally noted that those sources themselves contain a great deal of exegesis of the classical myths, which incidentally exhibits more consistency than the interpretations of the encyclopedic mythographers. In the following discussion of the literary history of mythological interpretation in the Middle Ages, I wish to emphasize two points: (a) that classical mythology was understood for many centuries through moralizing interpretation, and (b) that interpretation of the myths

51. Their teacher in this matter was Augustine; see especially *De Doctrina Christiana* II, 40, in which he likens the writings of the pagans to the "Egyptian gold" of Exodus 3.22, then says of this very interpretation that he offers it "without prejudice to any other equal or better understanding" of the text (trans. D. W. Robertson, *On Christian Doctrine* [New York, 1958], 76).

52. *Red. Mor.* XV, 8 (Engels 125).

53. Hirsch, *Validity in Interpretation* (New Haven, 1967), 184.

was practiced, not only by the encyclopedic mythographers, but by most of the significant writers of the Middle Ages, both early and late. In this preliminary survey we will not often encounter the Ovidian and Virgilian lovers whose tales furnish much of the *matière* of the medieval love-narratives; medieval interpretations of those tales will be the subject of the following chapters. We will, however, meet in passing certain other mythological characters—Ulysses and the Sirens, Circe, Proteus, the Furies, and the infernal sufferers Tantalus, Tityus, Sisyphus, and Ixion—who appear associated with the mythological lovers in those narratives. The basis of that association will, I hope, presently become clear.

The practice of mythographic interpretation arose not long after Homer wrote, and continued to flourish in Latin letters; the strength that the tradition had already acquired by early medieval times is shown in the fact that the Christian Fathers, to whom the old religion is the enemy, nevertheless follow the inherited intellectual habit of looking beneath the husk of the old fictions for the precious kernel of truth. Justin Martyr's *Cohortatio ad Gentiles* contains an entire chapter on the "Follies of the Greek Mythology," but he uses the *Testament of Orpheus* to demonstrate to the pagans that their own hero had professed faith in the One God, and he believes that the myth of Otus and Ephialtes expresses historical truth under the veil of allegory.[54] St. Ambrose, in the fourth chapter of his *Expositio in Lucam,* condemns the fables of the poets even as he locates Christian truth in one of them; of the myth of Ulysses and the Sirens, he writes:

> Figmentis enim poeticis fabula coloratur. . . . Compositum hoc specie, et ambitiosa comparatione fucatum est. . . . Quod autem mare abruptius quam saeculum. . . . Qui sibi vult puellarum figura, nisi eviratae voluptatis illecebra. . . . (*PL* 15, 1696D–97A)

Paule Demats explains how the Fathers justify finding moralities in the poets at the same time that they condemn them:

> [The fictions of the pagans] may present some appearance of truth, that is to say of agreement with Christian doctrine;

54. For Orpheus in Justin, see John B. Friedman, *Orpheus in the Middle Ages* (Cambridge, Mass., 1970), 4; on Otus and Ephialtes, *Cohortatio ad Gentiles* 28.

> there is not, then, as pagan apologists (Celsus, for example) maintain, borrowing by Christianity from pagan myth, but an unconscious participation by the poets in the mysteries of the true faith, of which they had knowledge perhaps from the Jewish prophets, perhaps from the spirit world, but in any case in too confused a fashion to be able to understand them.[55]

Such a belief gave Christian apologists licence to use the myths in whatever way they pleased, and indeed they found in them a rich source of doctrine. Clement of Alexandria invents and rearranges quotations from Homer to establish the sacredness of the seventh day (for *Od.* V, 262, "It was the fourth day, and all was finished," he substitutes "seventh"). In a figure that will become conventional, he uses the transformations of Proteus to signify the degrading changes wrought in man's rational nature by the passions. He not only uses *exempla* from the classics, but recommends their use. In a wonderful passage of the *Paidagogica,* he extracts three successive quotations from Hesiod as a gloss on Scripture to prove that "pagans are of no account."[56] Clement finds no contradiction in railing against the myths of the gentiles and even against the traditional allegorical interpretation of those myths while at the same time finding moralities in them, recommending that they be converted to Christian use, and stating his own theory of the myths as *integumenta,* or coverings for truth: "The ancients taught their wisdom by means of suggestive symbolism—and I am thinking when I say this of Orpheus, of Linus, Musaeus, Homer and Hesiod and of all other such men as were possessors of wisdom. For the great multitude their poetic psychagogy was like a concealing curtain."[57] He enunciates an esthetic of difficulty, defending the poetic veil as protecting the truth from the many who are unprepared to receive it.[58] Together with all these attitudes, Clement, like most of his contemporaries and successors, was a euhemerist.

For several centuries Christian orthodoxy on the pagan myths—if this hodgepodge of apparently conflicting attitudes and practices

55. *Fabula: Trois Études de Mythographie Antique et Médiévale* (Geneva, 1973), 18n62 (my translation).

56. *Strom.* V, 14 (noted by Felix Buffière, *Les Mythes d'Homère et la Pensée Grecque* [Paris, 1973], 565); *Paidagog.* III, 1 and 8 (*PG* 8, 556 BC and 612A–13B).

57. *Strom.* V, 4, quoted by Hugo Rahner, *Greek Myths and Christian Mystery,* trans. Brian Battershaw (New York, 1963), xviii.

58. *Strom,* I, 5 (*PG* 8, 717).

may be so called—remained essentially the same. Origen, Clement's student and a fierce antagonist of both pagan myth and pagan allegory, reveals that he nevertheless accepts the myths as *integumenta* when he attacks pagan religion as corrupting the unlearned, who do not have access to the allegories of the gods.[59] Eusebius, although he condemns the myths as religion, is a euhemerist who includes the tales of the gods in his *Ecclesiastical History,* and (through Jerome's later translation) establishes the "historical order" of the gods that was to persist into the Middle Ages. Though he vigorously condemns mythographic allegory, Eusebius finds in the myth of Orpheus, who tamed savage beasts with his lyre, a parallel to the word of Christ, who brought spiritual peace to men through the instrument of His humanity; and, like Lactantius and St. Augustine, he regards Virgil's Fourth Eclogue as a prophecy of the coming of Christ.[60] Lactantius himself, strongly euhemerist, seeks to discredit pagan "physical" interpretations of myth such as the traditional identification of Saturn with time, but he praises Ovid and Virgil, uses the *bivium* passage of the *Aeneid* to dramatize each Christian's choice between virtue and vice, and sees in Tityus's vulture a figure for the divine fire that consumes the bodies of the damned.[61] He also states unequivocally his belief that truth lies concealed beneath the fictions of poetry: "It is the business of the poet with some gracefulness to change and transfer actual occurrences into other representations by oblique transformations," thereby communicating a "truth veiled with an outward covering and show."[62]

Although the Fathers often protest against the mythographic interpretations of the pagans by objecting that no truth can be uncovered in accounts that are in every respect false and meretricious, such a conviction is not borne out in their actual practice. The belief revealed in their practice, and the belief they transmit to the Middle Ages, is that, although the pagans were unqualified to

59. *Contra Celsum* I, 18 (*PG* 11, 692C).

60. *De Laud. Const.* XIV (*PG* 20, 1409C–12C); his interpretation of the Fourth Eclogue is noted by John Sandys, *A History of Classical Scholarship,* 3 vols. (Cambridge, 1903–8), I, 634.

61. Demats (*Fabula* 54) notes his frequent praise of Virgil and Ovid; on the *bivium,* see Pierre Courcelle, "Interprétations Néo-Platonisantes du Livre VI de l'Énéide," in *Recherches sur la Tradition Platonicienne,* ed. W. K. C. Guthrie et al. (Verona, 1957): 94–136, p. 100; on Tityus, Courcelle 104.

62. *Inst. Div.* I, 2; quoted by Robertson, *Preface* 15–16, from Fletcher's translation.

detect the truth in their own poetry, Christians may do so, as long as the truth they discover is in harmony with Christian doctrine. The homily of Basil "On the Right Use of Greek Literature" in fact says as much, and so does Augustine.[63] Basil himself uses the myth of Odysseus and the Sirens to illustrate the way in which young readers should flee from all that is base in poetry, and the myth of Proteus in the way that Clement used it, as a figure for the moral transformation of men by vice.[64] Augustine repents the tears he shed over Dido and ridicules Porphyry's interpretation of the myth of Attis (as well as Varro's, of Saturn and others), but he is much inclined to finding Christian doctrine in Virgil—in the *City of God* he even puts into the mouth of God the words of Jupiter on the nature of divinity—and indeed to mining "Egyptian gold" wherever he can.[65]

There are even certain exegetical commonplaces in patristic moralizations of the myths: the Sirens stand for worldly temptations, the Centaur for the double nature of man (half bestial, half rational), the transformations of Proteus (and of the companions of Ulysses by Circe) for spiritual transformation by lust, the flight of Dedalus and Icarus for the sin of presumption, the gold showered by Jupiter into Danae's lap for corruption by avarice, the sufferings of the Homeric damned for the passions that beset men, the Homeric *bivium* for the choice between vice and virtue, the adventures of Aeneas for the temptations of life, and Ovid's reference (in *Met.* I, 84–86) to the upright posture of man as an allegory of man's higher spiritual nature. Although the Fathers are vocal in their opposition to finding deeper meanings in mythology, these "standard" interpretations are to be found in almost all of them, if one looks closely enough; certainly they are all to be found in the writings of Augustine. They use them uncritically, as it were unconsciously, and with complete conviction. Later, medieval mythographers, encyclopedists, historians, and poets adopt them and use them in the same spirit.

63. See *Essays on the Study and Use of Poetry by Plutarch and Basil the Great,* trans. Frederick Morgan Padelford (New York, 1902), 105, and *De Doctrina Christiana* II, 18: "Rather, every good and true Christian should understand that wherever he may find Truth, it is his Lord's" (trans. Robertson, *Christian Doctrine* 54).

64. See Padelford, *Plutarch and Basil* 104, 118–19.

65. On Dido see *Conf.* I, 13, 21; on Attis and Cybele, *De Civ. Dei* VII, 26, 22–28, and VI, 8. Edward K. Rand, *Founders of the Middle Ages* (Cambridge, Mass., 1928), 276, makes note of Augustine's use of the words of Jupiter.

It may seem that we have traveled far from the love-narratives of Boccaccio, Machaut, and Chaucer, but in fact late medieval understanding of the classical myths is merely an extension of attitudes and traditions that arose in antiquity and persisted through patristic times. Scholars who wish to trace the transmission of mythographic interpretations have generally done so, logically enough, by moving from one mythographer to the next; there is, after all, no more fruitful source of mythographic exegesis than the mythographers. This approach has, however, created the mistaken impression that interpretation of the myths was the special province of a few, a sort of backwater of scholarship that exerted little influence upon the literary tradition in general. That impression, in turn, has made critics of medieval literature reluctant, not only to consider the classical allusions of medieval poets in the light of the interpretations of the mythographers, but even to grant that medieval poets knew or cared anything about mythographic interpretation. R. R. Bolgar, who seems to have enjoyed medieval poetry, considered medieval mythography a bizarre "divagation of the human mind";[66] this opinion, unfortunately, is still widespread. In fact, the interpretation of the classical myths was, from ancient times through the Middle Ages, an activity of such great interest to so many people that one can construct a tolerably coherent survey of literary use and exegesis of the myths without even including the encyclopedic mythographers. This is certainly not to say that the mythographers were without influence; it is merely to say that, from the early to the late Middle Ages, all kinds of writers—mythographers, encyclopedists, historians, preachers, and poets—agree upon a single manner of approaching the myths: they seek in them the truths of morality and of religion. The implications of this fact for the interpretation of the literature of the high Middle Ages will be the subject of other chapters, but they will begin to emerge as we consider glosses on the myths by writers of early medieval times.

Macrobius is of special interest in such a consideration, as being greatly influential and, at least possibly, the first Christian to dedicate himself entirely to interpreting the classical heritage (though not, of course, in explicitly Christian terms). In doing so, he relies wholly upon the assumption that infallible truth is to be found beneath the veil of the classical fictions. In his commentary

66. *The Classical Heritage and Its Beneficiaries from the Carolingian Age to the End of the Renaissance* (Cambridge, 1954), 422.

on the *Somnium Scipionis* he objects to obscene or sanguinary myths (like the adulteries of the gods or Saturn's castration of Caelus) and maintains that truth inheres only in fables that "draw the reader's attention to certain kinds of virtue" or in a type of fable he calls the *narratio fabulosa,* which "rests on a solid foundation of truth . . . treated in a fictitious style." He offers as examples "the performances of sacred rites, the stories of Hesiod and Orpheus that treat of the ancestry and deeds of the gods, and the mystic conceptions of the Pythagoreans."[67] (The last, of course, are simply mythographic treatises.) In practice, however, he elaborates at some length, in the *Saturnalia,* the conventional Stoic exegesis of the myth of Saturn and Caelus, and does not scruple to allegorize the loves of Venus and Adonis.[68] Moreover, he believes both Virgil and Homer to be infallible—his word is "perfect"—and constructs elaborate interpretive edifices upon their most insignificant utterances. In the *Saturnalia* he asserts of the *Aeneid* that "we . . . shall not suffer the secret places of this sacred poem to remain concealed, but we shall examine the approaches to its hidden meanings and throw open its inmost shrine for the worship of the learned."[69] His glosses show that he interests himself mainly in literary, historical, and scientific curiosities, rather than in moralization. But he devotes a whole chapter of the *Somnium* (Bk. I, Ch. 10) to moralizing the Homeric Hades, identifying Hades itself as the body of man, in which the soul is imprisoned, and the sufferings of Ixion, Tityus, Sisyphus and the other Homeric damned as the passions.

Four enormously influential works of the early Middle Ages—Macrobius's commentary on the *Somnium,* Martianus Capella's *Marriage of Philology and Mercury,* the *Consolation of Philosophy* of Boethius, and the *Etymologiae* of Isidore of Seville—all show in different ways the importance of the interpretation of classical myth within the general literary culture. Martianus both repeats the traditional allegories on the nature of the pagan gods and makes use of them to assimilate classical learning to the medieval trivium and quadrivium. He reveals awareness that fable is not, in some quarters, considered an appropriate vehicle for serious philosophical

67. *Somn.* I, 2, trans. William Harris Stahl, *Commentary on the Dream of Scipio* (New York, 1952), 85.

68. *Sat.* I, 8 and 21.

69. *Sat.* I, 24, trans. Percival Vaughan Davies, *The Saturnalia* (New York, 1961), 156.

discussion; beginning his discussion of grammar, he announces that he will "put aside all fable and for the most part explain serious studies," only to take it all back again when the Muse reminds him, four lines later, that the fabulous *integumentum* is traditional: it is "a weakness of the poet to make straightforward and undisguised statements."[70] When Martianus, in his *persona* as a rather silly "gray-haired man living in retirement," comically objects that he has already given notice he will abandon fable for truth, the Muse laughs and tells him what, of course, every reader of his time would have known very well already: "Let us tell no lies, and yet let the Arts be clothed. . . . Why will you not admit that your work cannot be composed except by the use of imagery?"[71] The idea that fables are not lies, but a special category of the truth, was well established even in Martianus's time; it appears not only in the commentaries on the poets, but in the treatise *Contra Mendacium* of St. Augustine.[72] Homer and Virgil, having "attained celestial bliss and . . . earned temples in heaven," appear prominently at the marriage, and Martianus's Grammar herself explains the importance of *enarratio* as an intellectual activity when she says, "My duty in the early stages was to read and write correctly; but now there is the added duty of understanding and criticizing knowledgeably."[73] *The Marriage of Mercury and Philology* contains a very great deal of mythological lore, especially in the first (and most frequently read) books on the betrothal and marriage. Since it was, as H. O. Taylor puts it, "perhaps the most widely used schoolbook of the Middle Ages,"[74] it must have done much to acquaint medieval readers with the traditional domains and attributes of the gods.

We do not ordinarily think of the *Consolation of Philosophy* of Boethius, another enormously popular medieval textbook, as perpetuating the tradition of mythographic interpretation, but in fact the moralization of classical fable is one of Boethius' chief rhetorical resources. Precisely because it is not principally a work of mythography, the *Consolation* is a good indicator of the most current and widely used moralizations of its period. Lady Philosophy, in the

70. *De Nuptiis* II, 220, and III, 221, trans. William Harris Stahl and Richard Johnson, *Martianus Capella and the Seven Liberal Arts,* 2 vols. (New York, 1977), vol. II.

71. *De Nuptiis* III, 222, trans. Stahl and Johnson.

72. On Augustine's view of fables, see Robertson, *Preface* 337.

73. *De Nuptiis* III, 230, trans. Stahl and Johnson.

74. Quoted by Stahl and Johnson, vol. I, 21–22.

very act of banishing the Muses of poetry from Boethius's bedside—"Get out, you Sirens; your sweetness leads to death"—evokes the conventional identification of the Sirens with worldy temptations.[75] Speaking of the harmfulness of wealth, she borrows Ovid's myth of the former age (*Met.* I, 89–112), and near the end of her argument, in the fifth book, she repeats the familiar allegory on *Met.* I, 84–86, on the upright posture of man as a sign of his soul's sublimity (V, Mtr. 5). In her lecture on fate and free will the many-headed Hydra furnishes a symbol of the many doubts men conceive of God's providence, and Homer's words on Phoebus, the sun—"He sees all things and hears all things"—become the basis of a poem on God's omniscience (IV, Pr. 6; V, Mtr. 2). The extensive use made by Boethius of the myths of Orpheus and Eurydice, Ulysses and Circe, and the labors of Hercules is well known; his influence must be in some measure responsible for the growing conventionality of the moralities on these myths in the centuries that followed.

The mythological poems of the *Consolation* are all colored by allegory. At the point when Boethius accuses Philosophy of mocking him with a circular argument on the nature of evil, she responds with the tale of Orpheus, following closely the dramatic account of Ovid in *Met.* X. The morality she extracts from the story—that, having once raised their minds to celestial things, men must not look back with longing upon the world—implies the allegorical identifications made by later mythographers and poets, in which Orpheus represents a man seeking the *summum bonum,* Eurydice his soul, and Hades the world (III, Mtr. 2). Later, as part of her proof that evil is its own punishment, Philosophy sings the story, often moralized by the Fathers, of Circe's turning the companions of Ulysses to swine. She first discourses at some length upon the transformation of men into beasts by vice:

> Auaritia feruet alienarum opum uiolentus ereptor? Lupi similem dixeris. Ferox atque inquies linguam litigiis exercet? Cani comparabis. Insidiator occultus subripuisse fraudibus gaudet? Vulpeculis exaequetur. Irae intemperans fremit? Leonis animum gestare credatur. Pauidus ac fugax non metuenda formidat? Ceruis similis habeatur. . . . Ita fit ut qui,

75. Lib. I, Pr. 1, trans. Richard Green, *The Consolation of Philosophy* (Indianapolis, 1962). All translations from the *Consolation* are Green's.

> probitate deserta, homo esse desierit, cum in diuinam condicionem transire non possit, uertatur in beluam.[76]

In her moralization of the myth, she cites the patristic commonplace that demons (in this case, Circe) can alter appearances but cannot change the nature of things: "She had power over the bodies of men, but could not change their hearts" (IV, Mtr. 3). How much more powerful, she argues, are the temptations of the world, which corrupt the inner man.

Boethius gives to the mythological poems prominent places and important functions in the *Consolation*; the metre on Orpheus sums up his argument on the nature of true good, and at the end of Book IV he places the stirring call to action inspired by the mythological heroes, who set an example for lesser men by performing superhuman tasks: Agamemnon steeled himself to execute his own daughter, Ulysses outwitted the Cyclops, and Hercules won heaven with his labors. What, then, should be impossible to us? "Go now, strong men! Follow the high road of great example. Why slack off and turn your backs? When you overcome the earth, the stars will be yours" (IV, Mtr. 7). Here, as later in the mythographers, the heroes are presented, not just as overcoming difficulties, but as conquering evil itself; in Boethius's Hercules we may see the germ of Salutati's, the type of Christ.

Isidore of Seville, who in the *Sententiae* forbids Christians to read pagan literature, nevertheless considers it worth extensive consideration in the *Etymologiae,* where in fact Servius is one of his sources and the allegorical nature of classical poetry one of his explicit assumptions. Discussing the tropes, he writes:

> Allegoria est alieniloquium. Aliud enim sonat, et aliud intellegitur, ut (Virg. *Aen.* i, 184):
> Tres litore cervos
> Conspicit errantes
> Ubi tres duces belli Punici, vel tria bella Punica significantur. Et in Bucolicis (3.71):
> Aurea mala decem misi
> id est ad Augustum decem eglogas pastorum.[77]

76. Lib. IV, Pr. 3, 13–15, ed. Adrian Fortescue, *De Consolatione Philosophiae Libri Quinque* (New York, 1976).

77. *Etym.* I, 37, 22, ed. W. M. Lindsay, *Isidori Hispalensis Episcopi Etymologiarum sive Originum Libri XX* (Oxford, 1911).

Isidore seems to believe literally in the Ovidian transformations (he points out that matter is, after all, continually transformed in nature), and in a great variety of monsters from classical fable as well as from folklore, but he also believes that the monsters have meaning. Of the Furies, he says:

> Aiunt et tres Furias feminas crinitas serpentibus, propter tres affectus, quae in animis hominum multas perturbationes gignunt, et interdum cogunt ita delinquere, ut nec famae nec periculi sui respectum habere permittant. Ira, quae vindictam cupit: cupiditas, quae desiderat opes: libido, quae appetit voluptates. Quae ideo Furiae appellantur, quod stimulis suis mentem feriant et quietam esse non sinant.[78]

Here, the literal existence of the Furies appears far less important than the ideas they represent; Isidore does not even moralize their attributes, but imports, probably from Lactantius, a morality entirely unrelated to their characteristics in classical fiction. The increasing prestige of Ovid as a source of wisdom may be seen in Isidore, who, in addition to quoting him anonymously on many occasions, cites him by name as an authority on transformations, the origin of serpents, the minotaur, and the owl.[79]

Writers of the twelfth and thirteenth centuries also found ways to adapt classical materials to didactic purposes. Alanus de Insulis, an important source of Chaucer and of his French and Italian contemporaries, claims that in the best poetry (including his own) "the poetic lyre gives a false note on the outer bark of the composition but within tells the listeners a secret of deeper significance so that when the outer shell of falsehood has been discarded the reader finds the sweeter kernel of truth hidden within."[80] Of course he employs the myths in allegorical and exemplary fashion throughout both the *De Planctu* and the *Anticlaudianus:* Paris and the Ovidian love-heroines signify lust, Scylla, Charybdis and the Sirens temptation, Tantalus avarice, Lucretia, Penelope, and Daphne chastity, the Furies crime, and so forth.[81] (Raoul de Longchamp, in his

78. *Etym.* VIII, 11, 95–96, ed. Lindsay.

79. *Etym.* XI, 4; XII, 4, 38 and 48, and 7, 39.

80. *De Planctu* Pr. IV, 133–36, trans. James J. Sheridan, *The Plaint of Nature* (Toronto, 1980), 140.

81. *De Planctu* Mtr. I, 53; Pr. IV, 68–92; Mtr. V, 25–30; Pr. VI, 16–19 and 44–54; Mtr. VII, 1–14; Pr. VIII, 57–64; *Anticlaud.* I, 170–80; III, 450–68; VIII, 200–210; IX, 400–420, and passim.

commentary on the *Anticlaudianus,* uses the term "integumentum" to introduce his interpretation of the myth of Orpheus, a quite conventional one in which Orpheus represents *ratio* and Eurydice *caro,* or *sensualitas.*)[82] Walter Map begins his *De Nugis Curialium,* a wonderful compilation of quasi-historical tales and instructive *exempla,* with a comparison of court life to Hell, with the infernal sufferers of the classical Hades—Tantalus, Tityus, Ixion, Sisyphus—representing the vices of courtiers. In the epistle to Rufinus advising him against marriage, which he includes in the fourth part of the book, Walter makes use of other mythological figures we will meet again and again in discussions of love; the Sirens, the Ovidian and Virgilian heroines, the judgment of Paris, the ladies beloved of the gods, all are moralized, and Rufinus is advised to follow instead the chaste ways of Perictione, the aged virgin who became the mother of Plato. In justification of his copious use of *exempla* from mythology, Walter includes the following statement:

> Amice, miraris an indignaris magis quod in parabolis tibi significem gentiles imitandos, Christiano ydolatras, agno lupos, bono malos? Volo sis argumentose api similis, que mel elicit ex urtica, ut suggas mel de petra et oleum de saxo durissimo. Gentilium noui supersticionem; sed omnis creatura Dei aliquod habet exemplar honesti, unde Ipse tum leo tum uermis tum aries dicitur. Plurima peruerse agunt increduli, aliqua tamen que, licet in ipsis intereant, in nobis habunde fructum facerent.[83]

Ovidian manuscripts of the twelfth and thirteenth centuries were commonly accompanied by what Ghisalberti has called "encyclopedic" *accessus,* glosses, and marginalia of various kinds, so that schoolboys (and men of letters) were constantly exposed to the medieval moralities on Ovid whether they read the mythographic manuals or not. Often enough, of course, students were not offered the Ovidian text at all, but various moralizing substitutes for it such as the *Ecloga Theoduli* or the *Allegoriae* of Arnulf of Orleans. This universal exposure to the moralities on the myths shows in the

82. In the section "De Musica" VIII. See the edition of Jan Sulowski, *In Anticlaudianum Alani Commentum* (Wroclaw, 1972), 191–92.

83. *De Nugis Cur.* IV, 3, ed. M. R. James, *Walter Map* De Nugis Curialium: *Courtier's Trifles* (Oxford, 1983), 308.

productions of writers of all kinds. One devout thirteenth-century allegorist (Rand's anonymous "Friend of the Classics") converts Venus's address to Cupid in the *Aeneid* into a mystical treatise on the sonship of Christ.[84] The *Art of Love* of Guillaume Guiart begins with a summary of Ovid's *Ars,* proceeds to the *Remedia,* and concludes with a sermon on love of God. In the words of Louis Karl, who summarizes the poem: "L'auteur va montrer d'abord les vices du monde, ensuite il révèléra la vérité qui est dans le service de Dieu."[85] Brunetto Latini, in the *Tesoretto,* describes Ovid as the master of love who eventually frees the narrator from carnal passions and sets him back on the path "to God and the saints"; so, later, does Guillaume de Guilleville in the *Pèlerinage de la Vie Humaine.*[86] Such use of the classics—uncritical, ahistorical, moralizing—predominated for centuries.

That writers of the century of Chaucer approached the classical myths by seeking moral truth beneath the fictive integument has been well documented. Coluccio Salutati, a contemporary of Chaucer, begins his famous letters in defense of liberal studies by assuming that the language of poetry is figurative and that the Bible, which unlike poetry is literally true, has likewise figurative levels of meaning. Like the works of the poets, too, the Bible contains accounts of immoral behavior; should we not, therefore, even prefer the practice of the poets, whose accounts of such behavior are acknowledged by all to be mere fictions?[87] Richard Green translates the following passage from the first edition of Salutati's works:

> No one should suppose that the sacred poets . . . left us their fables of gods and men with the intention that their stories should be believed or imitated. For no poet wishes to do harm, and what greater harm could they do than persuade credulous men to mistake vain and false things for true. . . . Something wholly different was hidden (and is still hidden)

84. "A Friend of the Classics in the Times of Saint Thomas Aquinas," in *Mélanges Mandonnet* II (Paris, 1930): 261–75.

85. "L'Art d'Amour de Guiart," *ZRP* 44 (1924): 66–79 and 181–87, p. 72.

86. *TES.* 2359–2403, in the edition of Julia Bolton Holloway, ed. and trans., *Il Tesoretto* (New York, 1981). The second (1355) version of the *Pèlerinage,* which includes the reference to Ovid, is most easily accessible in the translation of Lydgate, ed. F. J. Furnivall for EETS, 1899–1904. In this edition, the words of Ovid to the narrator appear on pp. 620–21, just at the end of the poem.

87. *Epis.* XX; in the edition of Francesco Novati, *Epistolario di Coluccio Salutati* (Rome, 1896), this argument appears in vol. 3, 539–43.

> beneath the surface of the fables which they artfully composed, so that, although they may deceive the ignorant with a certain pleasure, they offer to wiser readers the fragrant odor and sweet taste of inner meaning. Whoever does not believe this should read Cicero's *De Natura Deorum* and *De Divinatione;* and let him read Macrobius, Lactantius, Fulgentius, Alexander, and the many other authorities who have discovered the hidden secrets of these fables. Let them read, too, the admirable work of my wise fellow countryman, Giovanni Boccaccio, *The Genealogy of the Gods,* in which Boccaccio wonderfully improved on the traditional interpretations of all the older writers on this subject. Unless I am mistaken, doubters will be ashamed of their incredulity and struck with admiration for the poets and their fables. Finally, those who deny allegorical meanings in the traditional stories of the poets do not, in the words of the great Lactantius, understand the way poetic freedom works and how far the poet may go in his art, since the office of the poet is to change what really happened into new forms by means of oblique configurations and a certain beauty.[88]

The "doubters" to whom Salutati refers are certain monks, notably the Camaldolese Giovanni di San Miniato and the Dominican Giovanni Dominici, who had expressed disapproval of the exclusively pagan content of the arts course. The overwhelming majority of writers of the Middle Ages did not disapprove. Not surprisingly, poets were consistently strong in their defense of the moral significance of the myths. Jean de Meun, whose use of the myths we will later examine more closely, discourses upon it in the speech of Reason objecting to the Lover's squeamishness about "coilles":

> Si dist l'en bien en nos escoles
> Maintes choses par paraboles
> Qui mout sont beles a entendre.
> Si ne doit l'en mie tout prendre
> A la lettre, quanque l'en ot.
> En ma parole autre sens ot,
> Dont si briement parler voloie
> Au mains quant de coilles parloie,

88. Green, "Classical Fable" 119–20.

Que celi que tu i vues metre;
Et qui bien entendroit la lettre,
Le sens verroit en l'escriture
Qui esclarsist la chose oscure.
La verité dedens repote
Seroit clere, s'ele ert espote;
Bien l'entendras se bien repetes
Les integumens as poetes.
La verras une grant partie
Des secrés de philosofie
Ou mout te vorras deliter,
Et mout y porras profiter;
En delitant profiteras,
En profitant deliteras;
Car en lor geus et en lor fables
Gisent profit mout delitables,
Sous qui lor pensees covrirent
Quant le voir des fables vestirent.
Si te convendroit a ce tendre
Se bien vues la parole entendre.[89]

Jean makes very extensive, often ironic, use of the myths and their traditional moralizations. As we will see, La Vieille is an encyclopedia of lore, most of it employed in a delightfully wrongheaded way; her perverse glosses on the myths are one of the chief ways in which Jean defines her character. He can, however, speak quite earnestly of the lessons concealed in the classical fables. Seeing the Lover preparing to subject himself to the vicissitudes of Fortune through "disordinate love," Reason speaks of proper understanding of the ancient tales as the only insurance against enslavement to Fortune. Evidently the lover has forgotten the examples of Croesus, Hecuba, and Sisigambis, mother of Darius:

D'autre part je tiens a grant honte,
Puis que tu ses que lettre monte
Et que estudier te couvient,
Quant il d'Omer ne te souvient,

89. Lines 7153–80. References to the *Roman* are to the edition of Daniel Poirion (Paris, 1974) and the translation of Charles Dahlberg (Princeton, N.J., 1971).

Puis que tu l'as estudié.
Mes tu l'as, espoir, oblié,
Et n'est ce pene vainne et vuide?
Tu mes en lire ton estuide
Et tout par negligence oblies
Que vaut quanque tu estudies,
Quant le sens au besoing te faut,
Et solement par ton defaut?
Certes touz jors en ramembrance
Deüsses avoir la sentence,
Si deveroient tuit homme sage,
Et si fichier en lor corage
Que jamés ne lor eschapast
Tant que la mort les atrapast.
Car qui la sentence savroit,
Et toz jors en son cuer l'avroit
Et la seüst bien soupenser,
Jamés ne li devroit peser
De chose qui li avenist
Que touz jors fers ne se tenist
Encontre toutes aventures,
Bonnes, males, moles ou dures.
(6777–6802)

Dante, too, is well known for his theoretical statements on the moral significance of the pagan myths. It is unnecessary to insist on his acceptance of Virgil's authority and his belief in the wisdom of the *Aeneid,* but his attitude toward Ovid is less well known. In the *Inferno,* of course, Ovid appears third among the four divine poets under Virgil; in the *De Vulgari Eloquentia,* Dante cites the *Metamorphoses* as a model of the highest style (something schoolmasters had been doing for centuries); and in the *Commedia* generally, he uses Ovid more often than any other Latin poet except Virgil.[90] His best-known comment on the importance of recognizing the hidden meaning in poetry occurs in the discussion of the allegory of poets and theologians in the *Convivio.* His ideas are entirely conventional; we have seen them before and will see them again many times. He

90. *Inf.* IV, 90; *De Vulg. Eloq.* II, 6. My assertion about Dante's use of Ovid is based upon the study of Edward Moore, *Studies in Dante, First Series: Scriptural and Classical Authors (New York, 1896).*

speaks of four senses—literal, allegorical, moral, and anagogical—and illustrates the allegorical sense with reference to Ovid:

> L'altro si chiama allegorico, e questo è quello che si nasconde sotto 'l manto di queste favole, ed è una veritade ascosa sotto bella menzogna: sì come quando dice Ovidio che Orfeo facea con la cetera mansuete le fiere, e li arbori e le pietre a sè muovere; che vuol dire che lo savio uomo con lo strumento de la sua voce fa[r]ia mansuescere e umiliare li crudeli cuori, e fa[r]ia muovere a la sua volontade coloro che non hanno vita di scienza e d'arte: e coloro che non hanno vita ragionevole alcuna sono quasi come pietre.[91]

Dante himself employs the art of concealing allegorical meaning in poetry (to Can Grande, he writes of the *Commedia,* "subiectum est homo"—the subject is man), and he expresses scorn for poets whose meaning is too easily accessible:

> E acciò che non ne pigli alcuna baldanza persona grossa, dico che né li poete parlavano così sanza ragione, né quelli che rimano deono parlare così non avendo alcuno ragionamento in loro de quello che dicono: però che grande vergogna sarebbe a colui che rimasse cose sotto vesta di figura o di colore rettorico, e poscia, domandato, non sapesse denudare le sue parole de cotale vesta, in guisa che avessero verace intendimento. E questo mio primo amico e io ne sapemo bene di quelli che così rimano stoltamente.[92]

The case of Dante is instructive, because like Boccaccio he is both a literary theorist and a poet. In his theoretical works, explications of classical poetry *per integumentum* are very plentiful, even when straightforward argumentation might have served as well. In addition to the above examples, he allegorizes the myths of Hercules and Antaeus in the third book of the *Convivio,* Polynices and Tydeus, Dido and Aeneas, and Aeacus in the fourth, and Hera in the *De Monarchia,* to take a few instances at random.[93] In his poetry,

91. *Conv.* II, 1, ed. G. Busnelli and G. Vandelli (Florence, 1968).
92. *Vita Nuova* XXV, ed. Alfonso Bernardinelli, *Dante Alighieri:* Vita Nuova (Milan, 1977), 50.
93. *Conv.* III, 3, and IV, 25, 26, and 27, and *De Mon.* II, ix.

in accordance with his stated understanding of the allegorical nature of learned fiction, he uses the myths in subtler ways. Sometimes the need for a gloss is very obvious, as in the case of the Siren of the *Purgatorio* or the Furies of *Inferno* IX, where Dante gives the reader a verbal poke in the ribs: "O voi ch'avete li 'ntelletti sani, / mirate la dottrina che s'asconde / sotto 'l velame de li versi strani"[94] (The Furies, as we have seen in Isidore, conventionally stood for certain destructive passions of men, in this case the emotions of Dante the pilgrim which threaten to impede his progress toward salvation.)[95] At other times, Dante's use of mythology approaches simile, as when he compares corrupt cardinals to Phaeton in a letter or himself to Phaeton in the *Paradiso*.[96] He does not appear to admit the possibility that mythology might serve as meaningless ornament; his reverence for the wisdom of the *auctores* is dramatically illustrated by his etymology of *auctor* in the fourth book of the *Convivio* (IV, 6, 1–6). We will see presently the importance of the conventional meanings of certain myths for our understanding of the *Commedia*.

Petrarch and his disciple Boccaccio are both said to have had "conversions" late in life which changed their attitudes toward mythology and the Roman poets, and it is true that Petrarch, in the *Vita Solitaria,* called Ovid "lascivus."[97] (He also declared that the ancient gods were demons, to the astonishment of de Nolhac, who calls the utterance "singulière."[98] It was, of course, a patristic commonplace.) As we have seen, none of this is inconsistent with the belief that moral instruction lies concealed within the myths, and Petrarch's own belief is well documented. He used the mythographic manual of Fulgentius, and in his discussion of the usefulness of poetry in the *Coronation Oration,* he wrote:

94. *Inf.* IX, 61–63, ed. John D. Sinclair, *The Divine Comedy of Dante Alighieri* (New York, 1939).

95. On the meaning of the Furies in the *Inferno,* see L. Jenaro-MacLennan, *The Trecento Commentaries on the* Divina Commedia *and the* Epistle to Cangrande (Oxford, 1966).

96. *Ep.* VIII, 4, and *Par.* XVII, 1–3.

97. G. Martellotti et al., eds., *Francesco Petrarca: Prose* (Milan, 1955), 532: "Ille (i.e., Ovid) michi quidem magni vir ingenii videtur, sed lascivi et lubrici et prorsus mulierosi animi fuisse, quem conventus feminei delectarent usque adeo, ut in illis felicitatis sue apicem summamque reponeret."

98. Pierre de Nolhac, "Les Scholies Inédites de Pétrarque sur Homère," *RPLHA* 11 (1887): 97–118, p. 110; on the gods as demons, see Demats, *Fabula* 40–45.

> I could readily prove to you that poets under the veil of fictions have set forth truths physical, moral, and historical. . . . Poetry, furthermore, is all the sweeter since a truth that must be sought out with some care gives all the more delight when it is discovered.[99]

(This esthetic of difficulty, a natural concomitant of belief in the fictive *integumentum,* was a commonplace, variously expressed over the centuries; a well-known expression of it occurs in the prologue to the *Anticlaudianus.*)[100] In addition, Petrarch wrote a famous letter to Aretino on the moral truths in the *Aeneid,* and in a letter to his brother he argued in the same vein as Mussato: "Poetry is in no sense opposed to theology. I might almost say that theology is a poetry which proceeds from God. . . . What are the Saviour's parables but allegories?"[101] His works are full of references to the myths and commentaries on them, sometimes tediously long ones. The *Secretum* contains glosses on Aeolus and the cave of the winds (which represent "anger and the other passions of the soul which seethe at the bottom of our heart"), the *bivium* passage of the *Aeneid* (the choice between the path of virtue and that of vice), Dido (the passion of lust), Orpheus and Eurydice (reason and the erring soul), and still more.[102] In the prologue to the *De Viris Illustribus,* he refers to the well-known allegory of the judgment of Paris as the choice among the three ways of life—contemplative, active, and voluptuary. But often, like other poets of his time, he does not tell us what he is about or that he is necessarily about anything in particular when he alludes to pagan mythology. He does not gloss mythological allusions in his *rime sparse* or other lyrics, where they are nevertheless very plentiful; we will reflect in later chapters upon the impli-

99. E. H. Wilkins, "Petrarch's Coronation Oration," *PMLA* 68 (1953): 1241–50, p. 1246.

100. R. Bossuat, ed., *Alain de Lille* Anticlaudianus (Paris, 1955), 56: "In hoc etenim opere litteralis sensus suauitas puerilem demulcebit auditum, moralis instructio proficientem imbuet sensum, acutior allegorie subtilitas perficientem acuet intellectum. Ab huius igitur operis arceantur ingressu qui, solam sensualitas insequentes imaginem, rationis non appetunt ueritatem. . . ."

101. Fam. X, 4, quoted by Ernst R. Curtius, *European Literature in the Latin Middle Ages,* trans. Willard Trask (Princeton, 1953), 226.

102. In Bks. II and III. See Martellotti et al., *Prose* 124, 150, 152, 172. The brief translation is that of William H. Draper, *Petrarch's Secret, or the Soul's Conflict with Passion* (London, 1911), 101.

cations of this fact for the interpretation of his lyric poetry and that of his contemporaries.

It should be unnecessary to establish the commitment of Petrarch's disciple Boccaccio to the revelation of the meaning hidden in the pagan myths, for he is himself the greatest mythographer of his age. His *De Genealogia Deorum* enjoyed enormous circulation and respect well into the Renaissance, when it was used by Spenser and Milton.[103] Boccaccio himself was greatly committed to it; it was his ambition to be remembered as a classical scholar, not as a popular poet. In the *De Genealogia* he assembles the wisdom of the Third Vatican Mythographer, Fulgentius, Alberic, Lactantius, Theodontius (who remains mysterious), Apuleius, Servius, Macrobius, Martianus Capella, the encyclopedists, the Fathers, and even Leonzio Pilato's notes on Homer. In the preface to this work, which takes the form of a dialogue between himself and a messenger of King Hugo IV, Boccaccio refers to his sovereign's request that he write the book:

> Addebas preterea, ut explicarem, quid sub ridiculo cortice fabularum abscondissent prudentes viri, quasi rex inclitus arbitretur stolidum credere, homines fere omni dogmate eruditos simpliciter circa describendas fabulas nulli veritati consonas nec preter licteralem sensum habentes trivisse tempus et impendisse sudores![104]

Boccaccio, of course, agrees with his king that learned men would not waste time telling stories that have only a literal meaning. In his account of bucolic poetry, he uses poetic allegory as a critical standard. As Rand summarizes his discussion, "There was first . . . Theocritus, who hid nothing under the rind of his verse; then there was Virgil, who hid much there; then came a string of ignoble and unmentioned writers, from whom the Pastoral Muse was happily delivered by his glorious Master, Franciscus Petrarca."[105] The fourteenth and fifteenth books of the *De Genealogia* are given over to a defense of poetry and an explanation of poetic theory; in the four-

103. On the longevity and influence of the *De Genealogia,* see the introduction of Charles G. Osgood, *Boccaccio on Poetry* (Princeton, 1930).

104. Vincenzo Romano, ed. *Genealogie Deorum Gentilium Libri,* 2 vols. (Bari, 1951), 1:4.

105. *Founders* 3.

teenth, Boccaccio describes the conversion experience of King Robert of Sicily, who thought the poets mere versifiers until he heard Petrarch discourse on the meaning hidden in the poetry of Virgil. Then ". . . he was struck with amazement, and saw and rejected his own error. . . . With wonderfully keen regret he began upbraiding his own judgment and his misfortune in recognizing so late the true art of poetry."[106] The extraordinary meaning which so amazed Robert (in which the adventures of Aeneas were made to correspond to stages in the moral development of man) was the same first set down—though probably not originated—in the sixth century by Fulgentius, then repeated and elaborated by Bernardus Silvestris in the twelfth century and Cristoforo Landino in the fifteenth.

Boccaccio's own use of mythology is sometimes abundantly glossed, as in the *Teseida,* for which he preferred to compose his own commentary rather than leave the matter to chance; in some of his works, though, his meaning in mythical allusions remains a matter of conjecture, as it has in the *Filocolo* and in the *Amorosa Visione.* I shall soon have occasion to discuss the interesting problems presented by the interpretation of mythology in Boccaccio's minor works; suffice it to mention here that in most of them he occasionally includes commentary on the myths he uses, much as Petrarch does. In the *De Mulieribus Claris,* several of the mythological tales function as *exempla:* the tale of Niobe against pride, that of Medea against "youthful wantonness and . . . corroding vices," that of Arachne against vanity.[107] In the *De Casibus* there are a variety of traditional glosses: we are told that the tale of Saturn consuming his children refers, "under the surface of the rough covering," to the fact that the passage of time consumes and destroys everything; that Danae, Phyllis, Scylla, and Iole (among others) illustrate the greed, choler, unfaithfulness and frivolousness of women; and, of course, that the failure of the Sirens to detain Ulysses refers to his resistance to worldly temptation.[108] Boccaccio's Fiammetta loves to derive moralities from the myths; in the *demandes d'amour* in the fourth book of the *Filocolo* she debates with her interlocutors entirely in terms of the wisdom or unwisdom of mythological figures:

106. *De Gen.* XIV, 22, trans. Osgood, *Boccaccio* 98.

107. *De Mul. Clar.* XVI, XVII, XVIII. The moralization of Medea is from XVI, 12; the translation is that of Guido A. Guarino, *Concerning Famous Women* (New Brunswick, N.J., 1963).

108. *De Cas.* I, 5 and 18; the translation is that of Louis Brewer Hall, *Giovanni Boccaccio:* The Fates of Illustrious Men (New York, 1965).

Byblis, Phaedra, Medea, Venus, Paris, Iole, a whole classical encyclopedia. In the work that bears her name, she moralizes her own plight (having loved passionately, she has been abandoned) by reference to their stories.[109]

It is natural enough to find such moralizations in a discursive work such as the *Fiammetta,* and natural enough not to find them very often in the lyrics of Machaut. He, however, along with Deschamps and Christine de Pisan, is likely to have used only the *Ovide Moralisé* as the source of his many mythological allusions. As de Boer taught us more than half a century ago, he probably did not use Ovid at all.[110] The *Ovide Moralisé,* a ponderous mythographic treatise, contains perhaps one-fifth narration to four-fifths commentary. A poet impatient with allegories would, at least, soon tire of reading such a work. When Machaut compares himself as a lover to Tantalus or Narcissus, or his lady to the image made by Pygmalion, or when he says that her *dangier* is as unvanquishable as the serpent Python, one recognizes the familiar terrain of the "enfer d'amour"; but the poet leaves it to his reader to assess this narrative voice. There is no ambiguity, however, in the case of the Furies, to whom in the *Confort d'Ami* he assigns the moral values of "orgueil, envie, tricherie," or when he moralizes Orpheus's looking back upon Eurydice as prompted by vain love.[111] The poem's conclusion therefore comes as no surprise: the reader is advised to reject vain love in order to "servir Dieu devotement."

The same conventions are observed by the other French poets of the fourteenth century. Deschamps, who also derived his mythological allusions solely or mainly from the *Ovide Moralisé,* writes swooningly of love in dozens of ballads and lays; he is especially fond of the idea of death for love and the list of love's martyrs from the *Heroides,* which he repeats again and again. He is threatened with death from a variety of sources: his lady's frown might be the end of him, or the necessity to part, or his long love-service without reward. His narrative voice changes, however, in the discursive *Miroir de Mariage,* in which he writes that the wisdom of the ancient

109. See Carlo Salinari and Natalino Sapegno, eds., *Elegia di Madonna Fiammetta,* in Vittore Branca, ed., *Tutte le Opere di Giovanni Boccaccio,* vol. 5 (Turin, 1976), 143–56 and passim.

110. Cornelius deBoer, *Ovide Moralisé: Poème du Commencement du Quatorzième Siècle,* 4 vols. (Wiesbaden, 1931), 1:28–43.

111. *Confort* 2299–2300, 2763–72, ed. Ernest Hoepffner, *Oeuvres de Guillaume de Machaut,* 3 vols. (Paris, 1921), vol. 3.

auctores (Juvenal, Catullus, Virgil, Ovid) is the only protection against foolish love:

> Car les exemples anciens
> Nous sont et cordes et liens
> De nous garder des grans perilz,
> Que nous trouvons par leurs escrips
> Et que nous veons clerement,
> Qui nous puelent mettre a tourment
> Du corps et de l'ame en la fin.[112]

Rare is the medieval poet who is not capable of such radical changes in tone. Modern critics have often tried to locate the genuine convictions of the poet by choosing one or another of the two voices; if you think the lover is the real Deschamps, you're "Romantic," if the preacher, you're an "historical" critic. In fact, the poet is writing in neither case in the confessional mode, but to a set of poetic conventions that, at bottom, dramatize a universal psychological conflict. The effete, mannered voice of the lover is one we no longer recognize, but it embodied the conventions governing the expression of the irrational, passionate, and impulsive side of human nature (a side which, fascinated by its potential for danger, medieval poets never tired of exploring). The rational voice is the one of which the poet, and everyone else, approves, but it is able only with great effort to achieve even temporary control over the passions. Medieval poetry is most often concerned with the struggle between these two forces within each human being, which characteristically it externalizes and compartmentalizes in the form of a psychomachia, with first one side speaking and then the other. What modern critics have not often understood is that both sides need not speak in every poem.

This point is important, as we will see, for our understanding of the uses made of mythography and mythographic techniques in medieval poetry. The truly traditional glosses can help to define context. I shall later demonstrate that there is not much doubt that a poetic voice that cites with sympathy or approval the Ovidian heroines Medea, Myrrha, Oenone, Hypsipyle, or certain others from the *Heroides* and *Metamorphoses* is the voice of the irrational,

112. *Miroir* 5565–71, ed. Gaston Raynaud and le Marquis Queux de St.-Hilaire, *Oeuvres Complètes de Eustache Deschamps,* 11 vols. (Paris, 1894), vol. 9.

impulsive lover. It should be obvious that, once one has determined that, simple dismissal or disapproval of the speaker are not appropriate responses. Writers of the Middle Ages had more respect for the passional and impulsive forces in human nature than we do; at least, they were more interested in analyzing them and fundamentally less sanguine about the possibility of "integrating" them successfully. The medieval psychomachia is not a sports contest in which one team or the other wins, but an ongoing drama in which rational and irrational impulses dominate in alternation.

This use of mythology as a characterizing device is one reason it is not often glossed in lyrics, though it is very often present. Thus in the lays and chansons of the fourteenth-century French poets the myths appear without a gloss, whereas the discursive *Trésor Amoureux* contains this passage in which "Congnoissance" responds to an argument of "Amours" by explaining her use of the myth of Io and Argus:

> . . . maintenant la verité
> Lui diray par moralité.
> Par Yo nous povons entendre
> La creature qui veult tendre
> A tous ses delis accomplir.
> Juno, pour ce fait raemplir,
> Doit estre en ce cas comparée
> A la voulenté separée
> De Raison, ma seur, et de moy;
> Et lors est elle sans esmoy
> Vache, et Argus la doit garder:
> C'est le monde, qui regarder
> La puet de cent yeulz, tout le temps
> Que ce fait li est delitans. . . .[113]

The gloss continues at some length: Jupiter, "qui Dieu signifie," sends his son Mercury ("le Saint Esprit"), who rescues the erring soul from the delights of the world and gives her into the governance of Reason. The poet of the *Trésor* (a contemporary of Froissart) clearly knows and respects the *Ovide Moralisé,* and shares the perspective of his contemporaries on the myths. If the lyrics of these

113. *Trésor* 2793–2806, ed. Auguste Scheler, *Oeuvres de Jean Froissart,* 3 vols. Brussels, 1867–77, vol. 3.

poets alone had survived, would we assume they drew only from the "text" of Ovid, if indeed that formulation has much meaning in the Middle Ages?

Not only the Italians and French, but also the English recognized the value of the myths as exempla. That is the whole method of Gower in the *Confessio Amantis*. Gower's method is complex, because of his need to make the moralizations credible as proceeding from Genius, the priest of Venus. They are not very often traditional, and sometimes they are so obtuse as to be wryly amusing, as when Genius uses the tragic passion of Pyramus and Thisbe to warn against "folehaste." (Pyramus should have waited a bit before concluding that Thisbe was dead [III, 1497–1501].) Obviously he knows the traditional moralizations of all or most of the well-known myths he uses; in fact, he glosses the Sirens as the temptations of the world, though he subtly alters the gloss to suit the character of Genius (I, 530–48). He does not discourse upon his method, probably because it is not really the wisdom of the ancients that Genius is offering, but a parody of it from the standpoint of one committed to Venerean love-service. Gower's *balades* contain mythological references which, in customary fashion, he does not explain; his *Traitié*, a treatise against love-service, uses the myths (mainly those of the *Heroides*) in conventional ways, as I shall later demonstrate, as does the *Vox Clamantis* (in which Gower cites the traditional gloss on metamorphosis as referring to the loss of reason in man [I, 10]). The essential medieval attitude toward the myths has not changed by the time of Lydgate, whose *Assemble of Goddes* is called by Purdon "the first attempt in English to present the gods in a reference list and to describe their attributes iconographically."[114] Ultimately, he allegorizes the gods as vices. In the *Temple of Glas* he presents the Ovidian heroes and heroines in a love-vision without comment, but he also translates the *De Casibus* of Boccaccio, in which they are moralized.

This brief survey of exegesis of the classical myths in medieval literary works has, I hope, established two facts: that medieval writers believed that the myths contained hidden meanings and that they most often interpreted them as allegories of the Christian moral life. In classical literature there is little or no connection between the myths of Proteus, Odysseus and the Sirens, Circe, the

114. Noel Purdon, *The Words of Mercury: Shakespeare and the English Mythography of the Renaissance* (Salzburg, 1974), 32.

infernal sufferers, the judgment of Paris, and the metamorphoses of Ovid—the myths we have encountered repeatedly in this chapter as they are reinterpreted and transmitted by medieval writers of all kinds. Throughout the Middle Ages, however, they are seen as related; modern critics are puzzled to find them occurring together in the love poems of Boccaccio, Machaut, Froissart, and Chaucer. They are seen as related because for centuries, as I have tried to demonstrate in this preliminary survey, they were wrested from their classical contexts and reinterpreted as allegories of the struggle between reason and the passions. They appear in the love poems of the high Middle Ages because that struggle forms the intellectual basis of those poems. I have still to deal with the group of myths that is most prominent in those poems, the lovers of Ovid's *Heroides* and *Metamorphoses;* although they are scarce in the earliest Christian literature, they too were later interpreted (as we have seen from time to time in passing) as *exempla* of successful or unsuccessful government of the passions.

Recognition of this fact is, I think, essential to intelligent reading of medieval poetry; although Ovid might have laughed at the notion that the transformations of Proteus symbolize the deformation of character by vice, it is important to our understanding of literature that learned men took such notions seriously for more than a thousand years. Today, many scholars object to applying the traditional glosses on the myths to the interpretation of serious medieval literature because they find the glosses themselves offensive as criticism. From a modern perspective, it is indeed difficult to acknowledge that poets of the stature of Jean de Meun, Boccaccio, or Chaucer might possibly have taken seriously the medieval moralizations of the classics. We are forced, however, to begin by admitting (1) that the most influential writers of the Middle Ages made use of the moralizations of mythology, and (2) that medieval mythographers, who devoted themselves to compiling entire volumes of such commentary, were among the keenest and most respected thinkers and writers of their day. Furthermore, among medieval literary figures at large, there seems to be no inverse relationship between the degree of a writer's distinction and the frequency of his use of mythographic commentary. The difficulty for readers today is that, as Theodore Silverstein has objected, the old moralizations "often [seek] to transform to something 'significant' a poetic *littera* already more profound than anything the interpreter can construct."[115]

115. "Allegory and Literary Form," *PMLA* 82 (1966): 28–32, p. 32.

That clearly was not the attitude of medieval writers (I can generalize because we have looked, at least briefly, at a fair number of them). What accounts for such a profound cultural difference? If they did not find the Sirens more useful and beautiful in Homer or Ovid than in Fulgentius, then why not? I suspect that the answer is that, for them, poetry "ethice supponitur"; one of its essential functions was instruction in morality. Everyone agreed that "solas" ought to accompany "sentence"; the powerful images that for us embody the very essence of poetry—Homer's gods dangling by a golden chain, or in Ovid a grieving mother, turned to stone by unutterable sorrow—must have been similarly pleasing to readers of the Middle Ages. But, as we have seen, the beauty of poetic images was conceived as a kind of husk, which even the most ignorant reader might gnaw with some enjoyment; the task of the intelligent reader was to extract the kernel of moral instruction within. The statements about the nature of classical fiction that we have seen abundantly illustrate the fact that the whole enterprise of literary criticism was envisioned differently in the Middle Ages. We will shortly have occasion to examine moralizations of the classical tales of love that are, in our terms at least, almost unbelievably unresponsive to every significant element of the tales they address. They ignore the requirements of narrative, change victims into villains, and outrage our sense of literary propriety—sometimes even our sense of common justice—by discovering virtue or vice in what seem to us precisely the wrong places. These glosses were nevertheless regarded during the Middle Ages as expressing important truths about the moral life of man that the classical *auctores* had deliberately concealed beneath the poetic integument. I have tried to demonstrate that such moralizations were used and transmitted, not only by the encyclopedic mythographers, but by many medieval writers of all kinds.

Certainly that is not to say that the mythographic manuals did not help to establish and perpetuate these literary traditions. The influence of the commentaries most often used in the schools—those of Fulgentius, Arnulf, and John of Garland—was great; in any case, their interpretations are often the same as the traditional moralities which the poets would have encountered as well in works of every genre: histories, poems, encyclopedias, florilegia, commentaries on Scripture. Men of letters would also have found marginal glosses, often very copious, throughout the manuscripts of Ovid and Virgil. Well-read men, such as the court poets were, would have known the commonest of the traditional moralizations—those that were repeated in one work after another in more or less the same form—almost reflexively. A poet who knows hows to use the moralities on the myths, then, need not necessarily have consulted the encyclopedic mythographers. I suspect that we often invoke Fulgentius, or the Third Vatican Mythographer, or Bersuire, to explain a poetic allusion that in fact has its immediate source in the historians, the encyclopedists, the Fathers, or another poet. I suspect also that we often invoke the mythographers to explain poetic allusions—like Chaucer's allusion to Marsyas—that have no really traditional interpretation *per integumentum* outside the narrow tradition of the mythographic manuals. Some myths and groups of myths, however, do have a well-established literary tradition of interpretation that can give us valuable insight into the intentions of poets who allude to them.

Such, I believe, is the case of a particular group of Ovidian lovers of the *Heroides* and *Metamorphoses*. It is this group of myths, some of which we have already encountered in early medieval writings, that appears again and again in the love-narratives of Boccaccio, Machaut, and Froissart. Like the myths of Ulysses and the Sirens, Circe, Proteus, the Furies, and the infernal sufferers, these myths of love—which are sometimes given imaginative and divergent interpretations by the encyclopedic mythographers—are interpreted quite simply and consistently within the general literary culture. The myths of love combine with those other well-known myths to form a body of mythological lore whose general outlines and conventional interpretations were evidently familiar to all of the educated writers of the High Middle Ages. This rather small body of "classical" knowledge—variously told and retold, interpreted and misinterpreted by assorted fictional speakers—takes up a great deal of space in the French and Italian love-narratives that are the sources of Chaucer's early poetry. In the forthcoming chapters, I shall try to show that this material is not "digressive," but most significant.

2

Classical Lovers and Christian Morality

The lovers of Ovid's *Heroides* and *Metamorphoses* are ubiquitous in the literature of the Middle Ages. In the late nineteenth century the grammarian Léopold Sudre accurately remarked, "Ubicunque carminum de amore disseritur, assidue recurrunt Pyrami, Narcissi, Jasonis, Cauni, Orphei, Thisbes, Echus, Medeae, Byblidos et Eurydices nomina."[1] There are others whose names occur almost as often: Phyllis, Myrrha, Ariadne, Dido, Scylla, Hero, Dejanira, Phaedra, Hypsipyle, Lucretia, Oenone, Pasiphae, Philomela. Often, too, they are joined by the mortals beloved of the gods—Daphne, Io, Europa, Danae, Adonis. These are the mythological figures wronged or disappointed in love, who in classical times served to embellish epithalamia and lovers' plaints. In patristic times, as we have seen in passing, the rhetorical emphasis changed; the classical gods became demons, and the classical heroines *meretrici*. Although these mythological figures have a long and continu-

1. *Publii Ovidii Nasonis Metamorphoseon Libros Quomodo Nostrates Medii Aevi Imitati Interpretatique Sint* (Paris, 1893), 21.

ous history, it is the French, Italian, and English poets of the High Middle Ages—Jean de Meun, Boccaccio, Petrarch, Machaut, Froissart, Chaucer—who allude to them most insistently, often even adding such allusions when their sources do not contain them. If they indeed believed that the tales of the *auctores* concealed moral instruction, what instruction do they find in the tales of the Ovidian lovers? Does allusion to them contribute anything to the meaning of their love poems, or is it mere classical window dressing? Editors have generally confined themselves to a brief note on the Ovidian story, when they have supposed it to be unknown to the general reader; critics have usually either compared the circumstances of the Ovidian heroine to those of the narrator or subject of the poem, or sought insight in mythographic commentaries probably known to the poet. None of these approaches is entirely satisfactory, as the poet may have known, or recalled, neither the Ovidian text nor the commentary. In any case, in making use of the allusion he has taken it out of the Ovidian or mythographic context and placed it into the context of a medieval love poem, within which we must try to understand it. In most instances, medieval writers do not interpret for us their allusions to the Ovidian lovers; but in some instances, they do. It may be well, then, to begin by trying to characterize the ways in which writers think of the classical heroes and heroines of love, and the uses to which they put them, on those occasions when they are obviously more than window dressing.

In both classical and medieval times, the heroes and heroines appear in poetry as members of Cupid's train, enslaved to love and at the mercy of its vicissitudes. The way in which poets regarded their situation, of course, depended upon their own perspective within each individual poem and upon the perspective of the age in which they wrote. In late classical poetry, the lovers of Cupid's train are often presented as tragic figures of great dignity, bowed down under the force of irresistible passions visited upon them by vengeful or capricious deities. As Christianity gains strength, this attitude changes completely; if carnal love is viewed as a defect of the will, there can of course be nothing heroic about the lovers. First to be attacked are the lovers of the gods, who are naturally criticized in the harshest terms by Christian apologists seeking to discredit the pagan pantheon. From the time of Justin Martyr, the human lovers of the gods are viewed as slaves of passion, subjugated by demons believed to be gods.[2] Athenagoras uses the scandalous love

2. See Justin, *Apol.* II, 5.

affairs ascribed to the gods to demonstrate that they were merely men, who became demons after death.[3] Clement of Alexandria rails against the "licentiousness" and "lewd delights" of the gods: ". . . if you but let him catch a glimpse of a woman's girdle, even Zeus is exposed and his locks are put to shame."[4] Minucius Felix feared that the loves of the gods might corrupt boys who read of them; Tertullian calls Homer the "dedecorator deorum," he who by his stories of their passions and crimes has stripped away the divinity of the gods.[5] Theophilus of Antioch, Eusebius of Caesarea, Lactantius, and Arnobius all recount the love affairs of the gods, with the implication that a mere recital of the myths ought to make their pagan readers ashamed.[6] Adultery, pederasty, and "unions contrary to the laws of nature and of society" furnish the Fathers with an unfailing source of material "contra paganos." Even Jerome, more liberal than the early Fathers in his attitude toward pagan literature, sees nothing redeeming in the love affairs of the gods. In his commentary on the book of Jonah, he addresses the probability of a man's surviving three days and three nights inside the belly of a whale, and concludes that it is intrinsically no less probable than the story of Daniel in the lion's den, or of the parting of the Red Sea—and a good deal more worthy of belief than the tales told of the pagans:

> Sin autem infideles erunt, legant quindecim libros Nasonis Metamorphoseos, et omnen Graecam, Latinamque historiam, ibique cernunt vel Daphnen in laurum, vel Phaetontis sorores in populos arbores fuisse conversas: quomodo Jupiter eorum sublimissimus deus, sit mutatus in cygnum, in auro fluxerit, in tauro rapuerit, et caetera, in quibus ipsa turpitudo fabularum, divinitatis denegat sanctitatem. (II, 2; *PL* 25, 1132B)

Augustine recalls the youth described by Terence who was incited to lust by a wall fresco depicting the ravishment of Danae: ". . . by imitating the gods—not, to be sure, true gods, but false and fabri-

3. *Legatio pro Christianis* XXI–XXX.

4. *Cohortatio ad Graecos* II, 28, trans. G. W. Butterworth, *Clement of Alexandria* (Cambridge, Mass., 1939), 66–67.

5. *Octavius* XXIII, 8, and Tertullian, *Apol.* 14, 4 (*PL* 1, 406A).

6. Theophilus *Ad Autolycum* I, 9; Eusebius *De Praep. Evang.* VII–VIII; Lactantius *Div. Inst.* I, 10; Arnobius *Contra Paganos* IV, 26.

cated gods—the most depraved of men become still worse."[7] With respect to the loves of the gods, he rejects allegory:

> At enim illa omnia quae antiquitus de vita deorum moribusque conscripta sunt, longe aliter sunt intellegenda atque interpretanda sapientibus. Ita vero in templis populis congregatis recitari huiusce modi salubres interpretationes heri et nudiustertius audivimus. Quaeso te, sicine caecum est humanum genus adversus veritatem, ut tam aperta et manifesta non sentiat? Tot locis pingitur, funditur, tunditur, sculpitur, scribitur, legitur, agitur, cantatur, saltatur Iuppiter adulteria tanta committens; quantum erat, ut in suo saltem Capitolio ista prohibens legeretur?[8]

This tradition continues into the early Middle Ages. Macrobius believes the myths of the gods' adulteries to be unworthy of the attention of a philosopher, John of Damascus concludes from them "neminem eorum deum esse," and Rabanus Maurus—who believes with most others of his time that the gods were men—nevertheless reproaches their unseemly behavior.[9] Later writers naturally show less interest in mounting full-scale attacks on the sins of the gods, but Danae, Leda, Io, and others become bywords for immorality in the works of Hildebert, Marbod, Petrus Pictor, and the preacher Amarcius.[10] John of Salisbury repeats Augustine's tale of the man tempted by the fresco of Danae, and condemns Adonis both for his hunting and for his lechery.[11] Alanus, in his *persona* as narrator of the *De Planctu Naturae,* is much troubled by the tales of Olympian *amours,* and even dares to question Nature's fairness:

> Miror cur poetarum commenta retractans, solummodo in humani generis pestes predictarum inuectionum armas aculeos, cum et eodem exorbitationis pede deos claudicasse legamus. Iupiter enim, adolescentem Frigium transferens ad superna, relatiuam Venerem transtulit in translatum. . . .

7. *Ep.* XCI 4; James Houston Baxter, ed. and trans., *Saint Augustine: Select Letters* (London, 1930), 157, 159.

8. *Ep.* XCI, 5 (Baxter, *Augustine* 158).

9. See p. 31; John, *Vita Sanct. Barlaam Erem.* XXVII (*PL* 73, 553B); Rabanus *De Univ.* XV, 6 (*PL* 111, 426ff.).

10. See pp. 61–64.

11. *Policrat.* VII, 9, 656a, and I, 4, 391a.

> Bachus etiam et Apollo, paterne coheredes lasciuie, non diuine uirtutis imperio sed supersticiose Veneris prestigio, uerterunt in feminas pueros inuertendo.[12]

Nature, annoyed at the ignorance of this "homunculus," launches into an oration on *integumentum,* then seems to make an exception of the loves of the gods, protesting that the poets were merely lying:

> Sed tamen, cum a poetis deorum pluralitas sompniatur uel ipsi dii Venereis ferulis manus subduxisse dicuntur, in hiis falsitatis umbra lucescit. . . . narratio uero illa, que uel deos esse uel ipsos in Veneris gignasiis lasciuisse mentitur, in nimie falsitatis uesperascit occasum. . . .[13]

Walter Map, in the *Dissuasio Valerii,* is unable to dismiss the matter so easily. For him, the shameful conduct of the gods as lovers serves as another instance of the baneful power of woman:

> Iupiter, rex terrenus, qui eciam dictus est celorum rex pre singulari strenuitate corporis et incomparabili mentis elegancia, post Europam mugire coactus est. Amice, ecce quem bonitas super celos extulit, femina brutis comparauit. . . . Phebus, qui sapiencie radiis tocius orbis primiciauit ambitum, ut merito solis nomine solus illustraretur, infatuatus est amore Leucotoes, sibi ad ignominiam et illi ad interitum. . . .[14]

The most spectacular love affair of the gods is of course that of Mars with Venus, in which the lovers are captured *in flagrante* and held by the cleverly contrived net of Vulcan, the wronged husband. First told by Homer, the tale is repeated in the *Metamorphoses,* and again in the *Ars Amatoria* as a comical *exemplum.* There is no use, says Ovid, keeping an eye on your girlfriend; if you once catch her cheating, she'll only do worse in the future. Everyone knows what happened to Vulcan, who became the laughingstock of the gods when he trapped Mars and Venus in his net. Later he cursed himself

12. Pr. IV, 115–22, ed. Nikolaus Häring, *De Planctu Naturae* (Spoleto, 1978).
13. Pr. IV, 139–41, 151–53, ed. Häring.
14. *De Nugis Cur.* IV, 3, ed. James 294.

many times for his stupidity! Truly, the only wise course is to let women behave as they will:

> hoc uetiti uos este: uetat deprensa Dione
> insidias illas, quas tulit ipsa, dare.
> nec uos rivali laqueos disponite nec uos
> excipite arcana uerba notata manu;
> ista uiri captent, si iam captanda putabunt,
> quos faciet iustos ignis et unda uiros.
> en iterum testor: nihil hic nisi lege remissum
> luditur; in nostris instita nulla iocis.[15]

Even pagans were uncomfortable with the myth; Plutarch, in the *Moralia* ("De Aud. Poet." 19), disapproves of the lovers and believes that Homer did, too, despite his concluding the tale with the laughter of the assembled gods. Early Christians, of course, utterly failed to appreciate the humor of the tale, and had recourse either to glosses based in "history" or physics or—more commonly—to outright indignation. Prudentius euhemerizes: ". . . the truth is that Venus was a woman of noble blood who cleaved to a low, common man in a forbidden deed of shame."[16] Martin of Bracara, who includes a passage on the gods-as-demons in the *De Correctione Rusticorum,* says of the affair:

> Alius etiam daemon Uenerem se esse confinxit, quae fuit mulier meretrix. Non solum cum innumerabilibus adulteris, sed etiam cum patre suo, Ioue, et cum fratre suo, Marte, meretricata est.[17]

In the eleventh century, Marbod moralizes the myth in the poem "De Fato et Genesi," and in the twelfth Abelard and Andreas Capellanus both use it as an *exemplum* of immorality, Abelard with reference to his own conduct. In the *Historia Calamitatum* he compares himself and Heloise to Mars and Venus:

15. II, 593–600, ed. E. J. Kenney, *P. Ovidii Nasonis* Amores, Medicamina Faciei Femineae, Ars Amatoria, Remedia Amoris (Oxford, 1982).

16. *Contra Orat. Symmachi* 172–73, trans. H. J. Thomson, *Prudentius,* 2 vols. (Cambridge, Mass., 1949), 1:362–63.

17. C. P. Caspari, ed., *Martin von Bracara's Schrift* De Correctione Rusticorum (Christiania, 1883), 9.

> Separatio autem haec corporum maxima erat copulatio animorum, et negata sui copia amplius amorem accendebat, et verecundiae transacta jam passio inverecundiores reddebat, tantoque verecundiae minor extiterat passio, quanto convenientior videbatur actio. Actum itaque in nobis est quod in Marte et Venere deprehensis poetica narrat fabula.[18]

Walter Map places Mars and Venus in final position in his sermon on the degradation of the gods by women in the *Dissuasio Valerii:*

> Mars, qui deus bellancium dici meruit triumphorum familiari frequencia, in quibus expedit maxime prompta strenuitas, nichil sibi metuens a Vulcano ligatus est cum Venere, inuisibilibus quidem cathenis, sensibilibus tamen; hoc autem ad applausum satirorum et derisum celestis curie. Amice, meditare saltem cathenas quas non uides et iam in parte sentis, et eripe te dum adhuc sunt ruptibiles . . . alligatus Veneri dolor fias et derisio uidencium, dum tibi applaudunt ceci.[19]

There is remarkable unanimity among the commentators, as well, on the interpretation of this and the other myths of the gods as lovers. Fanciful Christianizing equations are at a minimum, and simple moralization predominates among the mythographers just as it does among other writers of the Middle Ages. Every major medieval mythographer from Fulgentius to Christine de Pizan—that is, the Vatican Mythographers, Baudri, Arnulf, Giovanni del Virgilio, Bersuire, the *Ovide Moralisé,* and Walsingham—when dealing with the adultery of Mars and Venus, quotes some variant of Fulgentius's formulation, ". . . valor corrupted by lust is shamefully held in the fetterlike grip of its ardor."[20] Commentary on the other myths of the gods as lovers, though less ubiquitous, is similar; on the death of Adonis, the *Ovide Moralisé* comments, "Li pors l'ocist; ce fu l'ordure / De luxure et de lecherie, / Qu'il demena toute sa vie."[21] Giovanni del Virgilio, deploring Jupiter's fall from majesty to the status of a beast, writes of his courtship of Europa, "Maiesta-

18. *Ep.* I, ed. Victor Cousin, *Petrus Abaelardus Opera,* 2 vols. (Paris, 1849–59), 1:11–12.

19. *De Nugis Cur.* IV, 3, ed. James 294, 296.

20. *Myth.* II, 7, trans. Leslie George Whitbread, *Fulgentius the Mythographer* (Columbus, Ohio, 1971), 73.

21. *Ov. Mor.* X, 3733–35 (deBoer IV, 99).

tis honor, lascivo ductus amore, / Vilet, taurino subiciturque modo."[22]

In the literature of the early Middle Ages, the gods as lovers are understandably often treated separately from the other classical heroes and heroines, as part of the early Christian attempt to discredit the pagan religion. In the High Middle Ages, however, writers tend to conflate the two groups; to Jean de Meun, Boccaccio, Petrarch, and Chaucer, they are all simply the lovers of classical antiquity. We will shortly address later medieval treatments of the classical lovers (whose tales, by the twelfth century, writers had most often found in Ovid or a redaction of Ovid), but it is first necessary to establish—what is not surprising—that literary use and interpretation of the human lovers was, in the early Middle Ages, much the same as that of the divine. Even in classical times the lovers constituted a reliable resource for composers of misogynist tracts; Juvenal cites them as *exempla* in his Sixth Satire, and Propertius condemns them as oversexed.[23] In the *Deipnosophistae* of Athenaeus, a second-century cookbook, a chapter "concerning women" contains the following passage:

> Eubulus says in *Chrysilla:* 'To perdition go the wretch, whoever he was, who was the second man to marry a wife; the first man I will not blame. For he, I fancy, had had no experience of the evil, but the second must have learned what an evil a wife is.' And going on, he says: 'O most worshipful Zeus! Shall I then ever blame women? I swear, may I die if I do, she is the best of all our possessions. Even if Medea was an evil woman, yet Penelope, at least, was of great worth. Someone will say that Clytaemnestra was an evil woman; I match against her the good Alcestis. But perhaps one will blame Phaedra; surely there must have been *some* good woman;—yes, but who? Unlucky that I am, alas, the good women have given out all too quickly for me, while I still have many bad women to tell of.[24]

We may recognize in this a *topos* beloved to both the early and late Middle Ages, but of that more in time. The Fathers and the

22. *Allegorie* II, 14 (Ghisalberti 51).

23. Propertius Lib. III, #19.

24. *Deip.* XIII, 559, trans. Charles B. Gulick, *The Deipnosophists,* 7 vols. (Cambridge, Mass., 1950), 7:23.

early historians distinguished the classical lovers mainly by omission, sometimes conspicuous: Orosius sternly refuses to tell of Medea, but incidentally likens the soliders who sprang up from the dragon's teeth sown in the earth to the armies that rose up after the death of Caesar.[25] Gregory of Tours, like Augustine, scorns the sorrows of Dido.[26] Lucretia, Penelope and sometimes Alceste are praised in patristic and Carolingian literature: Julian the Apostate, Ausonius and his student Paulinus of Nola, and Odo of Cluny all mention them favorably, and Augustine's discussion in *The City of God* of the dilemma of Lucretia is well known.[27] In the eleventh and twelfth centuries, the heroines furnished *exempla* to a number of poets *de perversa muliere;* Hildebert, who begins promisingly, "Aufert, includit, fallit, nudat, dat, adurit, / Privat, monstrat, habet, exspoliat mulier," names Paris, David, Solomon, and Hippolytus as among the betrayed, and offers Danae as an example of corruption by gold; but he devotes a separate, laudatory poem to Lucretia.[28] Marbod, in his poem "De Meretrice," mentions Clytemnestra, Procne, and Leda, and—not wishing to omit any of the apt mythological commonplaces—likens women to Charybdis and the Sirens and adds that lust turns men to beasts as Circe transformed the companions of Ulysses.[29] Petrus Pictor in "De Mala Muliere" names Pasiphae, Phaedra, Byblis, Myrrha, and Scylla.[30] Bernard of Cluny, in his treatise on scorn of the world, includes Myrrha and Phaedra as villains and Hippolytus, Samson, and Solomon as victims in the section on the wickedness of women.[31]

John of Salisbury, in the *Policraticus,* clearly associates the classical heroines with various sorts of vice, especially the vice of lust; like all medieval commentators on the *Aeneid* he allegorizes Dido as lust and identifies Venus and Cupid with temptation to sin.[32] Bernardus Silvestris, in his commentary on the *Aeneid,* sees other classical heroines as *exempla,* as well: he associates Phaedra with

25. *Hist.* I, 12 and VI, 17.

26. In the preface to the *De Gloria Martyrum* (*PL* 71, 705–6).

27. Julian *Orat.* III, 104, 110, 112, 113; Ausonius *Ep.* XXXI, 192; Paulinus poem #10, 192; Odo of Cluny *Collationum* II, 11; Augustine *De Civ. Dei* I, 19.

28. *Carmina* CIX, XIV (*PL* 171, 1428A–1430A, 1447A).

29. See Walther Bulst, ed., *Liber Decem Capitulorum* (Heidelberg, 1947), 12–15.

30. See André Boutémy, "Quelques Oeuvres Inédites de Pierre le Peintre," *Latomus* 7 (1948): 51–69, pp. 61–64.

31. *De Cont. Mundi* III, 211–12, and II, 487–89.

32. *Policrat.* VIII, 6, and VIII, 11, 749c.

incest, Pasiphae with unnatural love, and Laodamia with obsessive love.[33] In Alanus, it is the classical lovers—Paris, Pyramus and Thisbe, Orpheus, Pasiphae, Helen, Myrrha, Medea, Narcissus, Byblis, Procne, Cleopatra—who are said to have rebelled against the rule of Nature by setting up immoderate sensual love in place of love of virtue. (Lucretia and Penelope, however, appear as part of the decoration on the garment of Chastity.)[34] Jean de Hauteville, whose goal in the *Architrenius* is to unite his wayward narrator in marriage with the virgin Moderantia, uses the lovers Pyramus and Thisbe, Myrrha, Byblis, and Iole in preaching against the temptations of lust.[35] Walter Map uses Myrrha, Scylla, Medea, Dejanira, and Paris in preaching against marriage, but he is not comforted by recalling the "good women": "Friend, there is no Lucretia, no Penelope, no Sabine left. Mistrust all."[36] Finally, an anonymous Venetian poet of the thirteenth century, in a poem said to be the oldest misogynist text in the Italian vernacular—the "Proverbia quae dicuntur super natura feminarum"—supports the proposition that "the more a man serves women, /The more I consider him foolish and crazy" by reference to Helen, Pasiphae, Dido, Medea, and Thisbe, among others.[37] We can be sure that this poet knows the *Heroides* of Ovid, which he mentions by name as a source of his poem.

Our best guide to twelfth- and thirteenth-century understanding of the old tales of love is the *accessus* tradition. Medieval *accessus* to the *Heroides* and *Metamorphoses* do not, of course, address all of the lovers, but the *Heroides* includes those most often mentioned in medieval European literature: Penelope/Ulysses, Phyllis/Demophoon, Phaedra/Hippolytus, Oenone/Paris, Hipsypyle/Jason, Dido/Aeneas, Dejanira/Hercules, Ariadne/Theseus, Canace/Macareus, Medea/Jason, Laodamia/Protesilaus, Hypermnestra/Lynceus, Helen/Paris, Hero/Leander. (Others included in the *Heroides*-Sappho/Phaon, Acontius/Cydippe, Hermione/Orestes—were often omitted from medieval manuscripts of Ovid and were thus less well known in the Middle Ages.) Glosses on the *Heroides* become common around the late twelfth century, at the time of their renewed

33. *Commentum* VI, 445–47.

34. *De Planctu* Pr. IV, 68–92; Mtr. V, 25–30 and passim.

35. *Architren.* IV, 255–71.

36. *De Nugis Cur.* IV, 3 (James 295).

37. See A. Tobler, ed., "Proverbia quae Dicuntur Super Natura Feminarum," *ZRP* 9 (1885): 287–331 (my translation).

popularity (I will not say of the renewed popularity of Ovid, for despite Traube's fixing the *Aetas Ovidiana* in the High Middle Ages, the popularity of the *Metamorphoses* seems never to have declined much). B. Nogara, Gustavus Przychocki, Heinrich Sedlmayer, R. B. C. Huygens, E. H. Alton, Ghisalberti, and others—including J. B. Allen in *The Ethical Poetic of the Later Middle Ages*—print *accessus* to the *Heroides* that show that, from at least the twelfth century to the time of Chaucer and beyond, the epistles were read as a guide to the proper conduct of love, a series of *exempla* offered for the instruction of Christian readers, who were to abhor the evil and imitate the good. I hope that the preceding discussion of medieval belief in the poetic *integumentum,* as well as the evidence we have seen of early medieval use and interpretation of the classical tales of love, effectively demolishes the argument sometimes advanced by scholars that medieval writers spoke of gathering moral profit from the myths only hypocritically, as a sop to the church. There is nothing in these *accessus,* or in other literary use and interpretation of the myths, to suggest a lack of earnestness; indeed, the earnestness of medieval poets and commentators is sometimes oppressive. They most often speak in terms that suggest their belief that they are describing the purpose in the mind of the classical author ("intentio est"), and that purpose is always instruction in morality.

Typical of glosses on the *Heroides* is a metrical one by a Goliardic poet, dated by Raby at about 1180:

> Actoris *[sic]* intentio restat condemnare
> Amores illicitos, fatuos culpare
> Et recte ferventium mentes condemnare [commendare]:
> Utilitas nostra sit iustum pignus amare.
> Nobis quis sit titulus, satis declaratur:
> Publius de publica fama nuncupatur
> Naso vel Ovidius satis declaratur,
> Si nasi species vel visere nomen agatur.
> Ethicae supponitur res libri praesentis
> Notetur intentio duplex: nam monentis
> Una manet, alia restat componentis
> Penelopes Naso commendat facta querentis.[38]

38. F. J. E. Raby, *A History of Secular Latin Poetry in the Middle Ages,* 2 vols. (Oxford, 1957), 2:214; quoted from Gustavus Przychocki, "Accessus Ovidiani," *Polska Akademia Umilietnosci,* ser. 3 (1911): 5–126, p. 117.

This early *accessus* treats the conventional *topoi—intentio, utilitas, parte philosophiae*—in a way that was apparently widely accepted at least through the end of the fourteenth century. The etymology of Ovid's name is likewise a conventional element of the genre. A fuller *accessus* from the time of Chaucer, preserved in Assisi and printed by J. B. Allen in *Ethical Poetic,* is similar in tone:

> Hiis visis dicendum de hiis que solent inquiri in primo cuiuslibet libri scilicet que materia, que intentio, que utilitas, cui parte phylosophie supponiatur (sic), quis libri titulus et que causa suscepti operis. Materia libri sunt mores et vicia dominarum. Intentio versatur circha matercam (sic). Intendit enim tractare de moribus et viciis dominarum et casto amore cum mendace et de incesto vituperare. Utilitas est duplex, scilicet communis et propria. Propria utilitas huius libri est quia cognito hoc libro cognoscemus dominas vel amicas nostras et cognantas (sic) caste amare. Utilitas communis est duplex, scilicet pulcritudo conditionum que sunt in hoc libro et pulcritudo vocabulorum. Cui parti phylosophie supponatur; supponitur ethice idest mortali (sic): tractat videlicet de moribus dominarum. Libri titulus dictus est Publii Ovidii hic liber incipit. Causa suscepi operis supradicta est, ut benevolentiam dominarum Romanarum caperet et has ystorias de greco in latinum transtulit.[39]

I cannot agree with Allen that the medieval critic intended his audience to use the *Heroides* to refine amatory technique, to "court by the book"; rather, he pretty clearly views the letters as lessons in charity whose end is chaste love. The ladies who love foolishly demonstrate vice, and constitute negative *exempla;* those who love virtuously instruct us in a Christian art of love. The irrelevance of this to Ovid's real art or intention is obvious; this is in no way historical criticism, but an attempt to mine pagan gold. Such attempts were common during and around the time of Chaucer; Carlo Figiovanni, in a translation of the *Heroides* dedicated to Andrea and Giovanni Pino de' Rossi about 1390, makes note "di quanto pericolo sia ne' giovanili petti il non moderato amore," and Meech has shown that Chaucer himself probably used an Italian translation of the

39. Allen, *Ethical Poetic* 28.

Heroides containing just such glosses.[40] Medieval manuscripts of Ovid were often glossed, and the glosses on the *Heroides* are remarkably consistent in their interpretations. It is unlikely that any reader of Chaucer's time could have known Ovid without having encountered the medieval glosses on Ovid.

Most of the *accessus* to the *Heroides* underline the lesson to be derived from the epistles by pointing to the virtue or foolishness of particular heroines. It is striking that, of all the heroines, the only one generally said to have loved virtuously is Penelope. Filippo Ceffi, author of the translation Chaucer is likely to have used, writes (in Meech's summary) that "in composing the letter of a virtuous woman, like Penelope, [Ovid's] intention was to recommend honest love; while in the case of an evil woman like Phaedra, it was to reprehend guilty passion."[41] An earlier *accessus,* printed by Przychocki, classifies the heroines according to the type of love they exemplify:

> Materia Ovidii est in hoc opere tam mittentes, quam quibus mittuntur epistolae. Intentio sua est legitimum commendare connubium vel amorem, et secundum hoc triplici modo tractat de ipso amore, scilicet de legitimo de illicito et stulto: De legitimo per Penelopen, de illicito per Canacen, de stulto per Phyllidem. Sed has duas partes, scilicet stulti et illiciti non causa ipsarum, verum gratia illius tertiae commendandi interserit et sic commendando legitimum, stultum et illicitum reprehendit. Ethicae subiacet quia bonorum morum est instructor, malum vero exstirpator. Finalis causa talis est, ut visa utilite quae ex legitimo procedit et infortuniis, quae ex stulto et illicito solent prosequi, hunc utrumque fugiamus, et soli casto adhaereamus.[42]

The *accessus* contained in MS. Laur. 36,27 and printed by Sedlmayer employs a similar division into types—this time, chaste, illicit, and incestuous: "Intentio est castum amorem commendare, illicitum refrenare et incestum condemnare. Utilitas est magna,

40. Quoted by Giovanni Pansa, *Ovidio nel Medioevo e nella Tradizione Popolare* (Sulmona, 1924), 55; S. B. Meech, "Chaucer and an Italian Translation of the *Heroides,*" *PMLA* 45 (1930): 110–128.

41. Meech, "Italian Translation" 111.

42. Przychocki, "Accessus Ovidiani," 81–83.

nam per hoc scimus castum amore eligere, illicitum refutare et incestum penitus extirpare."[43] MS. Vindob. 13685 gives examples:

> . . . intentio eius duo amore genera notare castum s. et incestum, ut Phedre et aliarum. Finalis causa sive utilitas est ut, dum castum amorem Penelopis intuemur, proderit instruendis moribus, ethicae suppositio, que in duas dividitur partes: in repulsionem s. et admissionem, repellimus enim turpia, admittimus honesta que utraque inveniuntur in hoc opere. . . .[44]

In alluding to "Phaedra and others," the writer indeed seems to include in his condemnation *all* the others except Penelope. The distinctions constructed in the *accessus* vary, as we have seen, but the heroines—with the single exception of Penelope—seem to be used almost interchangeably as *exempla* of foolish lovers. An *accessus* described by Monteverdi cites Penelope under "chaste love," Phaedra under "incestuous love," and Phyllis under "vain love."[45] Some of the *accessus,* like one cited by Huygens, retell portions of the heroines' stories in order to show their appropriateness to the moral: the love of Penelope may justly be called chaste, as during the seven years' wandering of her husband Ulysses she was courted by many men and yet continued to desire only her husband.[46] Though specific formulas may vary a bit—the love of Phyllis, for instance, is called "stultus" by one writer and "vanus" by another—there is great consistency in the moralities drawn from the separate epistles. Apparently, no one except Penelope is to be commended. An *accessus* from MS. Berol. Lat. 219, given by Alton, cites Phaedra, Phyllis, and Oenone:

> Materia ipsius est amor licitus et illicitus et stultus. Intentio sua commendare quasdam a licito amore sicut penelopem, alias reprehendere ab illicito sicut phedram, que dilexit ypolitum priuignum suum, alias etiam reprehendere a stulto amore, sicut phillidam et oenonem; stultitia enim est amare

43. Sedlmayer, "Beiträge zur Geschichte der Ovidstudien im Mittelalter," *Wiener Studien* 6 (1884): 142–58, p. 145.

44. Printed by Ghisalberti in "Biographies" 11n7.

45. Angelo Monteverdi, "Ovidio nel Medio Evo," in *Studi Ovidiani* (Rome, 1959): 65–78, p. 70.

46. *Accessus ad Auctores* (Leiden, 1970), 29–30.

> hospites sicut phillis, unde illud: certus in hospitibus non est amor; vel pueros diligere sicut oenone, quia solent esse inconstantes secundum etatis uariationem. Hec est principalis intentio. . . .[47]

That this emphasis upon the moral lessons to be derived from the epistles represents a genuine critical conviction of the writers, and not just a superficial attempt to sanitize Ovid for schoolboys, is demonstrated by numerous commentaries, histories, and poems—from the most distinguished writers of the High Middle Ages—that moralize the Ovidian heroines in precisely the same way. Medieval mythographic commentary on the *Metamorphoses,* at the same time that it reproduces certain of the old physical glosses on the myths of love and adapts them sometimes fancifully to Christian belief, perpetuates the conventional moralities as well. Bersuire says of Medea, "Istud potest dici contra maliciam malarum mulierum: quae arte mirabili sciunt homines incantare: in tantum quod suis incantationibus generant tenebras ignorantiae: ventos superbiae: choruscationes concupiscentiae vel contumeliae. . . .[48] Procne, Scylla, Dejanira, Byblis, and Myrrha (who do not appear in the *Heroides*) are likewise designated "mala muliere", in moralizations against *incestus, concupiscentia, luxuria, criminalem amorem,* and *fornicatio,* respectively.[49] Such moralizations are to be found as well in Giovanni del Virgilio, the *Ovide Moralisé,* Ridewall's *Fulgentius Metaforalis,* and in commentaries not specifically mythographic in nature, such as Pietro Alighieri's commentary on the *Commedia,* Boccaccio's gloss on the *Teseida,* and the gloss on the *Echecs Amoureux*. Encyclopedists, historians, and poets often derived their moralities on the myths from other encyclopedists, historians, and poets, but there is also ample evidence that the *accessus* and commentaries were felt to be relevant to other literary genres. In his (late thirteenth century) *Grande e General Estoria,* Alfonso X retells within the framework of Biblical and classical history many of the tales of the *Metamorphoses* and *Heroides,* borrowing the moralizations of John of Garland, the *Ovide Moralisé,* and the Ovidian *accessus*. On the letter of Phyllis, the commonest example of *amor*

47. E. H. Alton and D. E. W. Wormell, "Ovid in the Medieval Schoolroom," *Hermathena* 94 (1960): 21–38, and 95 (1961): 67–82, pp. 70–71.

48. *Red. Mor.* XV, vii (Engels 111).

49. *Red. Mor.* XV: vi, viii, ix, x (Engels 106, 123, 135, 145, 153).

stultus in the *accessus,* he comments: "Ovid's intention in this letter was to give example and chastisement to young noblewomen, . . . so that they would not lightly believe the claims of suitors. . . ."[50] Evidently regarding the moralizations as an essential part of the Ovidian stories of love, he appends advice against foolish love to the tales of Narcissus and Echo, Pyramus and Thisbe, Mars and Venus, Procne and Philomela, Theseus and Ariadne, Jason and Medea, and others.[51] We will see that the poets of the fourteenth century, although they may use the commentaries more subtly, continue to draw from them as well as from each other in writing of the Ovidian lovers.

Dante, who treats the lovers *sub specie aeternitatis,* naturally moralizes them. In *Inferno* V (ll. 38–39), Semiramis, Dido, Cleopatra, Helen and Achilles appear among "i peccator carnali, / che la ragion sommettono al talento," whirled about in a constant storm symbolizing the violence of their passions. Virgil identifies them for the pilgrim Dante:

La prima . . .
    fu imperadrice di molte favelle.
A vizio di lussuria fu sì rotta
    che libito fè licito in sua legge
    per tòrre il biasmo in che era condotta.
Ell' è Semiramis, di cui si legge
    che succedette a Nino e fu sua sposa:
    tenne la terra che 'l Soldan corregge.
L'altra è colei che s'ancise amorosa,
    e ruppe fede al cener di Sicheo;
    poi è Cleopatràs lussuriosa.
Elena vedi, per cui tanto reo
    tempo si volse, e vedi il grande Achille,
    che con amore al fine combattèo.
Vedi Paris, Tristano'; e più de mille
    ombre mostrommi e nominommi a dito,
    ch'amor di nostra vita dipartille,
(V, 52–69)

50. Ed. Antonio G. Solalinde, *Alfonso el Sabio* General Estoria, 2 vols. (Madrid, 1957), 1:2, 228 (my translation).

51. Solalinde 2:1, 172, 201, 207, 262, and 419; 2:2, 59ff.

When Dante speaks with one of these shades, it is with the gentle Francesca, who appeals to him with a commonplace of his own love lyrics: "amor, ch'al cor gentil ratto s'apprende," "amor, ch'a nullo amato amar perdona," has seized her so strongly that she is imprisoned yet. He replies simply, "Francesca, thy torments make me weep for grief and pity" (V, 116–17). Sinclair makes note of the "cumulative effect of passivity and helplessness" created by the verbs with which Dante describes the action of the storm—"borne on," "driven," "brought"—but one must note also that the active verb with which he characterizes their sin—"la ragion *sommettono* al talento"—is doctrinally correct. In the terms of medieval Christianity, the lovers have not been acted upon by an uncontrollable passion, but have freely willed to follow the promptings of their irrational natures. In the letter to Can Grande, Dante says of the *Commedia:*

> Est . . . subiectum totius operis, literaliter tantum accepti, status animarum post mortem simpliciter sumptus. Nam de illo et circa illum totius operis versatur processus. Si vero accipiatur opus allegorice, subiectum est homo prout merendo et demerendo per arbitrii libertatem iustitiae praemiandi et puniendi obnoxius est.[52]

Modern critics—Minnis comes to mind, speaking of the *Troilus*—have sometimes tried to argue that medieval writers refrained from criticizing pagans who devoted themselves to passionate love, on the grounds that, having lived before the Incarnation, they did the best they knew.[53] That argument would be vulnerable even without the evidence of Dante's practice, but his practice is worth noting: he holds everyone, both contemporary and classical figures, equally responsible in the afterlife. Certainly he does not shrink from using his contemporaries to exemplify the vices, so it is noteworthy also that he finds the classical figures most suitable to his discussion of lust. But his attitude suggests that he shares in some measure the weakness of the lovers; and we will presently see that he does not find the condition of lovers entirely irredeemable. In the ninth canto

52. *Ep.* X, 8, quoted from Paget Toynbee, ed. and trans., *Dantis Alagherii Epistolae: The Letters of Dante* (Oxford, 1966), 174.
53. Minnis, *Chaucer* 67–68.

of the *Paradiso,* the bishop Folco compares his passion as a youth to that of Dido, Phyllis, and Hercules as lover of Iole:

> Folco mi disse quella gente a cui
> fu noto il nome mio; e questo cielo
> di me s'imprenta, com' io fe' di lui;
> che più non arse la figlia di Belo,
> noiando e a Sicheo ed a Creusa,
> di me, infin che si convenne al pelo,
> nè quella Rodopea che delusa
> fu da Demofoonte, nè Alcide
> quando Iole nel core ebbe rinchiusa.
> (94–102)

The difference between him and the lovers he names, all of whom may be presumed to repose in the inferno, is that he ended by using his passionate nature as an instrument of transcendence. Praise, not repentance, is appropriate to this level of the heavens, and his tone in speaking of his old transgressions is, not indulgent, but Olympian:

> Non però qui si pente, ma si ride,
> non della colpa, ch'a mente non torna,
> ma del valor ch'ordinò e provide.
> Qui si rimira nell'arte ch'adorna
> cotanto effetto, e discernesi 'l bene
> per che 'l mondo di su quel di giù torna
> (103–8)

As Sinclair notes, Dante places Folco, a passionate soul and a repentant sinner, higher in paradise than the lukewarm or the inconstant in faith precisely because he values his passion, which with the right movement of will eventually turned to God.[54] In the *Convivio* Dante describes the operation of the heaven of Venus, which "conceiveth an ardour of virtue to kindle souls [on earth] to love, according to their disposition":

> E perchè li antichi s'accorsero che quello cielo era qua giù cagione d'amore, dissero Amore essere figlio di Venere, si

54. *Par.* p. 143.

> come testimonia Vergilio nel primo de lo Eneida, ove dice Venere ad Amore: "Figlio, vertù mia, figlio del sommo padre, che li darde di Tifeo non curi"; e Ovidio, nel quinto di Metamorphoseos, quando dice che Venere disse ad Amore: "Figlio, armi mie, potenzia mia."[55]

In the exposition of love in the eighteenth canto of the *Purgatorio,* Virgil has explained that not every love is good; the impulse to love is inborn and morally neutral, but also innate is reason, "the faculty which counsels and which ought to hold the threshold of assent" (62–63). A rational man curbs and directs the passions by right will: "Admitting then that every love that is kindled in you arises of necessity, the power to control it is in you; that noble faculty Beatrice means by freewill and therefore see thou have it in mind if she would speak of it to thee" (70–75).

The classical lovers are therefore condemned to the inferno, not by God, but by the force of their own gravity: "all natures have their bent according to their different lots, nearer to their source and farther from it" (*Par.* I, 110–11). In the twenty-seventh and twenty-eighth cantos of the *Purgatorio,* as Dante prepares to ascend to the heavens, evocation of the lovers serves to characterize the state of his mind, which is still earthbound. Acquiescing reluctantly to Virgil's command that he enter the fire that will purge him of lust, Dante reacts with longing to the name of Beatrice:

> Come al nome di Tisbe aperse il ciglio
> Piramo in su la morte, e riguardolla,
> allor che 'l gelso diventò vermiglio;
> così, la mia durezza fatta solla,
> mi volsi al savio duca, udendo il nome
> che nella mente sempre mi rampolla.
> Ond'ei crollò la fronte e disse: 'Come?
> volenci star di qua?'; indi sorrisse
> come al fanciul si fa ch'è vinto al pome.
> (XXVII, 37–45)

Virgil smiles because he sees that the "apple" that tempts Dante, his desire for Beatrice, is still the untutored desire of the young

55. II, 5, 14–15, ed. Busnelli and Vandelli. The brief translation is that of Philip H. Wicksteed, *The* Convivio *of Dante Alighieri* (London, 1912), 86.

lovers Pyramus and Thisbe; Dante loves her still for her own sake, not yet wholly for the sake of God. Later, entering the forest of the earthly paradise and catching sight of the fair lady beyond the stream, more lovely than the dream of Leah, Dante compares her beauty to that of Proserpine at the moment of her ravishment and of Venus as she was struck with love for Adonis; unable to cross the stream, he likens his frustration to that of Leander contemplating the Hellespont (XXVIII, 49–51, 71–75). Smiling, the lady responds to these images of profane love by suggesting that the psalm *Delectasti* will "give light that may dispel the cloud from your mind" (80–81). By evoking the psalm—"Thou, Lord, hast made me glad through thy work; I will triumph in the works of thy hands"—she gently reminds him that he is to rejoice in the paradise itself, and her work within it, rather than in the beauty of her person.[56]

In only three of the terraces of the *Purgatorio*—those devoted to the purgation of pride, anger, and lust—does Dante himself perform penance, and his penance is heaviest by far on the terrace of lust, where he must pass through a wall of fire so hot that he "would have cast [himself] into boiling glass to cool [him]" (XXVII,49–50). In this way he both implicates himself in the lovers' guilt and places emphasis upon atonement, rather than the fall. He is careful, however, to distinguish between folly and criminality, showing no quarter to the lovers who deceive, betray, and murder. Pasiphae, Procne, and Phaedra are all vigorously condemned, and Jason and Myrrha are consigned to the depths of the inferno, in the circles of traitors and falsifiers.[57] In all these instances it is clear that, for Dante, the old myths of love have moral significance—so much, indeed, that he tends less to explain the allusions by his arguments than to construct his arguments in terms of the allusions. I am not sure that Robson is correct in maintaining that Dante's reference to the darkening of the mulberry in the tale of Pyramus and Thisbe specifically evokes Giovanni del Virgilio's association of that event with the "stain" of carnality,[58] but in any case it is not necessary to go so far in order to establish that Dante read the old tales of love in the same spirit as his friend Giovanni. The terse couplets of the

56. See the discussion of Sinclair, *Purg.* 373–75.

57. *Purg.* XXVI, 41–42, and XVII, 19–21; *Par.* XVII, 46–48; and *Inf.* XVIII, 86–96 and XXX, 37–45.

58. C. A. Robson, "Dante's Use in the *Divina Commedia* of the Medieval Allegories on Ovid," in *Centenary Essays on Dante,* ed. Oxford Dante Society (Oxford, 1965): 1–38, p. 13.

mythographer—"Alba prius morus nigredine mora colorans / Signat quod dulci mors in amore latet"[59]—are very different in tone and purpose from Dante's sensitive, complex, and ramified allusions to the classical lovers, but the moral judgment is the same in both cases. Dante, however, includes himself in it, as we will see that the greatest medieval poets often do—and wish their readers to do.

Dante's intentions in referring to the myths of love are further clarified by the commentary of his son Pietro, who anchors his discussion of love in two great Augustinian commonplaces: (1) that love is the "foot" of the soul, which if straight inclines to charity, if crooked to cupidity; and (2) that disordered love ("amor inordinatus"), or vice, has its origin in overestimating the goods of the world, in underestimating the eternal goods, or in loving that which is evil.[60] Of those three errors, that of the "luxuriosi" is the first. It may be avoided through the proper exercise of free will: ". . . dicit Beatrix quod majus donum, quod a Deo habet homo, est liberum arbitrium, quod dicitur liberum quantum ad voluntatem, arbitrium quantum ad rationem. Est enim voluntatis appetere, rationis est videre quid sit agendum, vel non."[61] Those of the classical lovers who acted with honor—Penelope and Lucretia—are praised by both Dante and his son. In the eighth *bolgia* of the inferno, Ulysses blames his own *curiositas* for the suffering of Penelope; it seems to be the judgment of Dante as well (XXVI, 90–99). Among the virtuous heathen Dante sees Lucretia, together with other "great spirits by the sight of whom I am uplifted in myself": Brutus, Julia, Marcia, Cornelia (IV, 119–20). These two women are distinguished from the others, not by the nature of their actions themselves (Thisbe, Dido, Phyllis, and Lucretia all committed suicide), but by the fact that their actions were governed by the exercise of right will rather than by appetite.

Petrarch, who also makes much use of the lovers of antiquity, does not moralize them in his lyrics; what meaning they have there will be the subject of another chapter. In the *Trionfi,* however, more than thirty of the Ovidian and Virgilian lovers appear as a group, the captives of Cupid. The *Trionfi,* a series of six visions in *terza*

59. *Allegorie* IV, 4 (Ghisalberti 55).

60. *Inf.* I and VIII, ed. Vincento Nannucci, *Pietro Alighierii Dantis ipsius Genitoris Comoediam Commentarium* (Florence, 1845), 31, 113.

61. *Par.* V, ed. Nannucci 573.

rima, are hierarchical in their ordering: Chastity triumphs over Love, Death over Chastity, Fame over Death, Time over Fame, and finally Eternity over Time. Love therefore occupies the lowest position in the hierarchy; Fame, commonly said in the Middle Ages to be the last temptation of noble minds, stands higher. For all Petrarch's fame as a love poet, the tone of this poem is grim; it does not celebrate love. Like Dante, he notes its dominion over him; in fact, the *Triumph of Love* memorializes "that day / Whereon my love and suffering began."[62] (The following *Triumph of Chastity* is Laura's victory, not his own.) Throughout the poem, love remains coupled with suffering. Cupid appears, nude and winged, as a "cruel youth" on a "fiery car," surrounded by the lovers, all of whom are suffering: "Some of them were but captives, some were slain, / And some were wounded by his pungent arrows" (I, 29–30). The first words heard by Petrarch the dreamer are the *moralitas* on this scene from classical antiquity, pronounced by the "friend" who serves as guide: "These are the gains of those who love!" (I, 42). Looking around him, Petrarch sees the most celebrated figures of pagan story herded like cattle by a triumphant Cupid, transformed from heroes to mute prisoners whose spirits are chained to the earth. Their passion, far from augmenting their greatness, contrasts with it: Caesar, "though conqueror of the world, was vanquished"; Marcus is "worthy of all praise, / His tongue and heart full of philosophy— / And yet Faustina bends him to her will" (I, 100–102). The condition of the classical lovers under the dominion of Cupid is pitiable:

> Vedi 'l famoso, con sua tanta lode,
> preso menar tra due sorelle morte:
> l'una di lui ed ei de l'altra gode!
> Colui ch' è seco è quel possente e forte
> Ercole, ch' Amor prese, e l'altro è Achille,
> ch'ebbe in suo amar assai dogliose sorte.
> Quello è Demofoon e quella è Fille;
> quell' è Giasone e quell' altra è Medea,
> ch' Amor e lui seguì per tante ville;
> e quanto al padre ed al fratel più rea . . .
> Isifile vien poi, e duolsi anch' ella
> del barbarico amor, ch' 'l suo l'à tolto.

62. *Tr.* I, 2–3, trans. Ernest Hatch Wilkins, *The Triumphs of Petrarch* (Chicago, 1962). All translations from the *Trionfi* are Wilkins's.

Poi ven colei ch'à 'l titol d' esser bella.
  Seco è 'l pastor che mal il suo bel volto
mirò sì fiso, ond'uscir gran tempeste,
e funne il mondo sottosopra vòlto.
  Odi poi lamentar fra l' altre meste
Enone di Paris, e Menelao
d'Elena, ed Ermion chiamare Oreste,
  e Laodamia il suo Protesilao . . .
  Vedi Venere bella, e con lei Marte,
cinto di ferro i piè, le braccia e 'l collo,
e Plutone e Proserpina in disparte.[63]

Petrarch's attitude toward the lovers, like that of Dante, is both moralizing and compassionate: "Hark to the sighs and weeping, hark to the cries / Of these poor loving ones, who gave their souls / Into the power of him that leads them thus" (I, 145–47). The "innumerable bonds" that burden the lovers symbolize their spiritual bondage: "servitude / And death and torment wait for one who loves" (IV, 137–38). Penelope and Lucretia do not appear at all in this vision, but in the *Triumph of Chastity;* the other classical lovers are all moralized as *exempla* of vain and destructive conduct. Narcissus and Echo, Scylla, Pygmalion, Clytemnestra, Pyramus and Thisbe, Leander and Hero, Orpheus and Eurydice—it is difficult not to imagine that one of Petrarch's goals must have been to include them all! Semiramis, Byblis, and Myrrha appear together, "oppressed with shame / For their unlawful and distorted love" (III, 76–78). The plight of the lovers gives evidence of Petrarch's conclusion that Cupid "is held a god / By slow and blunted and deluded minds" (IV, 89–90). The solemn, didactic tone of *The Triumph of Love* never gives way to the mocking humor so often seen in medieval poems of love; Petrarch's aim is to show that love brings "ample grief and little joy."

That Petrarch's fundamental attitude toward the classical lovers is consistent, and not just a rhetorical feature of this particular poem, may be seen in his other writings. In the *Africa* Sophonisba, descending to Hades, is assigned to the plain of lovers, where she meets Byblis, Myrrha, Orpheus, Achilles, Paris and Oenone, and Pyramus and Thisbe, among others—all condemned to love and

63. *Tr.* I, 121–30; 133–42; 151–53, ed. F. Neri et al., Rime, Trionfi *e Poesie Latine* (Milan, 1951).

suffer through eternity as they did in life. Petrarch describes the plain:

> Non hic armorum strepitus studiumve frementum
> Cornipedum, non cura canum pecdumque boumque,
> Sed labor et lacrime et longo suspiria tractu,
> Et macies odiumque sui, pallorque ruborque
> Et malesuadus amor, scelus, ira, fidesque dolique,
> Furtaque blanditiis immixta, iocusque dolorque,
> Et risus brevis et ficto periuria vultu
> Crebraque sub raris habitant mendacia veris.[64]

In Petrarch's *Remedium Contra Fortuna,* "Reason" cites the lovers in a dialogue with "Joy" on love "for delight": announcing that he is in love, Joy will not heed Reason's warnings.[65] Admonished that there is no truth in love, that he should flee, that love is "servitude and weakness, which enervates and enfeebles even the strongest men," Joy nevertheless persists in embracing the condition of a lover. Reason counters: "Jupiter [was] transformed into various beasts, Mars imprisoned in a ridiculous net, and Hercules spun flax with his powerful fingers. . . . Furthermore Leander [perished by] the sea, Byblis by tears, Procris by her husband's arrow, Pyramus by his own lance, Iphis . . . by the noose . . . and Troy burned with flames."[66] The dialogue continues, but Reason has the last word—a very long one, filled with quotations from the *auctores,* and concluding with the reassuring reminder that old age and death will reform the errors of youth. In that part of the *Secretum* in which Augustine reproaches Petrarch with his love for Laura, Dido appears: "Aug. . . . Obstupuisti, credo, perstrinxitque oculos fulgor insolitus. Dicunt enim stuporem amoris esse principium; hinc est apud nature conscium poetam: obstupuit primo aspectu sidonia Dido. Post quod dictum sequitur: ardet amans Dido."[67] When Petrarch protests this indictment, Augustine shows less interest in his account of Laura's steadfast resistance than in his own spiritual condition: "Base desires, then, sometimes you felt. . . ? But it is the common folly of

64. VI, 43–50, ed. Nicola Festa, *L'Africa* (Florence, 1926).
65. *Remedium* I, 49.
66. *Rem.* I, 49, ed. Martellotti et al., 622 (my translation).
67. *Secretum* Lib. III, ed. Martellotti et al., 152.

lovers, let me say of mad folk."[68] And later: "Nothing so much leads a man to forget or despise God as the love of things temporal, and most of all this passion that we call love. . . ." Augustine goes on to ridicule the condition of lovers, who weep, sigh, lose sleep and neglect their business; at length, Petrarch acknowledges himself bested. Recommending flight as the only remedy, Augustine recalls the conventional allegory on Orpheus and Eurydice: "You, o man, must keep on in your flight for life, till you have escaped everything that might drag the soul back to its old passions; for fear lest, when you return from the pit with Orpheus and look back, you lose your Eurydice once more."[69] The seriousness with which Petrarch regarded the passion of love is shown in a letter to his beloved teacher Dionigi da Borgo San Sepolcro, written when he was thirty:

> Tempus forsan veniet, quando eodem quo gesta sunt ordine universa percuram, prefatus illud Augustini tui: "Recordari volo transactas feditates meas et carnales corruptiones anime mee, non quod eas amem, sed ut amem te, Deus meus." Michi quidem multum adhuc ambigui molestique negotii superest. Quod amare solebam, iam non amo; mentior: amo, sed parcius; iterum ecce mentitus sum: amo, sed verecundius, sed tristius; iantandem verum dixi. Sic est enim; amo, sed quod non amare amem, quod odisse cupiam; amo tamen, sed invitus, sed coactus, sed mestus et lugens. Et in me ipso versiculi illius famosissimi sententiam miser experior: Odero, si potero; si non, invitus amabo. Nondum michi tertius annus effluxit, ex quo voluntas illa perversa et nequam, que me totum habebat et in aula cordis mei sola sine contradictore regnabat, cepit aliam habere rebellem et reluctantem sibi, inter quas iandudum in campis cogitationum mearum de utriusque hominis imperio laboriosissima et anceps etiam nunc pugna conseritur. . . . O quanto studio laborandum esset, non ut altiorem terram, sed ut elatos terrenis impulsibus appetitus sub pedibus haberemus![70]

The "perverse and worthless inclination" to which he refers is of course his passion for Laura; if the formulation sounds harsh, it is

68. Trans. Draper, *Petrarch's Secret* 130.

69. Trans. Draper, *Petrarch's Secret* 148.

70. *Fam.* IV, 1, 149–67 and 251–53, ed. Vittorio Rossi, *Le Familiari,* 4 vols. (Firenze, 1933), vol. 1.

well to remember that it is not love for her that he repudiates, but that which he considers unworthy in his love for her, the carnal element which for him is represented by the classical lovers. Dante in the *Convivio* describes the passions he expressed in the *Vita Nuova* as inappropriate to mature age (in any case, he claims, the poems were allegorical),[71] but Beatrice nevertheless appears as the divine guide of the *Commedia*. Petrarch's Laura performs a similar function in *The Triumph of Death,* where she confesses her love for him only to lead him upward. Though I will later argue that the love poems of the Middle Ages are less autobiographical in nature than has often been supposed—they open onto the battlefields of great ideas rather than the secret chambers of the heart—it is plain that for Dante and Petrarch the classical lovers are associated with the love they wish to conquer in themselves. It is easy for modern readers to understand why the psychomachia described by Petrarch—the "insistent and uncertain battle" between his two selves—could never be permanently stilled by any effort, but he and other thoughtful men of his time set out quite seriously under the guidance of their spiritual teachers to discipline themselves to love perfectly. When they represent themselves in literature as failing, they liken themselves to the lovers of classical antiquity; when they represent themselves as succeeding, they reject the experience of those lovers, with a compassion that reflects their experience of the struggle between reason and will.

That does not mean that it is always easy to tell what the poets mean when they refer to the classical lovers; in the next chapter we will consider some of the difficulties. Their fundamental attitude toward them, though, remains essentially the same through centuries. So, as we will see, does the range of rhetorical uses to which the lovers may be put, though some of them are quite complex. But when the poets locate the lovers within the moral universe, they all do so in much the same way. Boccaccio, in his commentary on the *Commedia,* identifies the three beasts of the *selva selvaggia* with the three vices that impede Dante's progress from the dark valley of spiritual misery to the bright mountain of "dottrina apostolica ed evangelica": lust, pride, and avarice.[72] He then sets out to identify the characteristics of lust with those of the leopard that symbolizes

71. *Conv.* I, 1, 16–19.

72. *Esposizioni* I, 2, 92, ed. Giorgio Padoan, *Esposizioni sopra la* Comedia *di Dante,* in Branca, *Opere* 6 (Milan, 1965).

it, using the lovers of classical antiquity as *exempla* at each stage. Just as the leopard is light and swift, love is changeable: Dido forgot the long-beloved Sichaeus for an agreeable stranger, and Jason went quickly from Hypispyle to Medea, then to Creusa. Thus we may see the truth of what Dante says of women in the *Purgatorio:* "By this one may understand well enough how long the fire of love endures in woman, if eye or touch not frequently rekindle it."[73] Just as the leopard's skin is soft and spotted, so lovers adorn themselves to please the beloved: Paris was entrapped by the beauty of Helen, Caesar by that of Cleopatra. As the leopard is cruel, so love kills those who follow it, either by rendering them sick and debilitated or by driving them to suicide: Demophon led Phyllis to hang herself, and what was the "swine" that killed Adonis but outrageously excessive coupling with Venus?[74] Finally, like the leopard, carnal concupiscence is tenacious of its prey, using tears, promises, reproaches, and the whole repertoire of lovers' strategies to prevent one from leaving it to turn to divine things. Just so Dido tried to keep Aeneas back from his glorious enterprise, and so have many gone from a promising beginning to "the sad end of eternal perdition."[75]

Dante does not, of course, allude to the lovers at all at this point in the *Commedia;* Boccaccio introduces them simply because they were universally recognized as *exempla* against lust. He uses them in a similar way in the *De Mulieribus Claris,* where they exemplify lust (Venus, Clytemnestra, Helen), the power of love (Iole), and the ways of Fortune, to which all lovers are bound (Thisbe, Polyxena, Hypsipyle).[76] In the dedication to the work, however, he characterizes it as "a little book in praise of women."[77] In fact, many of the women are condemned in the strongest terms, and few are praised unqualifiedly. Boccaccio recommends to Andrea Acciaiuoli, Countess of Altavilla, to whom he dedicates the work, that she not be discouraged from reading it by the discovery of "wantonness intermingled with purity": "Rather persevere, just as on entering a garden you put out your ivory hands for the flowers after moving the thorns aside. Thus, putting aside offensive matters, consider the

73. *Esposizioni* I, 2, 94–98, ed. Padoan (my translation).

74. *Esposizioni* I, 2, 94–106.

75. *Esposizioni* I, 2, 107–8, ed. Padoan (my translation).

76. Boccaccio's method of exemplification is noted by Guarino, *Famous Women* xvii.

77. Trans. Guarino, *Famous Women* xxiii.

praiseworthy ones."[78] There is no apparent irony in the contrast between the actual nature of the book and his description of it; rather, he seems to "praise" women by constructing an ideal of womanhood out of the materials of history, as he understood it. Boccaccio extracts principles for the conduct of life from both the virtue of Lucretia and Penelope and the vice of Medea, Semiramis, or Helen. He values the old tales chiefly as *exempla.*

The same approach is visible in the *De Casibus Virorum Illustrium,* where his avowed purpose is to bring corrupt rulers to an understanding of "God's power, the shiftiness of Fortune, and their own insecurity"[79] by concentrating upon the downfall of the mighty. Among them are the lovers Hercules, Narcissus, Orpheus, Byblis, and Myrrha, who arrive in a large 'gathering of the mournful"—"Who can give all the names of those approaching?"—complaining of "the fires of lust and the great ignominy of their deaths."[80] The lovers reappear in a digression "in mulieres," one of two in the *De Casibus;* the other one appears very near the end of the work (VIII, 23), constituting as it were Boccaccio's last word on women. The first, and fuller, digression follows the story of Samson and Delilah. Boccaccio first enumerates the beauties of women and describes their skill in tending and increasing them; complains that "the reason of man is blinded by feminine wiles, for women know just how to walk, just when to show a little of their alluring breasts or their legs, how they ought to use their eyes in looking at a man. . ."; further mourns that "the person who works toward virtue finds that the object of pleasure is his greatest concern"; notes that Paris, Hercules, and Samson were all brought low by women; and offers Eriphyle, Danae, Phyllis, Scylla, Semiramis, Cleopatra, Medea and Procne in proof of the proposition that ". . . the female of the species is very greedy, quick to anger, unfaithful, oversexed, truculent, desirous more of frivolity than of wisdom." With rather crude sarcasm, he recommends that young men not listen to him, but go ahead and "let women capture you like blind men with their snares"; again sarcastically, he ends with the assertion that surely not all women are devious, but he himself has never met any who were good. "If I ever meet them, I will have to love, honor, and extol them beyond any man for their virtues."[81]

78. Trans. Guarino, *Famous Women* xxxiv.
79. Trans. Hall, *Fates* 2.
80. *De Cas.* I, 12 (trans. Hall, *Fates* 26–27).
81. *De Cas.* I, 8, 11–12, 17–18, 32–33 (trans. Hall, *Fates* 43, 44, 45–46).

The *De Mulieribus Claris* does not, of course, demonstrate that Boccaccio admired women, nor does this sort of rhetoric demonstrate that he despised them. Praise and blame of women were simply opposite sides of the same well-worn rhetorical *topos,* in which the classical lovers were very often employed as *exempla*. We have seen Juvenal, Propertius, and Athenaeus in classical times, as well as Hildebert, Marbod, Petrus Pictor and others in the Middle Ages, make precisely the same use of them. The discourse *in mulieres* and its counterpart, the oration in praise of women, was a common and accepted way for students to hone their persuasive skills in the classroom; in the Middle Ages, it became a division of sermons against overvaluation of temporalia in general (we have already seen Petrarch's Augustine use it in this way). Other such *topoi* (included, incidentally, in the *De Casibus*) were the themes of the operation of Fortune, the vices (pride, lust, and avarice were most popular), the virtues (chastity in particular), prophetic dreams, the deceptiveness of outer appearances, the overthrow of the mighty, the exaltation of the lowly, the fickleness of the multitude, the nature of true nobility, paradoxical events (a division of the operation of Fortune—example: "The greatest orator of them all was killed by a man he had earlier saved from the executioner"),[82] and of course the *ubi sunt topos*. These are the moralities derived by Boccaccio from the histories he recounts in the *De Casibus*. All of them are time-honored; put together, they constitute "wisdom," and they qualify the *De Casibus* as a book of wisdom. We will see that perhaps the most striking feature of the use of the classical lovers by medieval poets is its extreme conventionality. This is not to say that the poets always use these figures in the same way, but I will suggest that they use them in certain limited and prescribed, though at times fairly complicated, ways.

In the seventh chapter of the *Teseida,* the lovers Pyramus and Thisbe, Hercules and Iole, and Byblis and Caunus appear painted upon the walls of the temple of Venus (Chaucer, in the "Knight's Tale," replaces them with personified attributes, in the French style). Boccaccio does not moralize them within the tale, and in the gloss he simply retells the lover's stories. But he does moralize the attributes of Venus, thus furnishing a context within which the lovers are to be placed. Venus is said to be in the most secret part of the castle, accompanied by Opulence, because "a voluptuous life

82. Hall's summary of Boccaccio's history of Cicero, *De Cas*. VI, 12 (*Fates* 159).

cannot be obtained nor long pursued without riches." Her chamber is dark "because those who practice evil hate the light."[83] The gloss continues:

> Quindi disegna la belleza di Venere, la quale dice essere a giacere, in parte nuda e in parte d'una porpora sì sottile coperta, che appena niente nasconde di quelle parti che cuopre. Per lo giacere intende l'ozosità la quale è ne' voluttuosi, e il vivere molle; per la belleza di Venere, la quale sappiamo essere cosa labile e caduca, intende il falso giudicio de' voluttuosi, il guali da verissime ragioni leggierissimamente si convince e mostrasi vano. Per la parte ignuda di Venere intende l'apparenza delle cose, le quale attraggono gli animi di coloro la cui estimazione non può passare all'essistenzia; per quella parte de Venere che sotto la sottile copertura appare, intende di mostrare quale sia l'occulta estimazione di quegli che alle cose apparenti si prendono. . . .[84]

Thus the classical lovers are here intended to mean precisely what they mean in the *Esposizioni sopra la Commedia* and in the *De Mulieribus Claris* and the *De Casibus*. This interpretation is not an excrescence upon the text; nothing in it is inconsistent with conclusions one might naturally draw from the story of Palaemon and Arcites. It is the morality drawn from the tales of the classical lovers whenever they are glossed by writers of the Middle Ages.

That a similar tradition existed in France is shown of course by the *Ovide Moralisé,* but also by a less well-known, not exclusively mythographic commentary, the anonymous commentary on the *Echecs Amoureux*. The *Echecs,* an allegorical poem written in imitation of the *Roman de la Rose* at about the time of Chaucer's most productive period, has not been edited in its entirety, but was partially translated by Lydgate as *Reson and Sensuallyte*. The commentary—which is almost as long as the *Ovide Moralisé*—was translated by Joan M. Jones in her 1968 University of Nebraska dissertation. The *Echecs* itself is incomplete. It begins with the

83. *Tes.* VII, 50, trans. Bernadette Marie McCoy, *The Book of Theseus* (New York, 1974), 206.

84. *Tes.* VII, 50, ed. Alberto Limentani, *Teseida delle Nozze di Emilia,* in Branca, *Opere* 2 (Verona, 1964).

appearance of Nature, who scolds the poet for his slothfulness and bids him go out and find his way in life. She describes two roads he may take—one which begins in the east and goes west, then returns to the east, and another which goes from west to east, then west again. She reminds the poet that man is set apart from the beasts by reason, who prefers the road that ends in the east; then she departs.[85] Setting out on his way, the poet meets the three goddesses Pallas, Juno, and Venus, and is asked by Mercury, who accompanies them, to give his opinion of the Judgment of Paris. Observing the beauty of Venus, the poet says that he approves of it. Thanking him, Venus promises to make him her servant and to give him a lady more lovely than Helen of Troy. She directs him to the Garden of Deduit, but on the way there he meets Diana, who reproaches him for confirming the judgment of Paris (285). She warns him that he is in danger, and that there is bitterness beneath the apparent beauty of the garden. When the poet defends Venus and repeats his determination to see the garden, Diana departs. In the garden, the poet is welcomed by Oiseuse and Courtoisie, sees the God of Love and his meinie, and gazes into the fountain of Narcissus. Presently he finds a lovely lady engaged in a game of chess with Deduis; he plays with her, and loses. Cupid crowns the lady and counsels the poet in the rules of love. When he leaves the poet feels quite confident, but then Pallas appears to warn him: Venus is leading him astray, for love is full of fear and pain and often ends in disaster (285). Pallas will show him how to withdraw from the path he has taken by following the rules of the wise clerk Ovid. She describes the three ways of life, and advises him to choose the contemplative, or at least the active, but to flee the voluptuous (291). Then she quotes the *Remedia Amoris,* in full. Having advised the poet on the sort of life to choose, she offers him further counsel on a variety of matters: Paris and its university, the professions, the duties of husband and wife, child rearing, music, planning and building a house, and acquiring wealth. Here the manuscript ends.

Such an outline makes it obvious that the poem is entirely conventional, which is certainly not to say that it is not lively and amusing. There is nothing in it that is personal; none of its episodes describe, or could possibly describe, real experiences of the poet or

85. I refer in the following discussion to the summary of Stanley L. Galpin, *"Les Eschez Amoureux:* A Complete Synopsis, with Unpublished Extracts," *RR* 11 (1920): 283–307.

of anyone else. It is conventional because it uses situations and mythological personages whose significance in literature was well established to discuss ideas that were vitally interesting to writers and readers of the time. The poem purports to be about a young man who receives certain divine visitations and ultimately falls in love with a young lady in a garden over a game of chess; in fact, it is about the struggle between (to use Lydgate's words) "reson and sensuallyte" within the mind of each man. Even if Pallas's counsel did not occupy the bulk of the poem, there could be no real debate about which side the poet is on, or wishes us to be on; the materials of the poem are too conventional to allow for doubt. The poet's Nature is that of Alanus, principle of universal harmony, who predictably counsels reason and sets the poet upon the eastward road.[86] The judgment of Paris, which he ratifies, was interpreted at least from patristic times as a foolish man's choice of the voluptuous life.[87] Diana, goddess of chastity and the traditional rival of Venus, behaves characteristically in warning the poet away from the superficial attractions of the life he has chosen, and he behaves as a typical lover in ignoring her warnings. The fountain of Narcissus into which he gazes represents the temptations of idolatrous Venerean love, as it did from the time of Clement of Alexandria to that of Dryden.[88] One of the incidental attractions of the poem is the humorous way in which the narrator is made to display his ignorance, or misunderstanding, of conventional ideas and situations that the reader would recognize immediately: upon entering the

86. We will encounter this road imagery often in the medieval poems of love. It comes ultimately from Boethius, *De Cons. Philos.* III, Mtr. 9, and the commentaries on it, which derive from the *Timaeus*. Arnulf of Orleans refers to it in the *accessus* to his commentary on the *Metamorphoses* (see 176–77), and Chaucer and Dante both use it as well. Trevet discusses it fully in his commentary on the *De Cons. Philos.*, even providing a diagram of the rationally ordered universe in which reason (the *primum mobile*), tending always to the east, overrules the (westward) motion of sensuality (the planets) throughout the natural order and in the microcosm man (see Mark Science, ed., *Boethius:* De Consolatione Philosophiae *Translated by John Walton* [London, 1927], 367–71). The poet of the *Echecs* puts these ideas into the mouth of Diana, and the *Echecs* glossator in turn draws upon the Boethian commentaries in explaining them (Jones 91–97). Late classical works, the medieval commentaries on them, and the medieval poems of love are thus intricately linked.

87. The *locus classicus* for this interpretation is Fulgentius, *Myth.* II, 1.

88. For the interpretative history of the myth of Narcissus, see Louise Vinge, *The Narcissus Theme in Western European Literature up to the Early Nineteenth Century*, trans. R. Dewsnap et al. (Lund, 1967), and Frederick Goldin, *The Mirror of Narcissus in the Courtly Love Lyric* (Ithaca, N.Y. 1967).

garden he expresses delight at its beauty; how glad he is he did not take Diana's advice! He does not see why anyone ought to be frightened by the fountain of Narcissus, even though there are letters around its edge telling how he died. He reverently accepts Cupid's advice that he must be as changeable as Proteus if he is to please the lady (290) (we have seen repeatedly the traditional association of the metamorphoses of Proteus with spiritual degradation through loss of reason). He protests to Pallas that he does not understand why Diana slanders Venus and Cupid, who have been so friendly to him. This poet/narrator represents the perfect *naif,* which contributes to the comedic mock-tension surrounding his eventual decision; he listens just as uncritically to Pallas as he does to Cupid, saying that she speaks so *substancieusement* that he takes great delight in hearing her (297).

Within this framework the classical lovers appear repeatedly, both singly and in groups. Most significantly, they are listed by Diana and Pallas in their warnings against the love advocated by Venus and Cupid. Diana, who appears to the poet in a forest of evergreen trees and wearing a white garment, tells him that Venus has her name from *venin,* and her poisonous nature is illustrated by the old tales of love: think of the death of Narcissus, the loves of Jason and Medea, Pygmalion, Myrrha, Phaedra, Tereus, Scylla, Dido, Phaedra, Adonis, and the entrapment of Mars and Venus! The mulberry of Pyramus and Thisbe proves that love's sweets turn to bitterness. Pallas adduces the *exempla* of Aeneas and Dido, Paris and Oenone, Demophoon and Phyllis, to show that lovers cannot long be faithful (290). The commentary on the *Echecs* confirms the monitory force of the tales of love. It first retells them, then explains their meaning: "for there was never any doubt that [they] should not be understood literally,"[89] Several explanations, some euhemeristic or based on physical science, are offered for each fable, but the traditional moralities are offered as well. Pygmalion was said to love his image because the lover cherishes the image of the lady which he has constructed in his mind; Myrrha became a myrrh tree because she "wept her misdeed all the days of her life" (662, 666); Tereus, Philomela, and Procne were said to have become birds because "they fled, one here and another there, because of their confusion and shame," and Tereus became a hoopoe, which nests in

89. Jones 661. All references to the commentary on the *Echecs* are to this translation.

ordure, because of his indulgence in the vice of lust, "which is a stinking, excremental, and abominable thing" (674, 675). The tale of Pyramus and Thisbe reminds the glossator of that of Hero and Leander, which teaches that ". . . such mad loves commonly end in bitter sorrow and in some surpassing misfortune. And that is why the goddess Diana reminded the author in his youth, as he pretends, of the loves described above, so that he might take an example from them and be aware of the danger that lies in such loves" (606).

The glossator ends his work before arriving at the *exempla* offered by Pallas. His most illuminating comments are on the tale of Jason and Medea. He begins, apparently, in a "courtly" mode: ". . . we can properly enough say that the story of Jason and Medea signifies the condition and process of love and the steps by which the lover should pass who wishes worthily to acquire the love of a lady or maiden, which is ordinarily not an easy thing to do, but in truth requires great cunning and prowess, great care and trouble" (617). The fleece, then, represents Medea herself; the two cruel bulls are Danger and Refusal, "which should always be in every amorous lady and girl who wishes to keep her honor"; the serpent is "Evil Tongue, which never sleeps" (610). A wise and diligent lover will "give it to be understood that he does not think of that of which he is accused" (621), thus disarming Danger and Refusal and silencing Evil Tongue. The love of Jason and Medea is like that of Paris and Helen, in that both men risked dangers and from both affairs great evil resulted. Medea was a bad woman, one of those who "make in those whom they bemuse the darkness of ignorance, the winds of pride, the lightnings and thunders of burning concupiscence, the rains and sleets of grief and sorrow. . . . And briefly it is to say that these women cause men to be moved by various unreasonable motives and transform them from good morals to bad ones" (624). And finally:

> Now let us return to our purpose and say that it was not without reason that Diana compared the danger the author placed himself in, when, as he pretends, in his youth he undertook the path to the Garden of Mirth, to the danger Jason put himself in when he went to sea to conquer the golden fleece. For in truth those who follow the vanities and idleness of the world, which are meant by this garden, live in great danger, even if there were no other danger or evil in it than that delight and excessive games attract and hold them so that they cannot, at need, withdraw from them to under-

> take good work, because they are so deceived and deluded by bad habits, and in great uncertainty. (627)

This is indeed the condition of the lover in the garden, and in the poem as in the commentary the "courtly" level is simply a mirror of the delusions of the lovers and of their actions in pursuit of love, which are ultimately judged destructive and immoral.

Even the love poets Machaut, Froissart, and Deschamps, who do not often gloss their allusions to the classical lovers, offer the same kind of interpretations when they do. Machaut's *Confort d'Ami,* a consolation addressed to King Charles of Navarre during his year's imprisonment (1357–58) by King Jean of France, contains a section on love that makes use of the lovers. Machaut bases his *confort* upon *exempla* from the Bible and from classical mythology; early in the poem, he announces that:

> Par exemples te vueil prouver,
> Qui sont contenu en la Bible
> Et qui sont a nous impossible,
> Qu'adés cils qui en Dieu se fie,
> S'il a raison de sa partie
> Et s'il l'aimme, sert et honneure,
> Adés son fait vient au desseure.[90]

In the fashion common to writers of his time, he does not make much practical distinction between the authority of Holy Writ and that of Virgil and Ovid. He begins by offering *exempla* of faith in deliverance by God—the tale of Susanna, of Shadrach, Meschach, and Abednego in the fiery furnace, of Daniel in the lion's den, of King Manasseh (73–1548). Reminding Charles that he has lost only the goods of Fortune, upon which Boethius set no value, he suggests that perhaps the king followed vice in youth, for which he is now being punished (1904–2056). Perhaps, too, he is tormented in his imprisonment by love and desire. If so, he should not complain of desire, for it is sweet to feel the ills of love. He should have hope, as recommended by the *Remede de Fortune* (of Machaut). Without hope, lovers cannot accomplish great deeds: Orpheus would never have gone to seek Eurydice without it, nor would Paris have abducted

90. *Confort* ll. 46–52, ed. Ernest Hoepffner, *Oeuvres de Guillaume de Machaut,* 3 vols. (Paris, 1921), vol. 3. All references to the *Confort* are to this edition.

Helen, nor Hercules fought for Dejanira.[91] King Charles should cling to hope, and adore the precious image of his lady: "Sa grant biauté, son cointe atour / Et son gentil corps fait a tour." Abruptly, Machaut concludes:

> Mais, pour chose que je te die,
> Garde toy bien que t'estudie
> Soit adès tout premierement
> En servir Dieu devotement,
> Qu'il n'est amour qui se compère
> A s'amour, foy que doy saint Pere,
> Ne chose, tant soit pure, eu monde,
> Ne que riens contre tout le monde,
> Ou comme une ymage en pointure
> Contre une vive creature.
> (2763–71)

91. Lines 2103–2762. The formulation of William Calin (*Poet* 135) suggests that the biblical and mythological *exempla* are to be taken together as making the same point: "Job, Mattathias, Christ, Socrates, Orpheus, Ceres, Proserpina, Paris, Helen, and Hercules are cited for their loyalty to Hope." In fact, though, Machaut begins with a group of biblical *exempla* that illustrate faith in God (Susanna, Shadrach, Meschach, and Abednego, Daniel in the lion's den, and King Manasseh), moralizes upon them ("I have told you these four examples to comfort you. . . . You should note how God keeps those whom He wishes to counsel"), alludes briefly to Mattathias, Joseph, and Job as further *exempla* of God's grace, and then takes up the topic of love and the *exempla* from mythology. Within this division of the *Confort,* Hope is the deceitful lady we have already met in the *Roman de la Rose,* altogether different from the theological virtue that sustained the biblical characters. The Hope recommended by the *Remede de Fortune* will be a subject for another chapter; suffice it to say here that she is the same lady, though her identity is recognized neither by the lover to whom she speaks nor by modern critics of the poem. Douglas Kelly ("Inventions" 88), addressing the mythological *exempla,* writes that "Machaut compares the love of the prince for his wife to the love of Paris and Helen, Hercules and Dejanira, and Orpheus and Eurydice—while suppressing the tragic ending of each story. Machaut leaves Charles the choice between the truncated version that opens upon a happy future and the traditional one that reveals the sad effects of foolish love" (my translation). This interpretation, however, is difficult to support. There is no reason to infer a "happy future" on the basis of the poet's truncated version of the myths of love; a more natural inference is that the poet (who here playfully assumes the conventional narrative voice of a foolish lover) has suppressed the tragic endings in order to call attention to their absence, and his narrator's bias. Also, as Kelly himself notes ("Inventions" 90), there are difficulties in applying the poet's courtly love approach to the case of Charles and his wife, whom he had abducted. I believe that, as usual in the *dits,* the "lady" is a fiction, invented for rhetorical purposes.

Why would the *Confort,* which is fundamentally a religious document, first recommend that the king imitate Orpheus, Paris, and Hercules by serving his lady and then remind him that his duty is to serve God? The section on love is so brief and self-contained that, if the last ten lines are a palinode, the impression they create is odd indeed. In fact, the transition is abrupt and illogical only to a modern reader; if Machaut does not explain what he is about, it is because Charles would have known perfectly well. This discussion of love has basically the same structure that we have seen in the commentary on the tale of Jason and Medea in the *Echecs Amoureux,* and that we will see again many times in medieval discussions of love: passionate sexual love is first praised, classical *exempla* are adduced, and finally love is regarded *sub specie aeternitatis* and found wanting. Douglas Kelly has noted that Machaut's choice of classical *exempla* "is curious, since all the examples prove the unfortunate effects of desire despite the initial benefits of hope. . . . the tragic conclusion to each example suggests the misfortunes of immoderation in love or despair." He concludes that Machaut chooses to ignore the implications of these *exempla* in order to emphasize the benefits of Hope.[92] To the medieval reader, however, both the initial extravagant praise of love and the familiar classical *exempla* functioned as indications that he was within one of two possible rhetorical environments: either the speaker was a lover who would remain infatuated to the end of the poem (clearly not the environment of the *Confort*), or the speaker was preparing to remind him of the nature of such love from the standpoint of reason and religion. Medieval literature is rich in possibilities, but the very widespread and consistent tradition of interpretation of the myths of the classical lovers does serve to eliminate some of them. That a medieval poet would suggest seriously to his king that he ought to imitate Paris is not a possibility.

Deschamps, in the *Miroir de Mariage,* finds essentially the same *moralitas* in the classical myths of love, but his treatment of them is more straightforward. In this lengthy (over 12,000 lines, though never completed) consideration of the advantages and disadvantages

92. Douglas Kelly, *Imagination* 125. Kelly's comparison of Machaut's use of these *exempla* to Guillaume de Lorris's use of the fountain of Narcissus (he turned it "from a mirror of self-love to a source of *fin'amors*") is a good one, but as Kelly himself has seen these very commonplace mythological *exempla* stubbornly resist attempts to turn them to the good of lovers; in both cases, the purpose of the author is ironic.

of the married state, Deschamps depends chiefly upon *exempla* from the Old Testament. Though he begins the poem with a discussion of the goods of marriage, his perspective on it is never in doubt; his subject, Franc Vouloir, is counseled to marry by Desir, Folie, Servitute and Faintise.[93] In support of the doctrinally sound propositions that woman is a helpmeet, that God bade man multiply, and that even beasts mate, "Et non pas pour charnel delit, / Fors tant que son semblable lesse / En continuant son espece," the allegorical counselors adduce Sara and the wife of Tobias. Franc Vouloir, however, is inclined to consider "la franchise ou il est et . . . le servitute ou on le veult bouter," as well as the possibility that his wife may turn out to be ill-tempered, "jalouse, despiteuse, felle, ayrouse," or a spendthrift (572–1040). He decides to seek the opinion of his "vray ami," Repertoire de Science, who "cerche touz ses livres" and writes a letter of some 7,300 lines introducing some uncomfortable considerations: weddings are unsatisfactory whether modest or sumptuous, and wives whether rich or poor, ugly or beautiful, fertile or barren; it is easier to obtain accurate information about a horse for sale than about a prospective bride; children are a great risk and expense if healthy, and a shame to their parents if deformed; women are treacherous and will resort to any deceit to have their will; a poor husband, "envelopé de paroles," is sure to give in eventually (1129–8410). He advises Franc Vouloir to "soy desister et getter hors du flum de luxure par prier Dieu" and to embrace "les nopces espiritueles" (LXI, rubric). In his discussion of the treachery of women, Repertoire de Science cites, along with Samson and Delilah, Agamemnon and Clytemnestra, Paris and Helen, as well as Hercules and Dejanira. He demonstrates mastery of the customary rhetorical uses of the heroines; recounting with relish Clytemnestra's murder of her husband ("Savez vous encore qu'ele fit?"), he calls her "pecheresse," "luxurieuse," "putain" (2488–2722). The lesson he extracts from her story, and from those of Hercules and Dejanira, Paris and Helen, is the traditional one that "Belle femme est trop perilleuse" (2718). On account of Helen, "cent mille hommes xviii foys, / Et xxvi m. ensuivent" lost their lives; and Hercules, "qui tant de monstres surmonta," was conquered by an evil woman (2648–2702).

93. Rubric II (Raynaud IX, 4). All references to the *Miroir* are to the edition of Raynaud.

Lest the reader fail to detect his motive in including the classical tales, Repertoire de Science explains their importance. Listing the "saiges anciens" harassed or betrayed by women—Samson, Solomon, Hercules, Aristotle, Plato, Socrates, Cato, Juvenal, Ovid, and Virgil—he urges Franc Vouloir to heed their painfully acquired wisdom, as set down in their writings:

> . . . par leurs auctoritez
> Et les exemples de leurs livres,
> [ils] Conseillent que tu ne livres
> A telz maulx, puis que tu les sens;
> Tu seroies plus hors du sens
> Que ceuls qu'on maine a saint Acaire,
> Se tu veulz ouvrer du contraire,
> Car les exemples anciens
> Nous sont et cordes et liens
> De nous garder des grans perilz,
> Que nous trouvons par leurs escrips
> Et que nous veons clerement,
> Qui nous puelent mettre a tourment
> Du corps et de l'ame en la fin.
> (5558–71)

The *Miroir* is, quite obviously, a psychomachia, with Desir, Folie, Servitute and Faintise representing the appetitive faculties and Repertoire de Science representing knowledge guided by reason, which when presented with a problem looks to established authority for a solution. In this scheme neither appetite nor reason alone speaks for Deschamps or for any other man; the man is the battleground of their struggle. In the *Miroir,* after Repertoire de Science makes his report, the four foolish counselors return to rebut it, defending the virtue and chastity of women (using the Christian saints as *exempla*) and protesting that married men may come to heaven equally with the celibate (8411–10525). Even after Franc Vouloir, having considered all the arguments, decides in favor of spiritual marriage, he continues to be harassed by Folie; in terms of the allegory, that is, a wise decision taken does not exempt one from continued rebellion of the lower faculties. Here, it is not safe even to identify the classical heroines with Folie, as she herself does not defend them, but argues simply that not all women are evil as they are (9388–9750).

Froissart, in the dream vision *Joli Buisson de Jonece,* moralizes the folly of the classical lovers in a scheme much like that of Machaut, though on a larger scale: he first establishes his narrator as a servant of Venus, then introduces the lovers as *exempla*—if he suffers, how much more did they!—and finally rejects love-service altogether upon waking from his dream. The *Buisson* is an elaborate poem and an unusual one in certain respects, although its most important features are conventional. As the title suggests, it identifies love-service as characteristic of youth, though not, as we will see, really proper to it. The narrator, a man of 35, is accused of sloth by the lady Philozophie, who protests that he is wasting his talents: he must write. He objects that his inspiration is exhausted; he has already written *Le Paradis d'Amour, L'Orloge, L'Espinette Amoureuse, La Prison Amoureuse,* and "grant foison de dis et de lays."[94] Philozophie suggests that he draw inspiration from an old portrait of his lady that he has stored in a chest. When he finds the portrait and gazes upon it, he feels again the "ardent fu" that he felt as a youth, the same that Achilles felt when he first caught sight of Polyxena (615–26). At this point, the narrator interrupts his recital with the tale of Achilles and Polyxena, likening himself to the hero in that they both cherished portraits of a lady. He concludes the tale with the usual *moralitas* upon the classical lovers, applying it as well to himself: love was the cause of Achilles' death; in following love he followed Fortune, which was his undoing; and now the

94. Lines 102–452. All references to the *Buisson* are to the edition of Fourrier. This autobiographical material has led many scholars to read the *Buisson* simply as autobiography; in his summary of the poem, Fourrier refers to its narrator as "Froissart." However, any attempt to reconcile the "facts" of the poem with what we know of Froissart's life and work gives rise to contradictions. The *Buisson* is usually regarded as the companion piece of the *Espinette Amoureuse,* which tells of a youthful love-adventure; but the 25-year-old narrator of the *Espinette* is 35 in the *Buisson* whereas, to the best of our knowledge, Froissart really wrote the *Buisson* only three years after the *Espinette*. Freeman ("*Buisson*" 247n8) notes that "Froissart's *persona* in the *Buisson* is also ten years older than Guillaume de Lorris' lover-turned-poet"; it would seem, then, that the attributes of narrative *personae* in the *dits* are partly autobiographical and partly conventional, so that they are hybrid fictional creations. Fourrier, who identifies the narrators of both poems with Froissart, expresses surprise that the narrator of the *Buisson* possesses a portrait of the lady, whereas no portrait is mentioned in the *Espinette* (*Buisson* 32). Such difficulties vanish if we acknowledge the essentially fictional character of the *dits*.

narrator is foolishly pursuing the same course: ". . . je m'areste en grant folie, / Et se sçai bien que je folie; / Si n'en puis je mon coer retraire" (718–20). He reflects upon his age and the Last Judgment, hoping that he has not lost heaven by serving the lady instead of "celui que je doi servir." But the sight of the portrait has made a profound impression upon him, and when he sleeps Venus appears to him in a vision. He complains to her of having misspent his youth in profitless love-service—"elle m'a arrier rebouté / Pour autrui." She wastes little time denying it, but quickly suggests that they go amuse themselves in some pleasant place: "Tu os le rosegnol joli . . . / Lieve toi! Alons nous esbatre" (970, 980). He finds that in her company he cannot say his usual morning prayer, and so accompanies her without completing it; in return for a sight of the Buisson de Jonece, he promises not to complain of whatever fortune he may have.

The *buisson,* when they reach it, is an astonishing sight: round as an apple, more than a hundred hands high, and of an indescribable translucent bluish color. A young man, Jonece himself, replaces Venus as guide. He explains the meaning of the *buisson:* it is like the heavens, its leaves the stars, its seven branches the seven planets (1585–1707). The narrator, impatient with this lecture, protests that he wants only to enjoy himself, not to "parler de grant astronomie": "Mon esperit n'i poet entendre, / Car il ne voelt qu'a une tendre; / C'est a estre gais et jolis, / A amer solas et delis / Danses, carolles et esbas."[95] In his present mood, he would rather have a garland of flowers than all the wisdom of Paris or Sens. Jonece obediently brings him to a *locus amoenus,* where in a group of women he sees his lady, just as she was in youth. He does not dare approach her; considering the danger of intruding upon ladies, he rehearses the tale of Acteon (2242–88). After elaborate maneuvering to banish Dangier, Refus, and Escondit and bring forth Doulc Semblant, he is rewarded by a little smile, which inspires a *balade* in praise of the lady. Accompanied now by the full retinue of love—Beautés, Plaisance, Desirs, Maniere, Cognoissance—he complains to Desirs of his suffering: "J'ars tous et flame! . . . Dittes qu'on me

95. Lines 1740–44. Shears (*Froissart* 196–97) identifies these sentiments as the poet's own; describing Froissart as "our nonchalant and pleasure-loving poet," he quotes this passage as exemplifying the personality of this man who "demands of life pleasure and amusement, beauty, wealth, and power." The distinction between the poet himself and his conventional narrative *persona* is critical to the understanding of the medieval poetry of love. See note 94.

viegne secourre" (3059, 3068). Desirs replies with the classical *exempla;* many lovers, he says, have suffered as you do. He outlines the tales of Phoebus and Daphne, Proserpine and Orpheus (sic), Leander and Hero, Pygmalion, Narcissus and Echo, Paris and Helen, Achilles and Polyxena (among others), with emphasis upon their love-suffering and tragic deaths (3137–3392). The narrator still cries out for "confort," but Desirs impatiently replies that a priest doesn't blame his relics; he should feel honored that Venus allowed him the sight of the *buisson*. Desirs ultimately agrees to deliver a *balade* to the lady, and after he, Jonece, and Franchise speak on the lover's behalf she agrees to see him, on condition that he say nothing "oultrageuse." He speaks very prettily, and Jonece weaves the lovers a garland. The personified abstractions—Desirs, Humilité, Jonece, Maniere, Pités, Doulc Samblant, Franchise—express their good wishes in verse, each in turn, and Desirs suggests that the God of Love, "qu'on l'aimme et prise et serve et doubte" (5043), bestow the garland upon the one who has spoken best. Just as he is in hope of meeting the god at last, the narrator awakes, in something of the mood of Troilus in the eighth sphere. He marvels that he ever "fui de fu et de flame attains": "a present riens je n'en sens" (5755). Looking back upon his love-service in youth, he reflects that he will have to give account of the follies of the flesh, "qui n'est que cendre et poureture"; the sins of the body impede the upward progress of the soul. One's soul should be inflamed by Christ, not by carnal love. He offers a *lay* in praise of the Virgin, symbol of the real *buisson* of love, the bush that burns but is not consumed and whose flame gives light, not heat:

> C'est li Buissons / resplendissans
> Non amenrissans,
> Mais croissans
> Et edefians
> Tous biens par divine ordenance.
> Et ses Fils, ce dist sains Jehans,
> Est li feus plaisans,
> Non ardans,
> Mais enluminans
> Tours coers qui en Lui ont fiance.
> (5402-5411)

I have summarized this poem at such length for several reasons. First of all, the classical heroes and heroines of love appear here, as they have done in all the works we have so far examined, associated unequivocally with the love that is ultimately rejected. Second, it is not possible in the case of this poem to argue that its last 244 lines constitute a palinode, "tacked on" to disarm criticism of the five thousand lines devoted to the affair of the lovers. The poem's central symbol, the *buisson* whose center is everywhere, its circumference nowhere, is a convention not of fourteenth century French love poetry but of the Bible and Biblical exegesis. The final rejection of love stands as an integral part of the symbolic structure of the poem, closely tied to the revelation of the proper meaning of the *buisson*.[96] It does not, in fact, need a very alert reader to predict the eventual appearance of the burning bush from the title alone. Finally, although the rejection of love appears abruptly and is quite brief, it is foreshadowed throughout the poem by broad hints that the lover is behaving foolishly: he compares himself to Achilles, whose love for Polyxena ended in disaster; though he notes that he cannot pray in the presence of Venus, he nevertheless follows her; he does not wish to listen to an exposition of the meaning of the *buisson,* and in fact protests repeatedly that he is interested only in diversion; he says that he would rather have pretty flowers than great learning; he persists in love-service despite the fact that Venus, Desirs, and the lady herself offer slight reward, or none, and reply speciously to his questions, Desirs even offering the classical *exempla* as "confort" when their traditional significance is quite the opposite.[97] Considering, then, that both of the divisions of the

96. Alice Planche in her article "Du Joli Buisson de Jonece au Buisson Ardent: le Lay de Notre-Dame dans le *Dit* de Froissart," in *La Prière au Moyen Âge: Littérature et Civilisation* (Aix-en-Provence, 1980), after an excellent discussion of the six symbolic bushes of the *Espinette,* concludes, oddly, that the final rejection of love in the *Buisson* is too harsh and abrupt, "à la fin d'une oeuvre qui implique un jugement plus nuancé" (412). The rose and hawthorn bushes, traditionally symbolic of youth and love and a part of the characteristic furniture of love-allegory, give way first to the *Buisson,* an equivocal symbol which is not, of course, adequately described as the "buisson de jonece," and finally to the *buisson ardent,* which certainly preceded the others conceptually. Further, as Planche herself notes (411), the antithesis between the illusory and deceitful fire of love and the pure fire of the soul is present from the beginning of the work.

97. Froissart has been severely chastised for these mythological "digressions." Audrey Graham criticizes them as tediously long, and "extraneous to the principal subject matter" ("Classical Allusion" 29); Fourrier, Froissart's editor, regrets that

poem—the five thousand lines on love-service and the 244 lines in rejection of it—seem to have been carefully planned in their relation to each other, how shall we describe that relation? If the poet is ultimately to reject passionate sexual love in such strong terms—"cendre et poureture"—then why does he spill so much ink on it? If he is ultimately to recommend the love of God, why does he not write a long devotional poem, or at least a well-developed sermon, in conclusion?

There are, I think, at least two answers to these questions. The first one has to do with the great interest taken by Froissart, and by other poets of his time, in the dynamics of love. In the course of surveying medieval use of the classical lovers we have many times seen their spiritual condition related in various ways to the Augustinian notion of love as barometer of the soul's health. In the terms of medieval Christianity, men who concentrate their allegiance upon the things of the earth chain their souls to the earth, as Vulcan chained Venus and Mars in his net. In poetry and prose written before the thirteenth century, the lovers are straightforwardly condemned for their folly, most often in the context of sermons on disordered love. We will see that the impulse to examine and describe the dynamics of passionate love even as one criticizes it is

the poet "ait quelque peu abusé dans le *Joli Buisson de Jonece* du procédé de l'emprunt mythologique" (28), and believes that Froissart regards the fables as nothing more than a "magasin d'ornements poétiques" (27). Picherit perceives that, although Desirs intends to encourage the lover, the *exempla* he chooses are in fact premonitory tales of unhappy love ("Éléments" 503). Planche notes that the *exempla* do not relieve the lover's suffering, but only fan the flames ("*Buisson*" 410). They are both correct; we will see that situations of this kind, in which the lover is so infatuated that he is completely unable to penetrate the real meaning of the *exempla*, are a common source of humor in the *dits*. The *exempla* offered here are idiosyncratic in two ways: Froissart alters the tale of Narcissus so that he, and not Echo, becomes the grieving lover, and he cites Proserpine, rather than Eurydice, as the wife of Orpheus. These alterations are probably deliberate; he certainly knew the traditional version of the myth of Orpheus, as he retells it in the *Prison Amoureuse,* and later within the *Buisson* itself he alludes correctly to the tale of Proserpine (3183–84). Both Picherit and Douglas Kelly point out that the change in the Narcissus myth creates a closer analogy between Narcissus and the poet, although I do not think the tradition supports the inference that they are "good lovers" (as Kelly claims, "Inventions" 87). Fourrier suggests that Froissart may have borrowed Proserpine from Machaut's *Confort d'Ami,* where her tale appears inserted into that of Orpheus and Eurydice (*Buisson* 24); Picherit believes that, by evoking the Queen of Hell, Froissart may have wished to surround the love-journey to the *Buisson* with infernal imagery ("Éléments" 504).

first detectable in Jean de Meun. The *Roman de la Rose* certainly does not elaborate a new theory of love, or pioneer a new approach to it, but it does change the traditional proportions of discussions of love; instead of describing the lover's feelings and actions in bare outline as he preaches on the misdirection of *concupiscentia,* Jean externalizes and personifies them, so that the spiritual condition of the lover becomes the core of the poem.[98] This is a subtler, more artful, and potentially far more powerful way of communicating the accepted truths about love, and it brings us to the second answer to our questions about artistic proportion, which has to do with the requirements of effective teaching. Sermons on the vices and virtues had always concentrated on the vices; Chaucer's Parson finds roughly eight times as much to say about *superbia* as about its *remedium,* four times as much about *ira* as about *mansuetude,* and so forth. And, to remain with the Parson for a moment, the interest he shows in developing his discussion of the vices is much the sort of interest that Froissart shows in passionate love: he wishes to describe what men do and feel under the influence of certain emotions. In reading or hearing of what men do and feel, we recognize ourselves, a process that was, as we will see, more accustomed and less uncomfortable to medieval readers than to modern ones. The well-known medieval combination of *sentence* and *solas* has long been out of fashion; we take our preaching in church, where it had better be tactfully impersonal, and our literature is the exclusive preserve of *solas* (seasoned, at times, with *scientia*). It would not be possible for a modern poet to suggest to his political leader, as Machaut did to Charles of Navarre, that present hardship might be payment for sinful practices in youth. But there is considerable evidence that, in the Middle Ages, moral chastisement was viewed as both a benevolent gesture and an accepted feature of serious literature. Placebo the flatterer is no friend to the Merchant, or to anyone; a great poet, like a good friend, encourages one to

98. On Jean's innovations in allegory, see the excellent articles of H. R. Jauss, "Allégorie, 'remythisation,' et nouveau mythe. Réflexions sur la captivité chrétienne de la mythologie au moyen âge," in *Mélanges Offerts à Charles Rostaing,* vol. 1 (Liège, 1974): 469–99, and Karl Uitti, "From Clerc to Poète: The Relevance of the *Roman de la Rose* to Machaut's World," in Cosman and Chandler, eds., *Machaut's World,* 209–16. Jean alters the form of the traditional psychomachia so that the personified abstractions, instead of combatting each other in polarized pairs independently of a detached narrator, act in harmony with the impulses of the narrator, a particular individual within a fictional situation.

virtue, and he does it by means of *exempla* in which one can see one's own behavior as in a mirror. In that sense, all serious medieval poems, and certainly the *Joli Buisson,* are *specula.* Froissart's lover (like the classical lovers to whom he is compared) is a mirror for the reader, which reflects the more clearly the more his emotions and experiences are detailed and analyzed.

Because the poetry of love never developed as fully in England as in France and Italy, England contributed less to the tradition of moralization of the classical lovers; but when English poets do comment upon the lovers, they do so within the same rhetorical environments that we have seen constructed by their contemporaries on the continent. The works of Chaucer will be the subject of a later chapter, after we have reviewed more thoroughly the rather complex conventions governing medieval use of the lovers. The works of Lydgate in which the lovers are moralized—*Reson and Sensuallyte* and *The Fall of Princes*—are translations, the originals of which (the *Echecs Amoureux* and Boccaccio's *De Casibus*) we have already examined. In another medieval *speculum,* the *Mirour de L'Omme,* Gower places Pluto, Proserpine, and Venus at the head of the table at the wedding feast of the World with the Seven Daughters of Sin, and in his discussion of the sins Paris and Helen furnish an *exemplum* against *luxuria.*[99] But it is in a shorter work, the *Traitié,* that he moralizes the tales of love fully in traditional fashion. The title of the *Traitié* does not reveal much about its content, but it is followed by an explanatory rubric that begins by referring to the *Confessio Amantis,* which evidently preceded it in the manuscript:

> Puisqu'il ad dit ci devant en Englois par voie d'essample la sotie de cellui qui par amours aime par especial, dirra ore apres en François a tout le monde en general un traitié selonc les auctours pour essampler les amantz marietz, au fin qu'ils la foi lous seintes espousailes pourront par fine loialté guarder, et al honour de dieu salvement tenir. (Rubric, 379)

Much of the *Traitié* is devoted to an exposition of the Christian ideal of love and marriage. God gave man reason that it might rule over his body; the love of God is the love most natural to the soul, but

99. Lines 961–72 and 16700–716. All references to the French works of Gower are to the edition of G. C. Macaulay, *The Complete Works of John Gower,* vol. 1 (Oxford, 1902).

marriage is sanctified as a concession to the weakness of the flesh, and for *engendrure* (I, 1–2). Both body and soul are good, but the soul is a higher good; both the contemplative and active lives are good, but the contemplative is higher. God does not compel men to the perfection of the contemplative life; they may marry. If they do, however, they should be loyal, for honest love is essential to true marriage. It is against reason to choose a wife, confirm one's choice by marriage, and then betray her. Marriage is indissoluble and sacred; Christ himself was born to a married woman. Love outside of marriage ends badly, for God avenges adultery (III–V).

After this introduction, Gower offers the classical *exempla* in proof of the principles he has enunciated. Because his topic is adultery, he chooses married lovers unfaithful to their mates—Ulysses with Circe, Hercules with Iole, Jason with Creusa, Clytemnestra with Aegisthus, Helen with Paris, Tarquinius with Lucretia, Tereus with Philomela (VI–XII). He accompanies them with *exempla* from history and from the Bible: Anectanabus and Olympias, Paulina and Mundus, David and Bathsheba. The point of all the *exempla* is that adultery is punished by God. Ulysses was killed by his illegitimate son Telegonus, Anectanabus by Alexander, Clytemnestra by Orestes (VI–IX). The adultery of Hercules was avenged by the burning shirt, that of Jason by the death of his sons, that of Helen by the destruction of Troy. The sin of Tarquinius resulted in the death of Lucretia, and Tereus was transformed into a filthy and ignoble bird (XI–XII). Such dreadful punishments amply demonstrate that lovers are wrong to praise love: "Tiels chante, 'c'est ma sovereine joie' / Qui puis en ad dolour sanz departie" (XVIII, 1, 5–6). This approach to teaching by means of the classical *exempla* is anything but subtle; Gower summarizes the old stories because "bel oisel par autre se chastie," and in a Latin envoy to the poem acknowledges his hope that readers will refrain from adultery from fear of punishment: "Exemplo veteri poterunt ventura timeri" (XV, 7; XVIII, 4, 10). He concludes that there is no joy in illicit love: "Non ita gaudebit sibi qui de carne placebit, / Quin corpus flebit aut spiritus inde dolebit" (XVIII, 4, 12–13).

This sort of non-mythographic moralization of the classical lovers continues into the Renaissance and beyond in France, England, Italy, and Spain. Christine de Pizan, in the *Livre de la Mutacion de Fortune,* retells at length the story of Jason and Medea, reflecting parenthetically:

Si fait a noter comme Amours,
Meismes aux sçavens change mours
Et avugle si et deçoipt
Que le plus sage n'apperçoit
Sa follie, par trop amer.[100]

Robert Henryson, in his *Tale of Orpheus and Erudices his Quene,* concludes with an allegorical *moralitas* of 218 lines (to a poem of 633), quoting Boethius's identification of Orpheus with "the part intellectiue / Of mannis saule" and Eurydice with concupiscence, always ready to fall back into sin.[101] The fifteenth-century Spanish poet Juan de Mena, in the *Laberinto de Fortuna,* includes Myrrha, Canace, Pasiphae, and Scylla among the "ancients given to evil love":

Eran adúlteros e fornicarios,
e otros notados de incestuosos,
e muchos que juntan tales criminosos
e llevan por ello los viles salarios,
e los que en efectos así voluntarios
su vida deleitan en vano pecando,
e los maculados de crimen nefando,
de justa razón e de toda contrarios.[102]

He concludes with the pious wish that "los viles actos del libidinoso / Fuego de Venus del todo se maten, / e los humanos sobre todo caten / el limpio católico amor virtuoso."[103]

Perhaps the most remarkable production of the early Renaissance that places the classical lovers within the context of Christian morality is the *Blason de Faulses Amours* of Guillaume Alexis, prior of Bucy. This long poem takes the form of a dialogue on love between "un gentilhomme" and "un moyne" who are traveling together, the monk saying his offices as the gentleman sings lewd ditties. When the gentleman invites the monk to join him in song—"Car en

100. Lines 14685–89, ed. Suzanne Solente, *Le Livre de la Mutacion de Fortune par Christine de Pisan,* 3 vols. (Paris, 1959), vol. 3.

101. Lines 428–29, 431–34, ed. Denton Fox, *Poems of Robert Henryson* (Oxford, 1981).

102. Stanza 101, ed. Louise Vasvari Fainberg, *Juan de Mena:* Laberinto de Fortuna (Madrid, 1976).

103. Stanza 114, ed. Fainberg, *Laberinto.*

chantant / Et s'esbatant / Le temps se passe"—he is treated to a lecture on "amours folle."[104] I see, begins the monk, that you care for nothing but love; you are a good demonstration that love makes fools of those who are caught in his net. You praise vain love, but I can answer your songs: "Faulses amours, recullez vous / De moy, que jamais ne vous voye." Whoever thinks that love is pleasant deceives himself; the reward of love is sorrow, madness, and regret. You'd be better off as a bricklayer's helper![105] The pleasure of love is brief, but the evil that comes of it lasts forever. Can you think of a more terrible martyrdom than the life of a lover? To pursue the voluptuous life is to live as a beast, not as a man. In reply, the gentleman objects that one cannot ignore one's need for pleasure; love is proper to youth, and old age is soon enough to forswear it. Everything has its season. Do you want to deny us the company of women altogether? The debate continues in this vein, until the monk embarks upon a long misogynist diatribe in which the classical lovers figure prominently as *exempla*. "Pour ung bien que donne Amour," he warns, "Cent mille maulx vous y prendrez" (599–600). Think of Adam, Samson, and Solomon; think of Hercules, if you would know "Les grans excès / Qu'a perpetrez / Femme mauldicte" (628–30). Consider the death of Hippolytus, the cruelty of Medea who murdered her little children, the fate of Troy because of the vain love of Paris and Helen. The love of Pyramus and Thisbe led to tragedy; Lucretia died on account of the lust of Tarquinius; Clytemnestra, Cleopatra and Semiramis all came to a bad end. "De femme fine / Tost en ruyne / L'estat viendra, / Et qui s'incline / A sa doctrine / Mal lui prendra" (709–14). Once Venus takes hold of you, she will never let go; you'll be an old man, still trying out of evil habit to continue in the vices of youth. At length the gentleman himself, convinced at last (or perhaps only exhausted), finishes the lecture:

> Plaisirs muables,
> Fais importables
> Sont amours et telles les voy
> . . . .

104. Lines 37ff, ed. Arthur Piaget and Emile Picot, *Oeuvres Poétiques de Guillaume Alexis, Prieur de Bucy,* 3 vols. (Paris, 1896), vol. 1. All references to the *Blason* are to this edition.

105. Lines 85–120. To quote Piaget and Picot (190n): "On disait au moyen âge que rien n'est plus pénible que de servir les maçons."

Veu que savons
Que cy trouvons
Si briefve vie,
Et tost avons,
Se mal vivons,
Mort desservie,
Saige n'est mye
Qui porte envie
Aux vices que nous poursuyvons.
(1471–73, 1476–85)

In concentrating upon straightforward moralizations of the classical lovers by major poets in non-mythographic works, I have of course omitted mention of the mythographers. It is nevertheless true that the poets I have discussed must often have derived their attitudes toward the classical tales of love, wholly or in part, from one or more of them. The French poets of the High Middle Ages learned their Ovid from the *Ovide Moralisé,* which along with its elaborate allegories repeats many of the traditional moralities on love and the lovers. Of the fable of Mars and Venus, it comments, "Grief mort et grief destruction / Vienent par fornication," and "Amours toute vertu efface"; it identifies Leander with "fole amour" and Hero with "luxure"; it reproaches Pasiphae for "puterie et . . . grant honte," and Byblis, "trop bele et poi sage," for her "fol penser."[106] It also repeats the traditional allegory on Orpheus and Eurydice, associates Myrrha with "luxure" and the Judgment of Paris with choice of the voluptuous life of "fol voloir."[107] Almost all of the lovers are condemned for their folly, either in the narrative itself or in terms of the allegory. Giovanni del Virgilio, friend of Dante and author of an influential commentary on Ovid often used in schools, identifies the darkened mulberry of the tale of Pyramus and Thisbe with the death that lies hidden in love and the tale of Tereus and Philomela with "amor obscenus."[108] The Third Vatican Mythographer moralizes the loves of Pasiphae, Medea, Polyxena, Phaedra, Hero and Leander, Dido and Aeneas, Paris and Helen, and of course Mars and Venus in terms of "detestabili amore," "cupidi-

106. IV, 1640–41, 1717, and 3592–93; VIII, 1084; IX, 2533 and 2537 (DeBoer II, 47, 48, and 87, and III, 134 and 282).

107. X, 220ff and 3707; XII, 835 (deBoer IV, 16, 99, and 253).

108. *Allegorie* IV, 4 and VI, 32 (Ghisalberti 55 and 74).

tas," "turpitudo."[109] Bersuire, as well as repeating the familiar morality on the affair of Mars and Venus, makes use of Procne and Philomela, Jason and Medea, Byblis and Caunus, Scylla, Dejanira, and Myrrha in moralizing against *luxuria, concupiscentia,* and incest.[110] Boccaccio, the most distinguished and influential mythographer of his age, does the same in the case of Paris and Helen, Orpheus and Eurydice, Pasiphae, Narcissus, and Ariadne.[111]

The influence of the mythographers, and especially the pervasive influence of the *Ovide Moralisé,* the *Ovidius Moralizatus* of Bersuire, and the *De Genealogia Deorum,* has been established by such scholars as deBoer, S. B. Meech, Ghisalberti, J. Engels, and Lowes. Even without other evidence, we could be certain that Dante, Petrarch, Boccaccio, Chaucer, and their French contemporaries knew the traditional moralizations of the classical tales of love. A review of some of the evidence from their own works makes it clear in addition that they respected them enough to use them as props to some of their most serious arguments. What remains unclear, perhaps, is how those arguments are to be understood in the light of other works in which the same poets use the same classical figures in quite different ways. What we have thus far established is that there was a long-standing tradition of moralization of the classical lovers *sub specie aeternitatis;* that is, the lovers were conventionally used as *exempla* of disordered love. But they were used in other ways as well, which is to say that there are other conventions governing their use by medieval poets. A medieval poet might use them in preaching, but he might equally well compare himself to them, write in praise of them, express envy of them, or defend them against detractors. In doing these things, he may seem to us to contradict himself; how can Froissart reject the lovers in the *Buisson de Jonece* while seeming to admire them—and even defending his own behavior as a lover in terms of theirs—in his lyrics? Perhaps the first thing to consider is that in both cases Froissart is speaking through a *persona,* which we are dependent upon the literary work itself to define. None of his works, or those of any of the other poets we have discussed, are confessional in the modern

109. Lib. 11: 6, 24, 20, 4, ed. Georgius Henricus Bode, *Scriptores Rerum Mythicarum Latini Tres Romae Nuper Reperti* (Hildesheim, 1968).

110. *Red. Mor.* XV: 4, 6, 7, 9, 8, 10 (Engels 77, 106, 111, 145, 123, and 153).

111. *De Gen.* VI, 22; V, 12; IV, 10; VII, 59; and XI, 29 (Romano I: 304, 245, 168, 381, and II, 567).

sense; even the confessional tone of the lyrics is achieved by careful manipulation of conventional formulae. This is a poetry whose drama is all in the conflict of ideas, and our understanding of the ideas depends greatly upon our familiarity with the conventions through which they are expressed.

In an important way, then, a study of this kind approaches medieval poetry backwards, and although that is necessary under the circumstances it is a most undesirable way to read. In the light of the evidence we have surveyed, we can now see that, when we encounter an allusion to, say, the affair of Paris and Helen in a work that is clearly didactic in intent, we must expect the writer to discuss carnal and celestial love, or *amor legitimus* and *amor stultus*. If he does not do so right away, their very appearance constitutes a clue to his likely conclusion: he is practically certain to do so sooner or later. We know that, however, only because we have just examined a great many medieval works in which the lovers appear, seeking insight into the conventions governing allusions to the classical heroes and heroines of love. But the poets have not planned their works for readers seeking such insight; on the contrary, they have planned them carefully for readers who know the conventions very well already, which is to say readers of their own time rather than ours. They expect the allusions, in their particular context, to function as clues to the meaning of the poems, whereas we as modern readers are dependent upon other clues within the poems to interpret the allusions for us. Those clues may very well be inadequate, and we may miss the meaning both of the allusions and of the poems themselves. I have begun by addressing the moralizations of the lovers because the convention by which the lovers are moralized is the easiest to grasp of all the conventions governing their use in the Middle Ages; in addition, it is historically prior to the others and fundamental to understanding them. That frustrating process by which we struggle to understand classical allusions that ought to illuminate medieval poetry for us rather than complicating it is made much easier when the lovers simply stand for a sort of love that is rejected by the speaker. But it is now time to examine some of the other contexts in which the classical lovers occur. It will soon become apparent that, although they are different from the context of straightforward moralization, they resemble it in being limited and predictable, which is to say conventional. Once we have understood the range of contexts within which poets place these allusions, we can begin to use the allusions as clues to meaning, in the way that the poets intended.

3

The Theme of Spiritual Pilgrimage

The meaning of allusions to the classical lovers within medieval poems depends entirely upon the context in which they occur. We have already seen that medieval writers often allude to the classical lovers within the context of works involving spiritual pilgrimage. The *Consolation of Philosophy,* in which the speaker moves from a depressed and benighted state to philosophical enlightenment, is one such work; so are works in which the speaker is presented with contrasting moral choices, or given the opportunity to examine various ways of life, like the *Pèlerinage de la Vie Humaine,* Jean de Hauteville's *Architrenius,* the *Divina Commedia,* Petrarch's *Secretum* (and even the *Trionfi*), the *Echecs Amoureux,* and the *Joli Buisson de Jonece.* The speaker in such works does not in every case avail himself of the opportunity to pursue the highest good; because we have spoken so far only of works in which the classical lovers are definitively moralized, we have met only rather docile protagonists, who trot along obediently in the steps of their guides and counselors and end wiser than they began. That is one of the prescribed outlines for poems of spiritual pilgrimage, but there is another. Because medieval poets delighted in exploring the problem of spiritual allegiance from every possible perspective, they often created speakers who are naive, stupid, trivial, helplessly enmeshed in the sensual life, or just intractably resistant to *doctrina*. Froissart presents his narrator in that way throughout most of the *Joli Buisson,* and we have seen another such speaker in the *Echecs Amoureux,* though the poem breaks off before his reaction to the long speech of Pallas. Much of the *sentence* of these works lies in the example presented by the speaker himself. The classical *exempla* may be adduced as warnings by a wise counselor, praised by a foolish counselor, or praised and imitated by the lover himself. Except for Penelope, Lucretia, and Alceste, they are never praised by any spokesman for reason or religion.

Perhaps the most celebrated incorrigible narrator in all medieval literature is the Lover of the *Roman de la Rose*. In a work where, as Pierre Col pointed out, each character speaks according to his nature, we would expect to find the classical lovers praised or defended by foolish characters and used by the wise as *exempla* of fol'amors. That is precisely what we do find, but since Jean's technique is to exemplify rather than to preach, his intention in alluding to the lovers has not always been clear to critics. Ovid's *Art of Love,* on which the *Rose* is largely based, is indeed—as Christine de Pizan said, and as even her opponents agreed—an art of deceit and seduction that has nothing to do with real love.[1] This is the art of the Lover and of some of his counselors, and since Jean's main concern (as well as his main source of humor) is the description of the Lover's thoughts and experiences, this art is elaborated in detail. But Jean is at pains to place his discussion of the art of seduction within the context of Christian thought on love; in fact, he is so concerned to present alternatives to the behavior he describes that he has confused many readers by putting wise speeches into the mouths of foolish characters. Guillaume de Lorris begins this practice when he has the Lover (who has, as we will see, just done and said some very foolish things with regard to the Mirror of Narcissus) moralize upon the harmful effects of gazing into the mirror: "Out of this mirror a new madness comes upon men . . . intelligence and moderation have no business here, where there is only the simple will to love, where no one can be counseled. . . . now I have fallen into the snare that has captured and betrayed many a

1. *Epistre au Dieu d'Amours* 281–90.

man."[2] Later, the God of Love calls love a "disease" (2185) and warns the reader that "A lover will never possess what he seeks; something is always missing, and he is never at peace" (2419–22). Jean, probably wishing to distinguish more clearly the Hope which comforts lovers from the Christian virtue of the same name, puts into the mouth of the Lover (who ends by embracing Hope) the statement that ". . . he who draws too near to Hope is a fool . . . many have been deceived by her" (4083, 4088).[3] And the long speech of Faus Samblant, of course, alternates between boasting and condemnation of his own hypocrisy. Jean is not really violating his own decorum; the tradition by which vice may be condemned out of its own mouth was well established by his time. Kemp Malone calls it the "convention of self-characterization," one which "serves to make clear to the audience just who the character is and what kind of character he is."[4] It may be seen in the cycle plays, where Herod and Pilate plainly name their own evildoing at the same time that they boast of it and seek to justify themselves.[5] Chaucer himself uses this method in his presentation of the Pardoner, who details his own chicanery and then invites the pilgrims to kiss his false relics.

This is one way in which Jean reinforces the context within which he wishes the reader to view the behavior of the Lover, but there are other ways as well. The discourse of Reason supplies the broad context of Boethian and patristic thought on love, outlining the lover's predicament and offering him the means of escape from it. The world, she reminds him, is not the native land of men; Cupid turns them away from the road that would lead them back to their

2. Lines 1583–87, 1612–14. Quotations are from the edition of Poirion and the translation of Dahlberg.

3. Although she has not generally been perceived as such, Esperance is a consistently deceptive character in the *Rose* and in the *dits amoureux*. Roger Dragonetti, "Pygmalion ou les Pièges de la Fiction dans le *Roman de la Rose*," in *Orbis Medievalis: Mélanges de Langue et de Littérature Offerts à Reto Raduolf Bezzola*, ed. Georges Guntert et al. (Bern, 1978): 89–111, p. 104, speaks of the "espoir chimérique" that sustains "courtly" lovers, and Kibler, in his article on the *Espinette Amoureuse* of Froissart, points out the deceptive nature of Esperance throughout the poetry of the late Middle Ages (95); it is, in fact, a name given to the lover's self-delusion, and we will see that careful attention to the *dits* reveals that it is exposed as such in all of them.

4. *Chapters on Chaucer* (Baltimore, 1951), 178–79.

5. John Fleming (*The* Roman de la Rose: *A Study in Allegory and Iconography* [Princeton, 1969], 53) compares Jean's organizational principles to those of the morality plays, specifically *The Castle of Perseverance*.

real home. "That foolish love which inflames hearts and makes them burn with desire" will lead him to lose his sense, time, possessions, body, soul, and reputation if he does not flee; flight is the only remedy (4593–4628). Men become beasts through such love: "certainly I would consider anyone a big joke who said that you were a man." Foolish lovers bind themselves to Fortune, which is dangerous and unstable. Carnal delight was provided by Nature to ensure generation, but it should not be sought as the highest good. Wise men seek the *summum bonum* through love of reason, the daughter of God (4680–6413). This sermon is wasted on the Lover, for "Love prevented anything from being put into practice, although I heard the whole matter word for word" (4629–33). But neither the speech of Reason nor the occasional self-incrimination of foolish characters is the most important way in which Jean creates context for his presentation of the Lover. His method, and that of Guillaume, is mainly exemplary; that is, they teach by creating the spectacle of foolish characters doing and saying foolish things. We are to recognize their folly by a number of conventions, some of them drawn from classical antiquity. Let us look first at the non-classical conventions. In accordance with his established character as a seducer and traducer of unwary men, Cupid is, as usual, asking a great deal and offering very little in return. The Lover must cultivate certain qualities in order to increase his seductiveness—friendliness, humility, elegance, cleanliness, generosity—he must think unceasingly of love, and he must seek out his lady at every opportunity. In return he may, in time, receive a reward. Cupid shows little interest in the reward, but passes quickly on to certain other conventions of love-service: its uncertainty, its constant and arduous demands, and its devastating effects on the lover. "Serving me," he says, "is without fail painful and burdensome": lovers sigh, lament, and shiver in torment; they are miserable when the lady is absent, and frustrated when they are with her; they lose sleep, weep, keep vigils at the lady's doorstep in the wind and rain. They waste away: "love . . . leaves no color or fat on pure lovers." In short, "it is true that no woe measures up to that which colors lovers" (1926–2580). With characteristic illogic, Cupid nevertheless recommends that the Lover rejoice in the opportunity to serve Love, for "Love carries the standard and banner of courtesy."

It is amusing that, although the speech of Cupid really does not make love-service appear very inviting, the Lover is pathetically eager to embrace it anyway. One way the reader may know that he is making a mistake is the convention by which he congratulates himself upon actions well established in medieval thought as foolish. When Idleness, who professes "no other purpose than to enjoy myself and make myself comfortable, to comb and braid my hair," admits him to the garden, he reflects, "Idleness . . . [has] served me well. My love was due her when she unlocked the wicket gate of the branching garden" (686–90). Enjoying the beauty of the garden and its inhabitants, he exclaims, "He who does not long for such a life is a fool. He who could have such a life might dispense with a greater good, since there is no greater paradise than to have one's beloved at one's desire" (1296–1300). (The conjunction of "greater good" and "paradise" must irresistibly suggest the Greatest Good identified by the Fathers.) He is at first afraid to approach the fountain of Narcissus, but talks himself out of his fear: "But then I thought that I might be able to venture safely to the fountain, without fear of misfortune, and that I was foolish to be frightened of it" (1519–22). Asked by the God of Love for his surrender—for no one may make a choice of spiritual allegiance without deliberate consent of the will, a point conspicuously made by all the major medieval poems about love—the Lover reacts with comically excessive folly and servility:

Sire, volentiers me rendré
Ja vers vous ne me deffendré;
A Dieu ne plasse que je pense
Que j'aie ja vers vous deffense,
Car il n'est pas reson ne drois.
Vous poés ce que vous vodrois
Fere de moi, pendre ou tuer
. . . .
Tant ai oï de vous bien dire
Que metre veil tout a devise
Cuers et cors en vostre servise . . .
(1899–1905, 1918–2065)

Later, overwhelmed by despair, he blames only himself, for "a god is never deficient in any respect" (4191).[6]

6. It is therefore difficult to accept Calin's claim ("Le 'moi' " 241) that Guillaume's narrator, unlike Jean's, is worthy of our confidence.

We expect foolish characters to utter folly, but it is characteristic of Jean's subtlety that he finds ways to make use of the Ovidian convention by which they also misapply traditional wisdom. The Friend has at his command a great store of time-honored adages for the proper conduct of life, which he glosses perversely in the service of Love. He condemns trickery (tricksters, like the guardians of the Rose, deserve to be deceived), praises courtesy (always a clever tactic in love), deplores profligate spending (cheap gifts are best), and counsels that a wise man submits willingly to correction (the Lover should heed his advice in every point). In his long lecture on friendship, he utters the truisms that Fortune cannot rob men of that which is inherently their own and that poverty reveals who one's true friends are, but he concludes by recommending that the Lover hold onto his goods, for Fortune is rapacious and poverty is worse than death. Great wealth cannot protect men from damnation, but it very effectively protects against suffering on earth. Indeed one's only permanent possession is good sense, and the Lover should make use of his by pursuing Love according to the Friend's instructions. The best love is the loyal, pure love of the Golden Age of man, based upon personal freedom; therefore men should never restrict the freedom of their ladies, but keep their favor by pretending ignorance of their derelictions. The Old Woman, who also makes this argument, mis-glosses conventional wisdom in the same way as the Friend, even managing to turn a lecture on good table manners to the uses of seduction. She warns Fair Welcoming that youth and beauty are fleeting, only to recommend that he exploit them before it's too late; his only happiness in old age will come from the memory of carnal delights enjoyed in youth. One should, she preaches, learn good lessons in infancy and apply them throughout life; therefore she will teach him how to play the games of Love, while steering safely clear of love itself.

We recognize such counsel as vicious because it has its source in conventional truths, turned upside down by self-serving speakers. Of much that is said by the Lover, the Friend, and the Old Woman, precisely the opposite is true. Another way in which both Guillaume and Jean characterize speakers is by putting into their mouths perverse moralizations of the classical myths; these cannot be identified or understood, of course, unless we know the traditional moralizations that were known to the poets and their educated contemporaries. Guillaume and Jean intended their allusions to the myths to clarify the meaning of the poem by incriminating foolish characters who do not understand (or who misrepresent) the wisdom traditionally found in them. Jean even tells us, in several places, what he is about; we have already seen Reason's exhortations to the Lover regarding his neglect of instructive classical *exempla.* The Lover replies, significantly, ". . . as for the sentences, fables, and metaphors of the poets, I do not now hope to gloss them. If I can be cured and if my service, for which I expect so great a reward, is meritorious, I shall gloss them all in time—at least as much as is fitting—so that everyone will see into them clearly" (7190–98). In other words, the irrationality of the Lover is such that he cannot fittingly gloss the poets, an activity which was defined as rational. The metaphors of husk/kernel, nut/shell, rind/marrow occur several times in the *Rose,* and Jean repeatedly promises to reveal the meaning of the myths, and of the dream itself, in time: "You will have an adequate art of love, and if you have any difficulty, I will clarify what confuses you when you have heard me explain the dream. Then, if someone creates opposition, you will know how to reply about love, when you have heard me gloss the text" (15144–50). In the famous passage in which he defends himself against the charge of misogyny, he protests

> . . . m'escriture . . . toute est por enseignement;
> . . . .
> . . . por ce en escrit mëimes
> Que nous et vous de nous mëimes
> Pöissions connoissance avoir,
> Car il fait bon de tout savior.
> D'autre part, dames honorables,
> S'il vous semble que je di fables,
> Por menteor ne m'en tenés,
> Mes as actors vous en prenés
> Qui es lor livres ont escrites
> Les paroles que j'en ai dites
> Et celes que je en diré;
> Que ja de riens n'en mentiré,
> Ne li prodomme n'en mentirent
> Qui les livres anciens firent.
> . . . .
> Je n'i fais riens fors reciter
> Se par mon geu, qui pau vous couste,

Aucune chose n'i ajouste,
Si cum font li autre poete
Quant chascuns la matire trete
Dont il li plaist a entremetre:
Car si cum tesmoigne la letre,
Profit et delectation,
C'est toute lor entencion.
(15202–3; 15211–24; 15234–42)

Jean's insistence upon "instruction" and "profit" hints at a meaning in the text accessible only to those who can gloss it well, and indeed Guillaume began in the way that Jean was to continue by using perverse glosses on the myths as a device for characterization. Both Guillaume and Jean allude to the Sirens: upon entering the Garden of Deduit, the Lover compares the beautiful birdsong that fills it to the song of angels—and then, with hardly a pause, to the song of "the sirens of the sea, who have the name *siren* on account of their clear, pure voices" (672–74). (According to mythographic tradition, they were called "siren" from *sirene,* "to betray" in Greek;[7] we have already seen that allusions to the Sirens in connection with deceiving women are plentiful enough in early medieval literature so that readers of the *Rose* were likely to know that. Validating the tradition, the jealous husband in the speech of the Friend accuses his wanton wife of singing "like a siren" [8473]). But Guillaume's first substantial allusion to the myths of love occurs when the Lover encounters the fountain of Narcissus, with its inscription commemorating his death. He retells the tale in some detail, at first seeming to show some understanding of it: "Narcissus was a young man whom Love caught in his snares. Love knew so well how to torment him, to make him weep and complain, that he had to give up his soul." Narcissus was loved by Echo, "a great lady," who prayed that he might one day be tormented by a hopeless love as he had tormented her. He thereupon fell in love with his own reflection, so that he "could not accomplish his desire and . . . could in no way take any comfort." Becoming distraught, "he lost his reason and died in a short time." The Lover offers a *moralitas* on the fable: "You ladies who neglect your duties toward your sweethearts, be instructed by this exemplum, for if you let them die, God will know how to repay you well for your fault" (1507–10). This is, of course,

7. An interpretation first recorded by Fulgentius, *Myth.* II, 8.

precisely the opposite of the conventional *moralitas* on the classical tales of love and particularly on the tale of Narcissus, which preached against idolatrous love. Leaving aside the mythographers, Alain de Lille in the *De Planctu Naturae,* an important source of the *Rose,* names Helen, Pasiphae, Myrrha, Medea, and Narcissus as among the "great body of foul men" who "roam and riot along the breadth of the whole earth, by whose seducing contact chastity herself is poisoned." Of his sermon on them, he says, "In my indignation I belch forth such words so that men of restraint may revere the mark of modesty and that men without restraint may be kept away from trafficking in the brothels of immodesty."[8]

The Lover is thus characterized as one who cannot penetrate the integuments of the poets. Jean continues the characterization. When Cupid sends for Venus to reinforce the army attacking the castle of Jealousy, the Lover pauses to tell the tale of Venus and Adonis. As the two are hunting in the wood, Venus warns Adonis of the danger of fierce game: "Harts and hinds, he- and she-goats, reindeer and fallow deer, rabbits and hares—these are the ones I want you to chase. . . . But I forbid bears, wolves, lions, and wild boars," the animals that can kill or injure hunters. (The hunt of Venus, after timid, furry creatures, is of course the hunt of love.) Adonis, who "agreed to everything in order to have peace," did not believe her, and was later killed by a wild boar. Venus grieved sorely for him. The tale, the lover insists, is a valuable *exemplum:*

Biau seignor, quoi qu'il vous aviengne,
De cest exemple vous soviengne.
Vous qui ne crées vos amies,
Sachiés vous faites granz folies;
Bien les deüssiés toutes croire,
Car lor dit sont voir cum istoire.
S'el jurent: "Toutes sommes vostres,"
Creés les comme paternostres;
Ja d'eus croire ne recreés.
Se Raison vient, point n'en creés;
S'el vous aportoit crucefiz,
Nel creés point ne que ge fiz.
Se cis s'amie eüst creüe,
Mout eüst sa vie creüe.

(15751–64)

8. *De Planctu* Pr. IV, 96–98, trans. Sheridan, 137.

This is broad satire, but it is satire by means of perverse mythographic exegesis; we have already seen a number of early medieval interpretations of the tales of the gods as lovers and of the boar of Adonis. The tale of Venus and Adonis, traditionally used as an *exemplum* against lust, has been converted by the lover to his own purposes, which are precisely opposed to the tradition.[9] We are not, I think, meant to interpret this as ingenuity on his part, but as benightedness; his gloss on the tale is amusing, but it also serves to remind us of the fundamental irrationality of his point of view. He gnaws the husk of the tales, but misses the kernel altogether. Reason may well ask him, "What is the value of whatever you study when its sense fails you, through your fault alone, at the very time when you need it?" (6786–88)

At the point in the *Rose* when Venus aims her torch at the "sanctuary," Jean chooses to dedicate four hundred lines to a retelling by the Lover of the story of Pygmalion. Transported by contemplation of the "pillars" and the "sanctuary," the Lover compares them to Pygmalion's statue, finding them far superior in beauty: "If anyone, using reason, were to draw a comparison between this and any other image, he could say that this image was to Pygmalion's as a mouse is to a lion" (20811–17). Pygmalion, he goes on to explain, was "a sculptor who worked in wood, stone, and metals" and wished to put his skill to the test; "he therefore made an image of ivory and put into its production such attention that it was so pleasing, so exquisite, that it seemed as live as the most beautiful living creature." In love with the image, Pygmalion despairs and compares himself to Narcissus, who was likewise frustrated in his love. He embraces the image and offers gifts, but it does not respond. "Love had robbed him of his intelligence and wisdom, so that he was completely desolated" (20924–25). The Lover takes great care in telling how Pygmalion dresses and undresses the statue, brings it flowers, and finally weds it with a ring. At the wedding he sings, "instead of the Mass, songs of the pretty secrets of love." At length, in mad desperation, he prays to Venus to inspire the statue with

9. Of the affair of Venus and Adonis, Arnulf of Orleans moralizes: "Extincta igitur veneris dulcedine pre labore, mutatur in florem sui nominis i. qui adonim, quia dulcius foret amor caritativus quam amor venereus" (*Alleg.* X, 10–11; Ghisalberti 223); Bersuire equates Adonis with "aliquem . . . occasione temptationis" (*Red. Mor.* XV, x; Engels 154). We have already seen the similar moralization given by the *Ovide Moralisé* (see page 59 above). Alain de Lille mentions Adonis in his discussion of mad lovers in the fifth metre of the *De Planctu Naturae*.

life. Venus, "overjoyed because he was abandoning chastity and striving to serve her as a truly repentant man," grants his prayer. Returning home, Pygmalion finds his image alive and welcoming; he "gave himself willingly to her as if he were entirely hers," and she conceived Paphus, for whom the island of Paphos is named (21122–87). Continuing the genealogy, the Lover notes that the son of Paphus was King Cynaras, father of Myrrha, who deceitfully lay with him and fled in shame and fear before giving birth to Adonis. He does not offer an interpretation of these tales, but promises to do so later: ". . . all this is very far from my matter, and I must draw back from it. By the time you have finished this work you will know what it means" (21211–14). And he insists again that "as much as the mouse is smaller than the lion in body, strength, and worth, and less to be feared, so much was the one image less beautiful than that which I here esteem so greatly."

The alert reader, of course, would already know the meaning of the tales of love; the promise Jean puts into the mouth of the Lover is really just a reminder to give a moment's consideration to that meaning. His insistence upon comparing the two images has the effect of identifying the Lover with Pygmalion, whose passion was condemned throughout the Middle Ages as lustful and idolatrous.[10] We have seen that Myrrha was well established in medieval literature as an *exemplum* against irrational love, and mention of her at this point, though it is presented as fortuitous, is well-timed. The Lover goes straight from his retelling of these tales to a repetition of his identification of the "image": "the one which I have described, the one placed between the pillars, within the tower, right in the middle." Here is a humorous—but pointed—reduction of the adored lady to the status of a disembodied *pudendum*. He continues with a declaration of allegiance:

> Onques encore ne vi leu
> Que si volentiers regardasse,
> Voire a genoillons l'aorasse
> Et le saintuaire et l'archiere;
> Ja ne lessasse por l'archiere
> Ne por l'arc ne por le brandon

10. That that characterization penetrated from the mythographers to the poets is shown by Machaut's use of Pygmalion in the *Confort*, where he compares his idolatry to that of the biblical builders of graven images (1283–1307).

Que je n'i entrasse a bandon;
Mon pooir au mains en feïsse
A quelque chief que j'en venisse,
Se trovasse qui le m'offrist
Ou sans plus qui le me soffrist.
  Si m'i sui je pieça voés,
As reliques que vous oés,
Et se Dieu plaist je les requerrai
Si tost cum temps et leu avrai,
D'escherpe et de bordon garnis.
(21232–47)

The Lover's misapplication of religious language—"sanctuary," "adore," "relics," with even his *virilia* appearing as the "sack and staff" of a pilgrim—sets up a witty incongruity, but it also irresistibly suggests the object that within the terms of the poem he ought to be seeking, the object to which Reason has said all men are "dedicated by God." The intention he declares is precisely the intention of Myrrha and of the other mad lovers of classical antiquity: to consummate their loves whatever end they might come to.

Jean uses the same technique of characterization through perverse interpretation of the myths in the case of La Vieille, who loves to seek justification in the wisdom of the ancients. Her interpretations, too, are precisely opposed to the conventional ones, and serve as a warning that she is not be to believed. (It is only one warning among many, for she also turns the Apostles and the Commandments on their heads.) Explaining to Fair Welcome that he ought to accept gifts from any man who offers them, always assuring each one—"even if there are a thousand"—that he will have the Rose to himself alone, the Old Woman argues that it makes no difference if he perjures himself:

Diex se rist de tel serement
Et pardonne legierement.
Jupiter et li dieu rioient
Quant li amant se parjuroient,
Et maintes fois se parjurerent
Li Dieu qui par amors amerent.
Quant Jupiter asseüroit
Juno sa fame, et li juroit
La palu d'enfer hautement,

Il se parjuroit faucement.
Ce devroit mout asseürer
Les fins amans de parjurer
Saintes et sains, moustiers et temples,
Quant li dieu lor donnent exemples.
(13125–38)

Again, this is broad satire, but the Old Woman's choice of words reminds the reader that the loves of the gods have, indeed, traditionally served as "examples"—and not at all of the moral acceptability of perjury. She proceeds directly from the love affairs of the gods to those of the other classical lovers, this time in an attempt to demonstrate that women should deceive men. Dido clothed, fed, and loved Aeneas, and killed herself out of sorrow when he left; Phyllis "waited so long for Demophoon that she hanged herself"; Paris even carved his vow to Oenone on a tree, but abandoned her in the end for Helen; and Jason accepted help from Medea, then deceived her. "Briefly, all men betray and deceive women; all are sensualists, taking their pleasure anywhere. Therefore we should deceive them in return, not fix our hearts on one" (13173–13268). In fact, as we have seen, the moral traditionally attached to all the classical lovers, both deceitful men and deceitful women, is that both sexes ought to flee *amor stultus*. Such attempts to use the classical *exempla* to condemn one sex while exculpating the other are ubiquitous in medieval literature, and they are most often designed specifically for the use to which Jean here puts them—to reveal the carnal perspective of the speaker.

Not much later in her speech, La Vieille again has recourse to the gods as lovers, this time to the myth of Mars and Venus caught in the net of Vulcan. It is profitable, she advises, for a woman to pretend jealousy of her lover in order to convince him of her love. She should express suspicion when he arrives late to a rendezvous: "When the man, with his silly ideas, hears this speech, he will believe, quite incorrectly, that she loves him very loyally and that she may be more jealous of him than Vulcan ever was of his wife Venus, when he found her taken in the act with Mars" (13835–42). La Vieille then makes use of Ovid's satirical moralization of the fable of Mars and Venus. Vulcan was a fool to concern himself with the lovers—"he who thinks he can keep his wife to himself has very little knowledge"—and besides, Venus was justified in taking a lover because Vulcan was gross and ugly, and women are free by nature.

Therefore, "Venus deserves less blame for loving Mars." Like caged birds, like fish in a net, women seek the freedom given to them by Nature. All women are made for all men, and all men for all women; a mare will choose for her mate the first stallion she sees (13582–14076). The animal imagery serves as a reminder of the commonplace (cited three times by Alanus in the *De Planctu,* always in connection with passionate love) that men become beasts through irrational behavior. The Mars/Venus myth itself, which is ubiquitous in medieval literature from patristic times forward, was invariably interpreted in quite the opposite way as an *exemplum* against the sort of freedom advocated by the Old Woman.

Jean displays a finely tuned sense of just how each of his characters would interpret the old tales. The glosses of La Vieille and the Lover are frankly immoral, but those of Nature and Genius, when they address the myth of Mars and Venus in their discussion of mirrors, are simply amoral. Because these characters do not partake of the divine rationality, they appear altogether unconcerned with the moral dimension of the tale. Observing that there are marvelous mirrors that can make very tiny things—"thin letters, very narrow writing, and tiny grains of sand" (18048–49)—appear so large that one can see them from a long way off, Nature is struck by the fact that if Mars and Venus had had such a mirror they might have seen the net of Vulcan before they lay down on the bed. Then they would never have been caught, and Vulcan could not have proved their adultery. They might have gone to some other place to make love. Genius agrees that, indeed, such a mirror would have been most useful to the lovers, who could have satisfied their desire somewhere else; or perhaps, if they had preferred to use the bed, Mars might have cut the net with his sharp sword. And if by chance Vulcan had come by and caught them in the act, Venus could certainly have found words to convince him that he had not really seen them together—"she would have said that his sight had been dark and confused" (18061–18123). This Ovidian passage, which apparently inspired Chaucer's "Merchant's Tale," also demonstrates Jean's admirable logic. As he has defined the characters of Nature and Genius, they concern themselves only with the process of generation. Here, they reveal a wish to apply scientific ingenuity to the problem of getting the lovers together, an end which is threatened by the net of Vulcan. It is the only end they have in view; they are completely uninterested in the moral condition of the gods, the Lover himself, or the Rose, though of course their use of the *exem-*

plum inevitably reminds the reader of it. When they see two lovers—any two lovers—with the desire to come together, it seems to them intolerable that anything should interfere. This is a wonderfully amusing passage that incidentally shows us that Jean knows precisely what he is about in the matter of idiosyncratic mythographic exegesis.

Although later poets rarely treat the classical lovers with the same humor and subtlety as Jean, they continue to use them in spiritual-pilgrimage poems in which the narrator, always a lover, must make a choice of spiritual allegiance. The *Amorosa Visione* of Boccaccio is an important poem of this type; like the *Rose,* it takes the form of a dream in which the narrator, a somewhat distractible fellow not overendowed with the rational faculty, is confronted by alternative ways of life, and advised by a guide to seek the *summum bonum*. Like Jean's narrator, Boccaccio's is prevented by the attractions of the world from taking even the first step toward it. Unlike the Lover of the *Rose,* however, he is accompanied at every stage in his journey by a wise guide who reminds him constantly of his spiritual duty. Nevertheless the *Amorosa Visione* has most often been read as a poem which (in Branca's words) "has as its goal the exaltation of the lady and of love as the way to virtue."[11] Read in one way, that claim is correct; certainly Boccaccio here recommends love as the way to virtue, but not the sort of love that his misguided narrator, with comical persistence, feels for the lady right up to the end of the poem. In this poem, more than in any other, Boccaccio exploits what Dahlberg has called "the Augustinian ambiguity of the term *amor*."[12] The *Visione* begins with the lover/narrator's explanation of his condition at the time of the dream. The first words of the poem are important to its meaning, so I quote them in full, in Hollander's translation:

> A new desire moves my bold mind,
> lovely lady, with the wish to sing,
> telling what Love made known to me,
>   what he pleased himself to show forth in vision
> to my soul, captured and wounded by You
> with that delight which appears in your eyes.

11. *Opere* 3, 562 (my translation).
12. In "Love and the *Roman de la Rose*," *Speculum* 44 (1969): 568–84, p. 570.

> My mind, then, bewildered by Your power,
> bringing thoughts to my heart,
> which already feared for its feeble life,
> ignited that heart with such fervent ardor
> that my phantasy, issuing forth from itself,
> at once coursed into unfamiliar error.
> It nonetheless retained its former thought
> securely, and besides retained
> what is felt was most precious of the new things.[13]

As he sleeps, the guide, "a woman bright and beautiful to behold," appears to him and suggests that if he will follow her, "but only if you would go to that highest felicity of which mortal man cannot ever speak unimpaired," he will "repose in such agreeable festivity that your every desire will surely be fulfilled" (I, 29–34). (The identity of the heavenly guide is uncertain; because she wears violet and carries a golden apple, Hollander has suggested that she is the Uranic Venus.)[14] The lover affirms his wish to seek the sovereign good, and the two set out together. They soon arrive at a castle, "beautiful beyond the scope of any human art." Beyond it is a wall, within which the guide points out "the gate which your soul so desires to see." The lover objects; surely this dark, narrow, steep, uninviting path is not the one he seeks. Next to it he sees a wide, bright doorway and hears sounds of celebration, so he suggests, "It will be better to go this way, in my opinion, for I believe we shall discover that which we seek—I think I hear it already." His guide disagrees, explaining patiently that, because his spiritual sight is obscured by the fog of irresolution, he cannot see the heavenly brightness of the steep path. The inscription over it urges him to "conquer the slothful flesh" in order to earn "eternal repose"; at the top, she assures him, he will see a light a thousand times more lovely than that behind the wide gate (I, 159–88; II, 1–87). When he insists upon taking the wide way, the guide reproaches him—"You desire to rush down with grief to the wretched center"—and he counters with the argument that, once he has enjoyed the "fallacious good things" of the world, "the struggle for the true will then be more precious." But the guide fears the lure of worldly things: "If you but knew how tenacious they are, how they draw a man from

13. I, 1–15, trans. Hollander et al. All references to the *Visione* are to this edition.
14. *Two Venuses* 80.

the straight way, you would not speak as you do." At this point, two jolly young men emerge from the wide gate and take hold of the lover, pulling him and urging him to join them: "Solace and merriment, enjoyed by many, you will not lack, and you will still be able to climb on up at the end of your life" (III, 1–57). The lover is farcically held fast, with his guide pulling at his right hand and the young men at his left, but finally the guide gives way, saying that as long as he desires the true she will accompany him in his journey through the world.

The journey of the lover consists of a progress through four triumphs—of Wisdom, Glory, Wealth, and Love—followed by a vision of the house of Fortune. In these visions numerous mythological and historical personages appear and are described. Some of them appear in more than one of the triumphs; Glory and Love, in particular, share certain of the classical figures. The chamber of Wisdom is a lovely place, painted in blue and gold, in which the philosophers and poets are portrayed seated on each side of Lady Wisdom (IV–V). The sovereign poet Dante is shown receiving a laurel crown from the Muse of Poetry. The lover, enthralled by the sight, pauses to mourn Dante's death, but is rebuked by his guide, who does not wish to stay in the chamber: "to look on these is to lose time" (V, 81–88; VI, 1–36). They progress to the chamber of Glory, where the lover is overwhelmed by the splendor of Lady Glory and her retinue, most numerous of all: 152 exemplary figures from mythology, history and legend appear with her, including Nimrod, Aeneas, Alexander the Great, Solomon, Samson, Jason, Ulysses, Hercules, Hannibal, Charlemagne, Barbarossa, and the knights of the Round Table (VII–XII). Their aspects differ; some are rejoicing, some thoughtful, some sorrowful, angry, or in pain. Overcome by their grandeur and fame, the lover is "smitten by desire," and longs to see even more, but his guide hurries him on to the vision of Wealth. The avaricious, led by Midas, appear simply disagreeable, as they emit bestial noises while scratching desperately at a mountain of gold (XII, 61–81). Although the vision is not a very attractive one, the lover is transported by it as he was by Wisdom and Glory, and wishes ardently "to be one of such a company." Admitting that, "if only men thought of its value for salvation as they should," wealth would not be much sought, he nevertheless desires it greatly: "saying that wealth is evil would seem Hebrew to anyone of clear understanding" (XIV, 76–78).

As in the *Roman de la Rose,* the lover is made to say foolish things that reveal his state of mind; of his last statement, precisely the opposite is true. Both Boccaccio and Jean have to some extent the artistic difficulty that they must simultaneously represent the moral undesirability of the things that tempt the lover, their real attractiveness, and the lover's desire for them. Because it is difficult to represent all these things convincingly (and Boccaccio is really not as skilled in this respect as Jean), the foolish statements of the lover also appear defective in logic at times: who would want to join the avaricious, oinking and scrabbling away at their mountain with "infuriated and menacing haste," "insatiable baleful desire"? (XIII, 61, 52) But realism is not, finally, Boccaccio's object in this moral allegory, in which the perversity of the lover's reactions dramatizes the moral perversity of desiring worldly goods more than the *bene etterne*.

Next in the pageant is the triumph of Love, in which the classical lovers appear in a green meadow surrounding Cupid in glory (XV–XXVIII). Beside him sits the lady Maria, who is not, however, named at this point. Cupid gazes raptly upon her but hardly dares approach her, for reasons that later become clear. The first of the classical pairs to catch the lover's eye are the gods: Jove with Io, Leda, Semele, Alcmena, and others; Mars and Venus, Phoebus and Daphne, Pluto and Proserpine. Then come Pyramus and Thisbe, Jason with Hypsipyle, Medea, and Creusa, Theseus with Ariadne and Phaedra, Pasiphae with the bull, Myrrha, Narcissus, Orpheus, Leander, Byblis, Phyllis, Penelope, Dido, Paris rendering his judgment, and many others—53 couples in all. From the tale of Mars and Venus the lover draws the conclusion that it is foolish to expose illicit love; from that of Pyramus and Thisbe, that love knows no law (XIX, 31–33; XXI, 1–6). The tales are told fully, the ladies pleading with their lovers in extracts from the *Heroides*. Imagining their pathetic speeches as he looks at the images on the walls, the lover is moved to compassion; of Dido he says, "I do not know anyone who could have been so cruel as not to have wept with pity, seeing what I there gazed upon" (XXVIII, 1–3). Despite the many tragedies and the great sadness that he sees in the vision of Love, he remains convinced that the sweetness of love more than justifies the sacrifices it exacts:

Invidiosi alcun dicon stoltezza
esser seguire con ragion quel stile
che dà questo signor de gentilezza,

lo qual discaccia via ogni atto vile:
piacevole, cortese e valoroso
fa chi lo segue e più ch'altro gentile.
Superbia esclude, onde ciascun ritroso
nel suo triunfo intervenir non puote:
indi ogni dio gentile e ogni uom grazioso
vidi seguir le sue triunfal ruote—.
(XXIX, 79–88)

The argument that love increases virtue was a commonplace, and commonly refuted; the traditional interpretation given to the myths of the gods and heroes as lovers was not that they were ennobled through increased humility, but that they were humiliated and degraded by the dominion exercised over them by Love. Boccaccio knows this tradition, and as we will see he gives it great prominence in the *Filocolo.* The lover's argument to the contrary here is one of the things that identifies him as a lover *par amours,* for only one who had abandoned reason would argue in that way.

Turning to his guide, the lover then defends the visions he has seen: "Oh how worthwhile it has been, seeing these various things, which You said were full of great evil! Now what could ever be more worthy than they, what more wondrous to have or to consider or to hear about?" The lady, unimpressed, diagnoses his problem: "The good which you sought, does it seem to you that you see it painted here? And yet these things are fallacious and without truth. To me it seems that such looking has goaded your mind into false opinion, extinguishing all sense of duty in you" (XXX, 13–18). To return him to himself, she will show him the cruelty and arrogance of Fortune, governess of the goods he values so highly. Following her into a spacious chamber, the lover sees the awesome and horrible Lady Fortune, turning her wheel to which men cling desperately. His guide delivers a Boethian lecture of some four hundred lines, pointing to the miserable condition of the wretches who submitted themselves to Fortune and explaining that the goods the lover should seek are those over which Fortune has no dominion (XXX–XXXVI). Finally, at the end of it, he appears ready to accompany her to the strait path, and sets out docilely. On the way there, however, they pass a lovely garden, "flowering and green as if in springtime." Within, the lover hears merrymaking and song. When the two youths reappear and invite him in, he determines to follow them, but his guide reacts with impatience: "Overmuch does everything arouse desire in you. Let us go on our way while we still have time . . . what is in here is the vanity of this world" (XXXVII, 61–84). When he persists, she predicts he will come to no good and threatens to abandon him, but accompanies him nevertheless. Following in his steps, almost nagging him ("Where you go, as you have seen, lies the transitory and false good, which, if you have well understood, as your words indicated . . . you would not consider it, but, on the contrary, you would abandon it as a thing without value. . . ." [XXXIX, 77–83]), she trails the lover until he finally delivers an ultimatum: he will take the steep path "in due time and place," but right now he is going to go look at the pretty ladies he has seen on the riverbank. She may come along or rejoin him later. She stays, and "without a word I left her there; I do not know if I did well or ill" (XL, 20–21).

Wandering through the garden accompanied by the two youths, he sees several groups of ladies—sitting, dancing, singing the praises of Love—and recognizes many of them. At length he finds the lady Maria, who writes her name on his heart and places a ring upon his little finger. He declares his submission to her, and wishes ardently to "experience the ultimate power which the terms of love hold in their sway" (XLV, 1–66); he feels sure that the sight of his pain has aroused pity in her, so that she will soon yield to his desire. The lady, however, sends him back to his guide, "for she is the one who leads those in error back to the straight path." Disconsolate, he seeks out his guide and asks that she accompany him back to the lady, "for I believe I shall remain in the service of her beauty until my last day." She objects: "I well know where you want to lead me and what desire holds you fast." The lover protests that, if he loved the lady "to fulfill an earthly and violent desire," her objection might have force, but in fact he loves "with that true integrity with which one must love every rational being . . . because of her I raise my mind to lofty concepts" (XLVII, 1–75). Apparently convinced, the guide follows him, and when she sees the lady the two women greet each other with recognition and affection. The lady, says the guide, is her sister, who follows her counsel: "thus by her example bridle your desire and follow true pleasure." She commends the lover to his lady's keeping; he is delighted, and the two set off together. Wandering with her into a thicket, where she falls asleep, the lover has finally his reward in view: "Why, since I am here, do I not take from her the long and anxiously awaited pleasures?" (XLVIII, XLIX 1–15) When he wakes her with passionate kisses she protests at first, but finally seems to surrender. The lover feels such joy that the dream is broken and he awakes: "Alas, how transformed into bitter pain was that pleasure which sleep had brought me, giving remedy to my grievous woes!" (XLIX, 49–54)

Except for Hollander, who has well understood the poem, critics have not been kind to the *Visione*. Sapegno makes note of its "enorme e caotico apparato erudito e mitologico" and calls it "la più povera, scolorita e prosaica" of Boccaccio's works.[15] Battaglia designates it "la piú inerte respetto ai sensi artistici," and Branca describes it as "questo mediocrissimo poemetto."[16] Branca believes that the experience of witnessing the successive triumphs renders the poet "worthy of meeting Fiammetta and of her 'celestial' love, worthy, that is, of the winning of Virtue," and that the poet's abortive attempt to possess the lady symbolizes his achievement of virtue.[17] He speaks of the *Visione* with condescension, imagining that Boccaccio did not fully plan the work before sitting down to write:

> . . . the reader may often have a keen feeling that the artist has failed to define and design the moral sense of his work carefully enough from the outset. All too often Boccaccio seems to forget it, only then suddenly to take it up again, as though stung by an access of zeal; all too often contradictory elements obfuscate its flow, indicating a lack of clarity of perspective and of purpose. . . .[18]

The movement that Branca is describing here reflects, of course, the intellectual processes of the irresolute narrator of the *Visione,* not those of Boccaccio himself. The alternation between a strong sense of moral purpose and the mindless pursuit of worldly goods forms the basis of the poem's humor (which only Hollander seems to have appreciated):[19] much of the *Visione* is farcical, an amusing drama-

15. Sapegno, *Storia Letteraria* 305n1.
16. Battaglia, *Letteratura Italiana* 246; Branca, *Opere* 3, 20.
17. *Opere* 3, 747 (my translation).
18. "Introduction" in Hollander et al., xviii.
19. In *Two Venuses* (87), he writes of the struggle between the lover's celestial guide and the two youths at the gate of moral choice: "The irony (as well as the humor) of the entire situation becomes even more apparent in the opening *terzina* of Canto VI, which presents the guide as *following* the narrator in his leftward journey."

tization of the ongoing struggle between the spirit and the flesh that is at the center of Boccaccio's notion of human psychology.

That Branca does not clearly enough distinguish Boccaccio from the narrator of the *Visione* is evident, too, in his "autobiographical" analysis of the series of triumphs, which offer "precisely the goods to which (Boccaccio) has most anxiously aspired in his youth: wisdom, greatness, wealth, glory, love."[20] In suggesting that the ambitious and energetic poet must have found it difficult to generate a thoroughgoing scorn of these things, Branca seems not to understand that the difficulty of resisting the appeal of *temporalia* is precisely the point of departure of the poem: if Boccaccio, or any man, found it easy to depreciate the things of the world, the poem need never have been written. The *Visione,* however, like all the poems we will consider, is not in any sense a confession, but a tissue of literary conventions. (To say this is certainly not to deny to these poems substantial originality, which consists in the meaningful arrangement and development of conventions.) Even my bare outline of the action should reveal that, within the terms of the poem, the guide and the lady are speaking one language of love while the lover speaks another. He imagines that he and the lady understand each other and that they both want the same fulfillment of their love; before assaulting her, he reflects, "She and I both desire to do so, so why should we seek to delay any longer?" (XLIX, 20–21) It is the comedy of a lover *par amours,* held in thrall by a lady even Cupid fears because she represents a higher love. The well-established convention of the group of classical lovers is not employed to emphasize the "passionate devotion and generosity of the heroines of love," but—in an elaboration of the *moralitas* traditionally attached to that convention—to teach the pilgrim/narrator that "whoever / puts his hope, unwisely, in such things as these / has for company burdensome tribulations" (XXX, 37–39). The plaintive speeches from the *Heroides* cause both narrator and reader to pity the abandoned lovers, and thus enforce the moral by leading the reader to participate imaginatively in their suffering.[21]

20. "Introduction," in Hollander et al. xviii.

21. At a time before the invention of Romantic sentimentality in literature, enforcement of the moral was seen as the natural consequence of imaginative participation in the suffering of literary protagonists. The Fiammetta of the *Elegia* insists upon this effect; in her address to readers at the beginning of the fifth book, she writes: "In truth I do not wish to offer any comfort or to conceal from you any part of this sad story, because you will pity me more, the more fully you understand

Unlike the *Rose,* the *Visione* does not end with the dream; the guide reappears to the waking lover and offers him another opportunity to gain "that beauty which the soul shows always to your heart." He gladly accepts, and ends the poem with an envoy to his lady, the "only one who can further my virtue." We remember the first words of the poem: ". . . my phantasy, issuing forth from itself, / at once coursed into unfamiliar error. / It nonetheless retained its former thought / securely. . . ." Do these words mean that this time he will finally achieve a vision of the lady consonant with her celestial nature?[22] Or will he again end in frustration? It is impossible to tell. In any case, the *Visione* succeeds brilliantly as a tribute to Boccaccio's unattainable "Fiamma," implying as it does that she possesses all wisdom while he struggles to transcend carnal concupiscence in order to return her love in kind. Within the vision, the spectacle of the classical lovers, his misguided admiration for them, and his misguided conclusions about them, serve to dramatize his condition. Only a foolish lover would praise the sort of love they represent.

Medieval poems built around the idea of spiritual pilgrimage most often use the classical lovers in this way, as part of the symbolic landscape of error. Even where moralization is not the principal concern of the poet, allusion to the lovers helps to locate the love of which he speaks within the moral universe; and there are few

---

the wickedness of him through whom these things happened to me, and will be more cautious in committing yourselves to any young man" (Sapegno, *Elegia* 58; my translation). Madeleine Doran's article on Ovidian commentary in the Renaissance ("Some Renaissance 'Ovids'," in *Literature and Society,* ed. B. Slote [Lincoln, Nebr., 1964]: 44–62, p. 46) confirms that this conviction that heightened compassion reinforces instruction was still alive in the mid-sixteenth century. Georg Schuler, in his commentary on the *Metamorphoses* designed for use in the Academy of Königsberg, writes, in Doran's summary: ". . . the example of Pyramus and Thisbe teaches what a truly unhappy exit from life may be the lot of those who prefer their illicit loves to the charity of their parents. And so that this example may shine and be impressed on the minds of the young, the poet ornaments the fable with the sweetness of so many affections and figures that nothing sweeter can be imagined. The apostrophes especially—to the wall, to beasts, to their parents, to the tree—wonderfully move the mind of the reader." Cleary, in Schuler's view, they do not move the mind of the reader to wish to emulate the lovers, but to avoid their error.

22. As Augustine reminds Petrarch in the *Secretum,* it is possible to love a worthy object in an unworthy way: "It is unquestionably true that oftentimes the loveliest things are loved in a shameful way. . . . Were she a queen, a saint—'A very goddess, or to Apollo's self / Own sister, or a mother of the nymphs'—yet all her excellence will in nowise excuse your error" (Draper, *Petrarch's Secret* 119).

narrative poems of love in which the poet does not accomplish that in other ways as well. The *Espinette Amoureuse* of Froissart, for example, begins with a reflection on love by a speaker who, we will discover, is still a lover: many young men wish to follow love, but if they knew in advance what would be the cost, they would never try. The payment is so dreadful that it is too perilous an adventure. Still, love seems desirable to young people. Well, if they must, let them pay their debt in youth, for I excuse young people more readily than older ones; I myself fell in love in youth.[23] There is nothing "courtly" about this introduction; it is impossible to maintain that it either recommends or romanticizes love-service. But it is, I think, impossible as well to characterize the *Espinette* as a work of moral philosophy. Froissart does not preach, and he insists far less than Jean or Boccaccio upon attaching negative moral weight to the delusions and ritual deceptions of courtship. The work seems to exist principally as a graceful frame for his very accomplished lays, balades, and virelays, and as the forum for a leisurely examination of the pleasures, frustrations and baneful effects of love *par amours*. It is a genre of poetry, and an area of inquiry, that no longer appeals much to modern readers, so that we are tempted to ask what Froissart's "point" may be: is it to condemn love, or to praise it? One feels justified in saying that Jean's "point" is to preach against love, but Froissart seems to take for granted the well-established place of passionate love within the moral scheme of things and to wish mainly to describe the condition of lovers. It is not a happy one, for the most part, and we are certainly justified in drawing from that fact the conclusion that Froissart does not recommend love as a way of life; but then he begins the poem by saying that quite plainly. It is not a conclusion that we are to reach after much thought and labor, but the point of departure of the entire work. As we will see, the workings of the poem's mythological machinery confirm it at every turn, without however making it the principal emphasis of the work as a whole. That emphasis is placed upon the condition of the lover himself, and the beauty of the lyrical utterances that the passion of love calls forth from him. In no way does the love achieve transcendence through the poetry; Froissart is at pains to establish the lover as overwrought and self-deluded, and his lady as a cruel and trivial coquette. His efforts to keep untarnished the mental *idolum* he has constructed of her, in the face of her behavior, are

23. Lines 1–26. All references to the *Espinette* are to Fourrier's edition.

the source of the humor and pathos that give to the poem what interest it retains for modern readers. The point of the poem is the self-delusion and frustration of the lover; the point of the intercalated lyrics is their verbal ingenuity and melodic beauty.

Like the other *dits amoureux,* however, the *Espinette* has been read (by all scholars, I believe, except Kibler)[24] as a poem in praise of love. Older critics like Scheler and Whiting, of course, hold this view; but even the poem's most recent editor, Anthime Fourrier, believes that Froissart's intention in the *Espinette* is to establish love as "the source of all perfection."[25] Nancy Bradley-Cromey, like Kibler, suggests that classical myths function in the *Espinette as* "a figural parallel to the real experience of love," but nevertheless defends the idea that both Froissart and his audience "assumed the absolute value of love, the *summum bonum seculare* to be sought not only as a way to happiness, but to virtue and moral excellence."[26] We will see, however, that even the most determined exegete would be hard pressed to find in the *Espinette* any trace of those three *desiderata.* As Kibler has seen, its love-narrative presents a negative *exemplum.*

The *Espinette* is unusual in beginning its narration with the early childhood of the speaker, who soon begins to characterize himself by saying the usual foolish things: "We have only a short time to live; therefore, it is good to elect a way of life . . . a man cannot, it seems to me, employ his time better than by loving well" (ll. 72–79). A partial excuse for his dedication to love is that he was struck by Cupid's dart while still very young; love found him "moult . . . foible et tendre." There follows a digression on the games of young children "dessous douse ans" that has taught us some of what we know about games of the time; then, the speaker tells us, he had to learn Latin, and he was beaten if he did not know the lesson. Later, he began to read romances, "especiaument les trettiers d'amours" (315–16). The turning point in the pilgrimage of his life comes

24. Kibler's remarkable 1976 article, "Self-Delusion in Froissart's *Espinette Amoureuse,*" well explains the meaning of the narrative action and of the mythological episodes, although I am not sure that the latter are precisely "typological" in function (note the useful distinction made by Hollander, "Typology and Secular Literature: Some Medieval Problems and Examples," in *Literary Uses of Typology from the Late Middle Ages to the Present,* ed. Earl Miner [Princeton, 1977]: 3–19).

25. *Espinette* 29.

26. "Mythological Typology in Froissart's *Espinette Amoureuse,*" *RPLit* 3 (1980): 207–221, p. 209.

when, daydreaming under a hawthorn bush on a lovely day in May, he has a vision of Mercury, accompanied by three ladies. Calling him by name, Mercury appeals to him to give his opinion of the judgment of Paris, which has so annoyed Juno and Pallas. If he had given the apple to Juno, he might have had vengeance on the Greeks, but he threw it away, losing supremacy and dignity for a little vanity. Because of his decision his own mother, father, and brother, as well as thousands of men in arms, died cruel deaths; it was indeed an unfortunate apple for the Trojans, and dearly bought. What have you, asks Mercury, to say of this decision? (395–482) When the speaker, overwhelmed, protests his youth, ignorance, and poverty—how can he make so important a judgment?—Mercury insists that it is precisely those qualities he seeks, "car en eage et en avoir / Sont malisces, Haïnne, Envie." Well then, replies the youth, Paris didn't care for fortune or prowess, and no more do I; he cared only to love and serve the beautiful lady Helen. I uphold his judgment. Mercury, with curt cynicism, comments, "Che moult bien savoie! / Tout li amant vont celle voie" (523–24). He departs with Juno and Pallas, leaving Venus to exhort the speaker and promise him due reward for his judgment, if he will be her servant. He accepts: "Car je ne quier ne voel aler / Contre vous ne vostre parler; / Tant en vault la doulce ordenance / Que grant joie en mon coer avance" (605–16). Having received his promise, Venus departs, and he never sees her again.

The purpose of this mythological set-piece, of course, is not really to recount a dream but to define in a decorative and conventional way the spiritual allegiance of the lover and to prepare the reader for what is to come: as a follower of Venus, he will suffer a great deal and he will behave foolishly.[27] Like Cupid in the *Roman de la*

27. Bradley-Cromey ("Mythological Typology" 210) has correctly seen that Mercury's comment establishes the lover of the *Espinette* as similar to Paris, but her modernist view of the poem posits them both as types of "courtly" virtue. She has, I believe, (p. 217) simply misread Venus's comparison of the lover's lady to Helen, in which the goddess claims that he will be so infatuated with the lady that "Diras apartoi en ce temps / Plus de mille fois la semainne / Qu'onques tele ne fu Helainne, / Pour qui Paris ot tant de mauls" (572–75). Surely this means, not that the lady is completely unlike Helen, but that she is quite like her, only more so. Kibler's understanding of the function of the choice of Paris within the poem—that it exposes the lover's folly ("Self-Delusion" 83) and foreshadows ill fortune for the lover (84)—is, I believe, correct. In any case it is reinforced by several similar re-enactments of the episode which we have seen, and will see, in the late medieval Italian and French poetry of love.

Rose, Venus hints strongly that the love-service she recommends is full of fear ("Car amour ne vault nulle rien / Sans cremour, je le te di bien") and suffering (the lover will believe that no lady is so desirable, not even Helen through whom so much evil came to Paris), but her implied warnings in no way diminish the enthusiasm of the lover. He reassures himself with a dozen conventionally foolish reflections: Venus's beauty is so great that it must be right to serve her; all good things will come to me through her; since she honored me by appearing to me in person, I must obey her; why, she treats me just as well as she did Paris, who loved Helen. Clearly, all she says is true; I can't do better than to serve love (61978). We have seen the lover of the *Echecs Amoureux,* after ratifying the judgment of Paris, reason in precisely the same way. So when the youth meets a lovely girl (engaged, at the time, in reading the romance of *Cléomadès*), he is struck by the god of love. She herself is not, but the lover does not blame Cupid for that, "car sires ne se poet mesfaire / Aucunement viers son servant" (696–767). He reflects that he could not do better than to die for her love, if it came to that, and in fact his suit will prove so unfruitful as to leave him little choice. When she asks him to lend her a book, he encloses an amorous *balade,* which she returns, apparently unread, with the book. When he brings her a rose, she smiles a little, which inspires a lovely virelay of praise and *espoir* (822–1045). Soon he is accepted as one of her circle, but languishes in misery because of her neglect; she gives him only the same smiles she gives to everyone. Finally he resolves to tell her of his love, but in reply to his confession she asks only, "Esce a bon sens que me vodriés amer?" and invites him to dance (1046–1124). Matters do not improve, but the lover never tires of repeating that death for her sake would be an honor. However, "il m'a convenut soustenir / Moult de griefs, dont petit don ai" (1187–88). A lady who knows her well comforts him and agrees to deliver a letter to her, but upon reading it she responds only that he expects too much. The lover is thrown back upon the consolation of death; it would, after all, be a glorious death. Leander, Achilles, and Acteon died for love, and is their fame not glorious? (1309–22)

In this state, the lover recalls—"une heure ireus, l'autre liés"—he continued for some time, while his confidante comforted him. Then rumors arise of his lady's approaching marriage; chagrined, he secludes himself, and lies for three months with a fever, writing poems of despair. If her husband dares to touch her, he vows, he will kill him. In a long *complainte* he compares himself to Phoebus as lover of Daphne; how much luckier he would be if his lady were transformed into a laurel tree, so that he could kiss and embrace her at will! Didn't Pygmalion love an image? And Candace loved the portrait of Alexander. Changing his mood, he wonders how he could ever excuse himself if the lady knew that he had wished her "gent corps" transformed into a senseless tree; feverishly, he reminds himself that she is the source of all goodness, reflects upon the ills of Fortune, and repeats that he would prefer death to life without her mercy (1556–2018). Certainly, if he did not have Hope, he would not be worth a strawberry. Phoebus never felt such pain when he was refused by Daphne. Alas, he was shown two paths, the narrow and the wide, and to his sorrow he preferred the wide path of Plaisance. Like Tantalus, he is tortured by the sight of things he cannot possess. Lancelot, Tristan, and Paris were love's martyrs; like them, he renders himself up to Love, his god. After his death, may his name be inscribed in the book of true lovers (2035–2338).

These reflections are repeated again and again, but finally—after three and one-half months, we are told—the lover recovers from his fever and undertakes a journey. His comforter gives him a mirror belonging to his lady, in which while he is away he sees her combing her hair. The lady of the mirror expresses her love for him and praises his loyalty. She loves him more than Hero loved Leander, or Medea Jason; if he were false to her, she would be pierced by a sharper dart than that with which Acteon (sic) struck his lady as she spied upon him jealously from behind a bush. She will always be as true to him as the laurel is green, but it is not well to proceed too hastily in love. He must accept her promise of eventual reward (2366–2990). After the image fades, he returns home, where the lady indeed shows him more attention than before; but as soon as she agrees to allow him to serve her, Male Bouche appears and takes away all his joy. The lady refuses to see him any more, and when he places himself once in her path she tugs roughly at his forelock, pulling out a tuft of hair, and says she is no friend of his (3145–3786). The lover laments, but manages to cheer himself in an impressive exhibition of lover's reasoning: the course of love, he reflects, is never smooth, and I could see that she was not in a good mood, so I should not have approached her. The hair-pulling was, after all, just an "amoureus tour," a piece of coquetry. Such reflections please him so much that he gives voice to a loving *balade,* whose sentiments are, in summary, as follows: My lady, all the good I have comes from the memory of you. I have experienced much sorrow in love, but I do not hold myself deceived, rather lucky; I would have been nothing without love, which turns vice to virtue. Love is not loss of time; one is advanced through love. I have had much pain through you and will have more, for the longer I live the more I love you. Venus promised me this when I first saw you, and I cannot choose better. I could never love another; you were the first and will be the last. The poem concludes with a *lay* expressing substantially the same sentiments and ending with an acrostic of the lovers' names. The lover trembles, he says, at mentioning hers, but does so at the urging of Desir and Plaisance (3798–4192).

It is easy to recognize in the utterances of this lover the convention we have seen many times already by which, once a speaker has identified himself as a lover *par amours,* he begins to talk nonsense about love. The lover's assertion at the beginning of the poem that one should elect a way of life in order to make the most of the time on earth is philosophically correct, but his election of the voluptuous life (symbolized by his ratification of the judgment of Paris) is foolish, as we are warned in advance by Mercury, here the spokesman for reason. The lover later laments it explicitly in his metaphor of the two paths, but he remains unable—or unwilling—to change his course. His formal oath of fealty to Venus, his willful disregard of the warning implied in her speech, and a dozen perverse utterances of a conventional sort—that Venus's beauty testifies to her virtue, that he is honored to be treated as well as Paris (!), that Venus cannot lie, that Cupid can do no wrong, etc.—all signal his mistaken spiritual allegiance. So do his many utterances in defiance of the plain evidence of his own story: that love is the source of all good, that it increases virtue, that a suffering lover ought to consider himself lucky, rather than deceived, that love is not loss of time, that it is an honor to die for love. Froissart's use of the classical lovers tends toward the same conclusion. The deaths of Leander, Achilles, and Acteon were not, as we have seen, "glorified" by poets and commentators of the time of Froissart; the deaths of "Love's martyrs" were regarded in a very different light from those of Lucretia or Alceste. In the terms of philosophy and religion, the "martyrs" to love allowed a misconceived passion to lead them to a foolish despair. Hero and Medea, with whom the lady seeks to identify herself in her speech of comfort to the lover, do not improve her case with the alert reader acquainted with medieval interpretations of the *Heroides* and the disposition of these ladies by serious poets from Jean de Meun to Dante to Petrarch.

The controlling myth of the *Espinette,* that of Phoebus and Daphne, has a history slightly different from that of the other myths of the gods as lovers. Like them, it was commonly viewed as evidence of Ovid's principle, "Non bene coveniunt maiestas et amor," but unlike the ladies of the other myths Daphne was often praised for her successful resistance, so that the laurel became a symbol of perpetual virginity (later exploited by Petrarch). In Alanus, who as we have seen disapproves thoroughly of the gods as lovers, the image of Daphne (with those of Penelope, Lucretia, and Hippolytus) forms a part of the decoration on the garment of Chastity.[28] Arnulf of Orleans speaks of the laurel crown as the reward of virgins after death, and explains that Daphne was said to be the daughter of the river Peneus because virgins are cool by nature, like flowing water.[29] Giovanni del Virgilio and Bersuire both associate Daphne and the laurel with Christian virginity; Giovanni writes, "Per laurum signatur virginitas eo quod semper est virens et redolens."[30] The gloss on the *Echecs Amoureux* praises Daphne's preservation of her virginity and describes the laurel as "a tree that is almost divine"; and the *Ovide Moralisé,* one of Froissart's sources for the tale, explains that Daphne, who is of cold temperament, represents virginity, which is fittingly symbolized by a tree because perfect purity remains unmoved by carnal desire. The tree is a laurel, which, like perpetual virginity, remains always green and bears no fruit.[31]

How does the lover of the *Espinette* use this tale? He begins by comparing himself to Phoebus, who ardently pursued the beautiful Daphne. Like the lady of the *Espinette,* she fled; like the lover, he suffered from her rejection and addressed to her extravagant speeches of love: he would die, he said, if she did not show him mercy (1572–1683). One day he surprised her in the forest as she was deer-hunting and chased her until she fell exhausted. In despair, she prayed for help to her mistress Diana, who suddenly transformed her into a laurel as Phoebus watched in amazement. The transformation did not dampen his ardor, for he embraced and

28. *De Planctu* Pr. 8, 57–64.

29. *Allegoriae* I, 9 (Ghisalberti 202–3).

30. Giovanni *Allegorie* I, 9 (Ghisalberti 46); Besuire *Red. Mor.* XV, 1 (Engels 41).

31. Jones 571; *Ovide Moralisé* I, 3185–3200. Froissart may have used both the *Metamorphoses* and the *Ovide Moralisé* in composing his account of Apollo and Daphne; although the narrative appears indebted to Ovid, certain words of the lady's *confort* (2863–65) seem to have been taken from the *Ovide Moralisé,* the usual source of Ovidian tales and commentary for French poets of the High Middle Ages.

kissed the tree many times, adopted it as his own, and granted it the gift of evergreen foliage. Oh, prays the lover, that my lady might be so transformed! Then I could at least be assured of seeing her. It is not so foolish to love an inanimate thing; Pygmalion loved his image, and Candace her portrait of Alexander (1690–1803). Praise of Pygmalion's image was well established as a commonplace of infatuated speakers from the time of the *Roman de la Rose,*[32] and here it appears as especially apt; the lover's wish that the lady be transformed reveals that it is really his *idolum* that he loves, and not the lady herself. His onanistic desire for her to stand still so that he can make love to her contrasts strikingly with the *Ovide Moralisé*'s equation of treelike stillness with moral steadfastness. In other words, this lover, like others we have seen, is turning the conventions of mythographic exegesis upside down. By using the myth of Daphne, which conventionally signified laudable resistance to carnal desire, to construct a fantasy in which his desire is fulfilled *malgré* the lady, the lover unintentionally defines the nature of the love which tortures him.

Like the *Amorosa Visione,* the *Espinette* has most often been misread and undervalued by scholars. Poirion regards its narrative as autobiographical, and characterizes Froissart as an amorous clerk.[33] Shears, who attempts to read the poetry of Froissart as solemn and didactic in tone, is troubled by certain elements of farce. How, he asks, are we to take seriously the poet's 800-line outburst of grief at the impending marriage of his lady, or his naive interpretation of her hair-pulling as a gesture of affection?[34] Most signifi-

32. Comparison of the lady to "l'image que fist Pygmalion" is a convention of the lyrics; in addition, Pygmalion appears in some form in almost all the *dits,* including the *Fonteinne Amoureuse* and *Voir Dit* of Machaut and the *Prison Amoureuse, Paradis d'Amour* and *Joli Buisson de Jonece* of Froissart.

33. *Poète* 206–7: "Le clerc peut connaître aussi, qu'il se destine à la cour ou à l'église, une vie amoureuse dont on ne songe pas a s'inquiéter: Froissart se vantera de servir Venus. Il fera dire à la déesse: '. . . x. ans tous entiers / Seras mes drois servans rentiers, / Et en apriès, sans penser visce, / Tout en vivant en mon servisce.' " It is essential to recognize that these are the words of Venus, who must be distinguished from the protagonist of the poem, who must in turn be distinguished from Froissart himself, who (it is pretty certain) would not have been likely to "boast" *in propria persona* of serving Venus. See note 93 and note 34 below.

34. He protests (*Froissart* 204), "We are unmoved . . . by [the poet's] grief, occasioned by the news that his mistress is about to marry, when that grief is depicted in an outburst of 800 lines, and especially when the poet, after a digression of 200 lines on the adventure of Phoebus, has to remind us of his subject!" Later, he

cantly, though, few critics of the *Espinette* have made any real attempt to account for Froissart's liberal use of mythology. In the introduction to his 1972 edition of the poem, Fourrier objects that its narrative line is so slender that it required extensive padding; Froissart thus introduced the mythological digressions, which add narrative interest to the work but render it rather shapeless.[35] Audrey Graham criticizes Froissart severely for the "irrelevance" of the mythological episodes of the *Espinette,* even claiming that the poet clearly admits digressing.[36] I hope that the foregoing discussion of the function of the mythological episodes—the imitation of the judgment of Paris and the tale, retold and alluded to at several points in the poem, of Phoebus and Daphne—has demonstrated their function as a gloss on the narrator's story and lyrics about his frustrated love. We will see that many of the poems of Machaut and Froissart, far from being shapeless, have this characteristic shape in which a rather inconsequential central love story is surrounded by far more lively and well-developed mythological "digressions." Just as the tales in a medieval manuscript of Ovid are often framed by much fuller commentary, so these slight tales of a lover who approaches a lady and suffers greatly for love of her, only to be rejected or ridiculed in the end, are framed by the classical tales of

suggests tentatively that "possibly Froissart does not intend us to take his poem too seriously" (205). Of the hair-pulling, Shears asks (205), "Are we to imagine that the poet is as naive as he would appear when he interprets this gesture as a mark of affection? He seems more sincere in his opening lines where he warns us that love is not worth the price one pays for it!" Precisely. Wimsatt's summary of the *Espinette* in *Chaucer and the French Love Poets,* 127–29, is occasionally ironic in tone, but he never suggests that the irony might be inherent in the poem itself. Peter Dembowski ("La Position de Froissart-poète dans l'Histoire Littéraire: Bilan Provisoire," *TLL* 16 [1978]: 131–47, p. 135) accurately describes the love story of the *Espinette* as an *exemplum,* though he does not hint at its *moralitas*.

35. *Espinette* 35.

36. Graham, "Classical Allusion" 29. She refers to lines 1764–65: "pour retourner au droit pourpos / De mon plaint, de quoi je pourpos," a common type of formula with which Froissart and Machaut make their way from a mythological episode back to the narrative. It does not, of course, undermine the relevance of the myth to the narrative; in fact, in an indirect, witty way, it points it up. The mythological tales, by providing a sort of commentary upon the love-narrative, are in fact a clearer window upon the author's "droit pourpos" than the narrative itself. There has been no thorough analysis of Froissart's use of classical mythology in the *Espinette*. Bradley-Cromey takes an ahistorical approach, and Kibler, although he has well understood the function of the myths, does not bring to bear the evidence in other *dits*.

love, whose very misuse by the lover/narrator constitutes a commentary on his emotions and actions. The lover of the *Espinette,* like those of the *Rose* and the *Amorosa Visione,* shows himself a bad reader of the old *exempla,* whose traditional exemplary function he ignores or perverts. For the reader, the episode of the judgment of Paris serves to define his love at the outset, while he himself sees in the divine visitation not a warning, but an opportunity to declare his allegiance to Venus, who will introduce him to a pretty lady. He constructs around the tale of Phoebus and Daphne an elaborate poetic edifice that not only fails to approach any of the meanings traditionally assigned to the Ovidian story, but systematically outrages them all. Far from deploring Phoebus' fall from the dignity of divinity, he expresses envy of his victory over Daphne, which was generally interpreted in precisely the opposite way as her victory over him. The tales from mythology, and the lover's failure to understand their meaning, introduce into the *Espinette*—in indirect, or, better said, in conventional fashion—considerations of reason and morality that would otherwise be suggested only by the spectacle of the lover's disordinate behavior and unrewarded labor. They are not digressions at all, but closely linked to the problem of choice of spiritual allegiance that is at the heart of the poem.

In indicating certain similarities in the ways in which medieval poets treat the myths of the classical lovers, I do not wish to understate the real and substantial differences between the poems in which they appear. The speakers of the *Roman de la Rose,* the *Amorosa Visione,* and the *Espinette* resemble each other in one essential respect: they all pursue a kind of love which the poet (and, presumably, his audience) recognizes as spiritual error. As we have seen, they are almost entirely unindividuated; the foolish things they say and do, and which identify them as passionate lovers, are quite conventional and do not serve to establish them in any way as separate personalities. But the ways in which they are used within the poems by the poets differ considerably. In the *Rose,* the dominant technique is irony, and the question of moral choice—which, to be sure, concerns Jean just as deeply as it does Boccaccio—is posed through the filter of the lover's exemplary antics and those of his foolish counselors. The lover of the *Visione* takes his moral pratfalls to the accompaniment of insistent reminders that life is fleeting and the choice of spiritual allegiance a matter of great urgency. The *Espinette* and other poems of its time and type represent a development of the tradition begun by the *Rose,* but they are different from it in important ways; Froissart recognizes—even, at times, insists upon—the folly of the lover, but within the poem the moral and esthetic emphases are balanced. Although we have seen that Froissart can preach, preaching has no place in the *Espinette,* in which the obsessive love-suffering of the speaker becomes the matter of graceful and highly disciplined verse. The poet's concern with the moral orientation of his speaker, which is clearly enough defined, is ultimately subordinated to his concern to create beautiful artifacts out of what we may regard nowadays as distinctly unpromising material. The convention, however, by which he chooses love-suffering as his theme—and indeed the impulse that animates medieval poets, early and late, to write about love—stems ultimately from the Augustinian and Boethian tradition of right love as the basis of all moral virtue.

This tradition established the choice of spiritual allegiance—earthly or heavenly—as the most crucial decision of every man and the most fitting theme of serious poetry. Medieval poets of love most often establish explicitly a moral framework for their discussions of love, but even where they do not, the two sorts of love are identifiable by the conventions associated with them, including of course the convention of correct or perverse exegesis of the classical myths of love. It is easy to define the moral preoccupations of Jean in the *Rose* and Boccaccio in the *Amorosa Visione,* but the *Espinette* presents an interesting case because it begins by presenting the lover as confronted by moral choice, shows him choosing wrongly, and then goes on to elaborate his love affair in the manner often called "courtly." The fact is that, although Jean's tone is ironic, Boccaccio's serio-comic, and Froissart's "courtly," the motives, techniques, and arguments of their lovers are strikingly similar, and all three poets take care to locate the love of which they speak within the moral universe. The "courtly" tone, then, should not be interpreted to mean that the poet is enraptured, but that his speaker is infatuated. This does not, however, imply that there is irony beneath the surface of all the love poems of the High Middle Ages. The poets seem to have taken just as lively an interest in the process of error as in the mechanisms of redemption, and they delight in detailing the state of mind of the lover. Irony is certainly a possibility, but so far we have seen fully developed irony only in Jean. It is not difficult to understand the complexity of tone that we find in this love poetry if we consider the importance that the issue of spiritual allegiance had for the poets and their audiences. The poetry dramatizes and exemplifies the difficulty of a correct choice of allegiance, of adhering to that choice once made, and of living within, or extricating oneself from, the miserable condition brought about by incorrect choice. These were difficulties that both the poets and their audiences had experienced, and continued to experience, themselves. There is an enlightening passage in the correspondence of Christine de Pizan and Pierre Col in which Pierre objects to the treatise of Gerson against the *Rose* on the grounds that Gerson was not an intelligent reader of the poem, being unable to participate imaginatively in the experience it describes. Pierre writes:

> . . . par my foy je tiens qu'ainsy come il meismes, quant il prescha en Greve le jour de la Trinité, dist que icelle Trinité nous veons et cognoissons en umbre et come par ung mirouer, ainssy voit, entent et parle d'ung fol amoureux; car je panse qu'il ne le fut onques, ne n'y ot onques pensee: en tant que je oseroie dire qu'il contoit mieulx la Trinité qu'il ne fait Fol Amoureux, aussi y a il plus pansé. Et pour yce j'eusse cause assés de dire a tout celle plaidoirie, qu'il n'y fault point respondre: car tout le plaidoié est fondé sur ung fol amoureulx, et l'aucteur ne sceit qu'est fol amoureux. Et ne vault riens de dire que ja soit ce qu'il ne soit fol amoureux, si entent il par aventure mieulx que tel—l'est ou a esté—; ce puet estre, mais j'ose bien dire que s'il meismes l'eust esté et ne le fust a present, il entendist mieux la moitié qu'il ne fait: car trop plus a experience de ne say quelle puissance que n'a meismes l'effait de vive voix. . . . presupposé encore que le dit Meung eust esté fol amoureux par aucun temps.[37]

Christine replies that she can cite many examples to show that "It is never necessary to have experience of a thing in order to speak properly of it."[38] She is right, of course, but she has missed Pierre's point, which is really a literary one: in order to be understood aright, a poem must be read with imaginative sympathy. What Pierre is saying is that, if Gerson had been able to feel sympathy with the condition of the Foolish Lover, he would also be able to see that Jean condemns his behavior very effectively within the poem, so that he would not have objected to the poem itself. Gerson's

37. Quoted from Eric Hicks, *Le Débat sur* Le Roman de la Rose (Paris, 1977), 91–92.

38. Quoted from Joseph L. Baird and John R. Kane, *La Querelle de la Rose: Letters and Documents* (Chapel Hill, 1978), 120.

argument, and Christine's, is not that Jean seems to recommend carnal love, but that he describes it in such detail and with such gusto that the unwary may be led astray despite clear warnings. As Christine writes,

> Rayson fist a l'Amant ainssy come se je parloie a une fame grosse ou a ung malade, et je luy ramentevoye pommes aigres ou poires nouvelles ou autre fruit, que lui fut bien apetisant et contraire, et je luy disoie que se il en mengoit, ce luy noirroit moult. Vraiement je tiens que mieulx li souvendroit et plus luy aroit penetré en son appetit les choses nommees que la deffence faicte de non en mengier. . . .[39]

Pierre contends that a reader fully acquainted, by personal experience or imaginative participation, with the condition of the foolish lover will not find his appetite whetted, but will be better warned by his example precisely because of his own knowledge of the consequences of incorrect spiritual choice. Thus the attitude of the intelligent reader of this poetry of love is not one of scornful superiority, but one of constant awareness of his own vulnerability to temptation. Certainly Dante would agree; so would Boccaccio and Froissart. It is only in modern times—and only because of great changes in the philosophical orientation of intelligent readers—that Christine's argument has gained widespread assent. Because the great medieval poems of love are founded upon the problem of spiritual allegiance, the poets feel free to explore the condition of erring lovers for the amusement and instruction of an ideal reader who "has been, but no longer is, a foolish lover," but who continues to struggle with the problem of maintaining correct allegiance.

No work illustrates this better than the *Ameto* of Boccaccio, a meticulously constructed pastoral allegory in which the "simple hunter" Ameto advances from a carnal to a Christian understanding of love while the narrator of the tale apparently fails to do so. On a superficial level, the *Ameto* appears as a collection of love-stories told by seven lovely nymphs gathered in a spring meadow where the lustful Ameto—who can scarcely believe his luck—has come upon them by chance. The tales themselves are frankly lascivious: most of the nymphs seem to have been married to unsuitable husbands and to have cultivated the acquaintance of toothsome young men

39. Quoted from Hicks, *Débat* 125.

who introduced them to love, for which they come together to give thanks to Venus. The nymphs unblushingly retail the crudest confessions, telling how they pursued their lovers with bribes, threats, striptease, and ambush in the marital bed, primed by frustration with the unwelcome demands of young husbands or the "eroded ploughshares" of old ones.[40] Throughout the tales the nymphs and their lovers invoke, and compare themselves to, the classical lovers in a way that suggests they serve the carnal Venus. The narrator introduces the collection by remarking that the various categories of men under the dominion of Fortune like to hear tales corresponding to their own conditions: soldiers enjoy tales of battle, the rich tales of the downfall of powerful men, and lovers tales of Helen of Troy, Dido, Hypsipyle, and Medea. Such tales not only recall past loves, but kindle new ones in their hearers; the narrator thus offers them in honor of Cupid, "master and norm of the good life" (I, 7). Cupid's sublimity can hardly be described; he comforts lovers who serve him, frees them of all vices and cultivates in them all virtues, makes even the gods humble, maintains the very spheres in motion. If at one time—"perhaps mistakenly"—the narrator complained of love, he now sings the praises of Cupid and of his lady, "a woman whose equal neither wise nature nor industrious art have ever set their divine hands to form" (I, 11). His book is for lovers: "let whoever loves listen; to the others, I pay no regard; their cares can keep them all." Finally, he praises Venus and calls upon her aid in the name of her own well-publicized passion for Mars and Adonis (II, 1–12).

We recognize this context as similar to others in which an infatuated speaker sets out to praise love. Such praise, as we have seen, may be "framed" in several ways: it may be counterbalanced by the appearance of a spokesman for reason, it may be undermined by the spectacle of the lover's foolish and self-destructive behavior, or it may be accounted for by a later identification of the speaker that defines praise of love as an essential feature of his point of view. In some cases it may persist to the end of the work, with only certain literary conventions (statements about love contrary to wisdom and experience, like those above, and praise of, or identification with,

40. *Com. Ninfe* XVIII, 34–35, XXXV, 60–70; XXXII, 15–16. All references to the *Com. Ninfe*—more commonly called the *Ameto*—are from the edition of Antonio Enzo Quaglio, *Comedia Ninfe,* in Branca, *Opere,* vol. 2 (Verona, 1964); translations are those of Judith Serafini-Sauli, *Giovanni Boccaccio:* L'Ameto (New York, 1985).

the classical lovers) to indicate the moral valence of the speaker's passion. The *Ameto* seems at first to fall into the last category. The standpoint of the hunter Ameto, who admires and pursues the nymph Lia, is the same as that of the narrator. Indeed Ameto is a very funny fellow, distracted to the point of insensibility by the physical charms of the nymphs, unable to listen to their tales at all for trying to peek between gaps in their clothing, busily extrapolating the beauties of the hidden parts from those that are revealed (XII, 16). He compares the loveliness of the nymphs to that of Daphne, Medea, Semiramis, Dido; when he prays that he may always be in their company, he wishes that his prayer might be answered, as were Daphne's and Myrrha's.[41] As the nymph Agapes tells of the incapacity of her aged husband Ameto curses his destiny, wishing that he might take the place of the old man or else persuade Agapes to imitate Helen and Briseida, who wisely abandoned old husbands for young lovers (XXXIV). The nymphs identify themselves, too, with the classical lovers: Mopsa compares herself, in pursuit of the young Affron, with Phoebus in pursuit of Daphne, and Hero receiving Leander; despairing of his love, she recalls the despair of Byblis (XVIII, 20, 31). The friends of the once reluctant nymph Acrimonia urge her to love with the argument that love dominates all: even Apollo, Hercules, Medea, and Venus herself succumbed to love's power. Agapes is introduced to love by being immersed with Venus in the fountain of Narcissus.[42] The classical lovers occur again and again in speeches of the nymphs in which they, or their lovers, seek precedent for their passion. Ameto also invokes the infernal sufferers, another conventional feature of medieval poems about love *par amours:* if Tantalus or Tityus could see the nymphs, he declares, they would forget their pain (XVI, 10). (As we have seen, the denizens of Hades appear frequently in the love poems, not so much for the sake of their suffering as for the sake of their well-established association with the irrational passions.)

There are, however, hints throughout the work that the tales conceal Christian meaning. The name "Agapes" sits oddly on a young woman who has enthusiastically received baptism by Venus into a career of adultery. The songs of the nymphs, in which they praise their particular goddesses, accord ill with the tales them-

41. *Com. Ninfe* XII, 16; XV, 12; XVI, 70.
42. *Com. Ninfe* XXIX, 19–25; XXXII, 41–56.

selves: Mopsa, having bared her flesh to attract the reluctant Affron, then sings of the influence of Pallas and "how down here each man must overcome all desire of false goods and pursue virtue for his own good"; Emilia praises Diana, who "checks wild and unbridled cupidity"; Acrimonia sings of Bellona, who "will carry us with her to a well in the heavens, away from the sins that are contrary to our salvation"; and the song of Fiammetta reveals that the heavenly crown of Ariadne, reward of those who fight against evil without despairing, would have remedied the iniquitous life of Dido and enabled the soul of Byblis to conquer the flesh.[43] Here is a reproach of the classical heroines most uncharacteristic of the speech of a lover. The tale-telling begins, too, with the debate between the shepherds Alceste and Acaten (XIV), whose "flocks" represent, respectively, the pious and the lustful. The allegorical nature of the whole is confirmed by the song of Lia, or Faith, who tells of the birth, life, death, and second coming of Christ. Ameto, never quick of apprehension, concludes only after the appearance of Venus in a column of fire that this is not the goddess he had thought to serve, but the Uranic Venus: "he deemed that she was not that Venus whom fools call a goddess for their disordered lust, but she from whom true, just, and holy love descends among mortals."[44] The nymphs, in their capacity as the four cardinal and three theological virtues, baptize Ameto and remove from his eyes "the dirty fog that had hindered him from seeing Venus." Ameto now finds that, "whereas the nymphs had pleased more his eye than his intellect, they now delighted his intellect more than his eye." He is transformed: "from brute animal he watched himself become a man" (XLVI, 5). The narrator, however, has apparently witnessed his experience without grasping its meaning, for he continues to praise

43. *Com. Ninfe* XIX, XXIV, XXX, and XXXVI. Battaglia, on the other hand, (*Letteratura Italiana* 245) views the allegorical "veil" of the poem as being "cosí leggero che sembra inesistente." That judgment would, I think, astonish Boccaccio, who included in the work many details inconsistent with a literal reading.

44. *Com. Ninfe* XLII. In its allegorical structure, the *Ameto* is not unlike the elaborately moralized *Messe des oisiaus et plais des chanonesses et des grises nonains* of Jean de Condé, in which Venus entertains love-questions from the two bickering orders and then Jean provides the proper allegorical identification of each of the participants; "He has hidden morality in this way, Jean explains, so that he may please both the wise and the fools—the wise may take example and the fools will be solaced by the humor. In closing he adds that both the canonesses and gray nuns do wrong in loving outside marriage, for all who enter into religious lives should put their hearts wholly on God" (Wimsatt, *French Love Poets* 67).

the nymphs, in the same terms as the unregenerate Ameto, for their physical attractions, and to long for carnal union with them. How happy, he reflects, must Ameto be, "seeing himself surrounded all of a sudden as the subject and the high lord of so many ladies, such as today he had before him"; and how miserable is the narrator himself, forced to return to a dark house, longing for death, "since I see no other way reserved for ending my long suffering" (XLIX, 95). His condition is precisely that of Dido and Byblis, a condition for which the nymphs offered a remedy, if he had been able to receive it.

Few works illustrate as well as the *Ameto* the ease with which medieval poets move between the realms of carnal and celestial love, and the inevitability with which the one suggests the other, even where the carnal vision is developed in considerable detail. Again, we see that references to the classical lovers provide a reliable index to the attitude of the speaker; Fiammetta's condemnation of Dido and Byblis cannot be reconciled in any way with her established character as a speaker in praise of love, and remains a discordant note in the poem until Lia's song reveals the real identity of the nymphs. Ameto declares himself more satisfied with this resolution of the poem's contradictions than a modern reader is likely to be; finally understanding the speeches of the nymphs in their proper sense,

> . . . discerne quali sieno i templi e quali le dee di cui cantano e chenti sieno i loro amori, e non poco in sé si vergogna de' concupiscevoli pensieri avuti, udendo quelli narrare; e similemente vede chi sieno i giovani amati da quelle e quali per quelle sieno divenuti. Ora gli abiti e i modi d'esse donne nota in se medesimo, debiti a così fatte. (XLVI, 3–4)

Ameto discerns, perhaps, more than we do, for the question "of what nature their loves were" remains a problem for modern readers. One is tempted to seek precise allegorical correspondences that probably do not exist: when Mopsa, who represents Wisdom, bares her breasts to entice Affron, does that somehow portray Wisdom revealing herself to men? And what could be the allegorical signification of the aged husband's disabled generative apparatus? Clearly, no possible answer to these questions could be really satisfying to the modern sensibility; an analogous problem is posed by Froissart's lengthy, painstaking, and often agonizing descriptions of the lover's behavior, which both he and we have already identified as foolish. That medieval poets did not share our distaste for these kinds of details is attributable, perhaps, to their stronger interest in the movements of the soul prompted by love. In any case, Boccaccio's central interest is in Ameto's conversion from carnal to celestial love. Among modern critics, however, belief in the ennobling power of love *par amours* dies hard. Sapegno believes that Ameto's carnal attraction to the nymphs helps to prepare him for the beatific vision: "Ameto raffigura l'umanità incolta e selvaggia, che si rinnova e si ingentilisce per l'influsso dell'amore, si purifica e si esalta nell'esercizio delle virtù e si rende alfine capace di contemplare la Divinità nella sua essenza segreta."[45] This view is reminiscent of Branca's belief that the narrator of the *Amorosa Visione* is made worthy to attain virtue by witnessing the successive worldly triumphs. In both poems, however, carnal love is explicitly rejected as error, and the protagonists are figures of fun as long as they pursue it. Despite his pastoral surroundings, Ameto seems, in fact, to represent a kind of medieval *homme moyen sensuel,* who becomes ever more deeply involved in carnal concupiscence until he is granted a vision he has done nothing to deserve, and which initially he does not even understand. His progress from carnal to celestial love is a matter of conversion, not of evolution.

A similar movement from carnal to spiritual love takes place in the *Filocolo,* a vast romance based on French and Italian versions of the tale of Florence and Blanchefleur. That movement has not often been noted, again because most of the narrative energy of the work is expended upon its carnal aspect; the passionate attachment of the forcibly separated lovers and their efforts to be reunited under the aegis of Venus. The *Filocolo* has been criticized even more severely than the *Espinette* or the *Amorosa Visione* for the shapelessness of its narrative. Koerting, Battaglia, de Sanctis, Perella, and others have deplored the apparent disorder of the work and the intrusiveness of its mythological machinery.[46] Even Quaglio, in the

45. *Storia Letteraria* 299.

46. Koerting and Perella are quoted by Hollander, *Venuses* 158n41 and 149–50n4; note also Sapegno, *Storia Letteraria* 288, and Battaglia, *Letteratura Italiana* 241–42: "La critica suole deprezzare quest'opera, perché la guidica tenedo gli occhi al *Decameron,* rispetto a cui la struttura del *Filocolo* resulta senza una sicura disciplina." Without really mitigating this judgment, Battaglia attempts to make a virtue of disorder: "Ma è proprio questa sua composizione apparentemente disordinata e convulsa che ne costituisce la novità."

introduction to his thorough edition, seems to regard the *Filocolo* as at best a "pastiche," "ove nessuno dei piani s'accorda strettamente all'altro, ma tutti collaborano a un superiore, talvolta discorde, effetto d'insieme."[47] Whatever the superficial impression created by the poem's dizzying succession of episodes, however, there can be no doubt that Boccaccio in fact planned it carefully; Victoria Kirkham's numerological analysis of the "questioni d'amore" gives ample proof of that.[48] Like the other poems of love we have examined, the *Filocolo* proceeds in accordance with a plan that depends upon literary conventions, including strategically placed references to the classical lovers. This, however, has not been perceived, and the poem has been severely criticized for its many classical allusions. In 1895, John Symonds objected that the "sudden and imperious intrusion" of mythology into the region of romance "renders the reading of *Filocopo* [sic] at the present day well-nigh intolerable," and more than half a century later Nicholas Perella—who attempts to read the *Filocolo* as psychologically realistic—finds its mythological allusions "the most annoying feature of all" in a poem full of irritating divagations.[49] In fact, though, mythology plays an important role in the *Filocolo*; if there were no other indication of Boccaccio's intention (and, as we will see, there are many), the contexts of his frequent allusions to the lovers of classical antiquity serve to characterize the love of Florio and Biancifiore in each of its stages.

The identity of Biancifiore, and her personal history, are critical to the story's meaning. Child of Christian parents, conceived in response to her father's prayer to St. James, her father's death in battle and her mother's in childbirth leave her to be raised in the household of King Felix of Spain, her father's pagan enemy. Taught together with Florio, the king's son born on the same day, she naturally learns only pagan lore; and when the children come to read "the holy book of Ovid, in which that supreme poet shows how the holy flames of Venus should be carefully lighted in cold hearts," they receive a visitation from Cupid and fall in love.[50] (The perspec-

47. Antonio Enzo Quaglio, ed., *Il Filocolo,* in Branca, *Opere* 1 (Milan, 1964), 49.

48. "Reckoning with Boccaccio's 'Questioni d'Amore,' " *MLN* 89 (1974): 47–59.

49. Symonds, *Giovanni Boccaccio as Man and Author* (London, 1895), 30; Perella, "The World of Boccaccio's *Filocolo,*" *PMLA* 76 (1961): 330–39, p. 330.

50. *Fil.* I, 45-II, 2 (trans. Donald Cheney, *Il Filocolo* [New York, 1985]). All references to the *Filocolo* are to the edition of Quaglio and the translation of Cheney. Monteverdi takes this passage literally as reflecting Boccaccio's own view of the *Ars Amatoria;* his opinion on the "santità dell'amore" is quoted by Janet Levarie Smarr,

tive on the *Ars Amatoria* is that of the narrator, a servant of love who writes at the command of his lady.) The sort of love that troubles the two young people is unequivocally described: they gaze at each other, sigh, and abandon their studies, and they are compared to Paris and Helen, Pyramus and Thisbe (II, 7 and 9). Dismayed by their growing passion, King Felix and his queen determine to separate them. When the king announces his decision to his son, there ensues the first of the book's many speeches and debates on love. The narrator first laments the king's decision, arguing that love only grows stronger through hardship: "Why else did the mulberry turn red, if not through the burning flame constrained in it, which took greater force in two lovers who could not meet? What made Byblis become a fountain if not the sense of her desire being frustrated?" (II, 9, 4) The king, better instructed in the meaning of the *exempla,* warns his son not to "love a woman beyond measure":

> Non udiste tu mai dire come miserabilmente Narcisso per amore si consumò, e con quanta afflizione Biblide per amore divenne fontana? E ancora gl'idii sostennero noia di tal passione. . . . e in brieve, niuno non è a cui questo amore non dissecchi le medolle dell'ossa. (II, 14, 4)

Florio promptly resorts to the opposing argument that

> . . . né il sommo Giove né il risplendente Appolo, da voi ora davanti ricordato, ne alcuno altro iddio ebbe all'amorevole passione resistenza. . . . Adunque, se io giovinetto contra così generale cosa non ho potuto resistere, certo non ne sono io sì gravosamenta da riprendere. . . . [Biancifiore] ha in sé una singular bellezza, la quale passa quella che Venus tenea, quando ignuda si mostrò nelle profonde valli dell'antica selva chiamata Ida a Paris, la quale, ognora che io la veggio, m'accende nel cuore uno ardore virtuoso sì fatto, che s'io d'un vile ribaldo nato fossi, mi faria subitamente ritornare gentile. . . . Sieno del loro amore ripresi la trista Mirra e lo scelerato Tireo e la lussuriosa Semiramis, i quali sconciamente e diso-

Boccaccio and Fiammetta: the Narrator as Lover (Urbana, Ill., 1986), 244n60. Smarr correctly points out that failure to distinguish author from narrator vitiates any reading of Boccaccio's works (236n19).

> nestamente amarono, e me più non riprendete, se la mia vita v'aggrada—. (II, 15:1–2, 11, 14)

Here are the characteristic conventions of a lover's argument: defense of the gods as lovers (and, by implication, of the judgment of Paris), and the assertions that love conquers all and confers all virtues on the lover. We will shortly see precisely such an argument effectively refuted, but at this point the narrator concludes that Florio has had much the better: "The king made no further reply to Florio, since he could see that the other had his arguments so well prepared that if he wanted to talk further with him he would lose by a wide margin" (II, 16, 1). Instead he sends Florio packing to tutors in nearby Montoro, deceitfully promising that Biancifiore may join him in time. Biancifiore, who has eavesdropped upon the exchange from a hiding place, redeploys the classical lovers in a long lament: Florio has let himself be tricked more easily than Hypsipyle; her own sorrow is greater than that of Ariadne or Phaedra, whose lovers at least abandoned them intentionally; his undertakings to her must be as false as those of Demophoon to Phyllis, since he leaves her so lightly; indeed she envies Arethusa, Hecuba, and Meleager, who escaped their sorrow by being changed into another form. When the lovers can speak together, she threatens to follow the course of Dido, and he praises her by comparison to Apollo, Venus, and Orpheus, and undertakes never to prove deceitful, as did Jason (II, 18–19). Giving him a magical ring and promising to bite off the nose of any other lady who attracts him, Biancifiore makes the idolatrous declaration: "You alone will be my pantheon, to whom I must pray for my felicity" (II, 21, 9). And so Florio leaves to begin the exotically colorful pilgrimage that will culminate in his discovery of a higher love.

The classical lovers continue to appear in conventional contexts: praised, excused, or appealed to by devoted lovers, maligned by disillusioned ones. Reflecting that he should never have left Biancifiore, Florio fears she may fall in love with another, and moralizes in misguided fashion the *exempla* of Paris and Clytemnestra:

> E qual cagione recò Elena ad innamorarsi dello straniere Paris se non la follia del suo marito, che, andandosene all'isola di Creti, lasciò lei assediata da' piacevoli occhi dello innamorato giovane? Né mai Clitemestra si sarebbe innamorata di Egisto, se Agamenon fosse con lei continuamente stato:

il quale poi lei insieme con la vita per tale innamoramento perdé. (II, 26, 12)

Later, hearing from the young knight Fileno that he loves Biancifiore and believes she returns his love, Florio laments:

> O dolore sanza comparazione! O miseria mai non sentita da alcuno amante che è la mia! Avvegna che io non sia il primo abandonato, io son solo colui che sanza legittima cagione sono lasciato. La misera Isifile fu da Giansone abandonata per giovane non meno bella e gentile di lei, e per la salute propia della sua vita, la quale sanza Medea avere non potea. Medea poi per la sua crudeltà fu giustamente da lui lasciata, trovando egli Creusa più pietosa di lei. Oenone fu abandonata da Paris per la più bella donna del mondo. . . . Oh quanti essempli a questi simili si troverebbero! Ma al mio dolore niuno simile se ne troverebbe, che un figliuolo d'un re per un semplice cavaliere sia lasciato. . . . (III, 18, 22–23)

Florio's folly (he himself has previously argued that true gentility has nothing to do with rank, and he is deceived in his belief that Biancifiore loves another) is soon answered by the hard-won, but only partial, wisdom of Fileno, who—finally understanding that Biancifiore feels nothing for him—curses Cupid, allegorizes his attributes in traditional fashion (his wings represent inconstancy, his youth immaturity, his blindness unreliability), and makes use of many of the heroines of classical antiquity in a bitter misogynist diatribe. Semiramis, Clytemnestra, Pasiphae, Helen, Procne, Medea, Myrrha, Byblis, Cleopatra, and Phaedra are all convicted of "libidinous fury," "unbridled lust," and horrible cruelty: "in such a multitude not a single good woman is to be found" (III, 35). A young man passing by overhears the words of Fileno, agrees, and comes forward to offer him comfort, having himself been abandoned by a lady. The source of his comfort, he says, is "the helpful advice of [his] reason," which has taught him that one cannot lose that which one truly possesses (III, 36, 10). The love they both followed is the inevitable cause of sorrow: "who would be so foolish as to love the poisonous hemlock and try to draw sweet juice from it?" Fileno laments his exile, but in fact "there can be no such thing as exile, since the world is a single city for all people." Concluding his Boethian lecture, the young man urges Fileno to "leave these complaints and rise, come with me, and think of living virtuously . . ." (III, 36, 15). But Fileno has not the fortitude to follow this advice, and weeps until at length he dissolves into a spring, to be reconstituted later by a pitying Biancifiore.

This debate about the proper meaning of the classical *exempla* of love is clearly an important subtext of the romance, with obvious implications for our understanding of the passion that unites the two lovers. It is finally resolved by Fiammetta in the section of the *Filocolo* usually called the "Questioni d'Amore." The importance of this part of the romance has been noted by Kirkham and, more recently, by Hollander in his book *Boccaccio's Two Venuses;* my own findings are complementary to theirs. The "Questioni d'Amore" occur as an interlude in Florio's journey (under the alias "Filocolo") to recover Biancifiore, who has been sold by his father to Eastern merchants. Forced by inclement weather into the port of Parthenope, he and his company join a party of youths and ladies in a garden. The setting is "courtly." Fiammetta/Maria, an amorous lady of marvelous beauty, serves as judge in deciding such questions as which indicates greater love, the giving or accepting of a garland; which rightly feels more sorrow, a lady who has lost a lover or one who longs for one she cannot attain; which is more to be loved, a wise, generous, or strong man; and the question borrowed by Chaucer in the "Franklin's Tale," whether more generosity is shown by one who honors an improper oath or one who excuses him from performing it (IV, 10–68). The classical lovers appear as *exempla* throughout the *questioni:* Dido's gifts to Aeneas are adduced as proof that giving shows more love than receiving, Medea's grief at losing Jason that it is a greater sorrow to have loved and lost, the loves of Dejanira, Clytemnestra, and Lucretia that certain persons are most attracted by certain qualities, the passion of Byblis, Pasiphae, and Leander that desire overcomes reason, the actions of Byblis, Phaedra, Hercules, Paris, and Pasiphae that love makes the lover timid and fearful.[51] The young knight Caleon, who has struck up a friendship with Florio, must be urged by Fiammetta to speak when his turn comes, so rapt is he in admiration of her. When he does speak, his question is fundamental: "Gracious queen, I desire to know if every man, for his own well-being, ought to fall in love or not. And I am moved to ask this by the various things seen and heard and maintained by the varying opinions of men" (IV 43, 16).

51. *Fil.* IV: 20, 24, 29, 42.

Fiammetta, who (as in Boccaccio's later book of that name) possesses wisdom she has not the strength to act upon, answers reluctantly, "It is necessary for us to speak against that which we follow with desire." Asking Cupid's forgiveness, she explains that there are three kinds of love: virtuous love, by which God and his creatures are bound together; love for pleasure, which she and her company follow and of which the question is asked; and love for utility, the commonest of all, which loves only where there is advantage and ought by reason to be called hatred. It is the second, she says, of which she will speak:

> . . . al quale, veramente, niuno, che virtuosa vita disideri di sequire, si dovria sommettere, però che egli è d'onore privatore, adducitore d'affanni, destatore di vizii, copioso donatore di vane sollecitudini, indegno occupatore dell'altrui libertà, più ch'altra cosa da tenere cara. Chi, dunque, per bene di sé, se sarà savio, non fuggirà tale signore? Viva chi può libero, seguendo quelle cose che in ogni atto aumentano libertà, e lascinsi i viziosi signori a' viziosi vassalli seguire—. (IV, 44, 8–9)

Caleon, objecting that her speech bids fair to spoil the festivities, interrupts to sing the praises of the second sort of love: it makes the proud humble (as witness Mars lover of Venus) and the stingy generous (Medea), spurs men to glorious deeds (Paris, Menelaus, and Perseus), and calms wrath (Achilles and the song of Orpheus in Hades) (IV, 45). "He who pleased the gods and the mightiest of men ought similarly to please us: may such a lord be followed and loved and served, and may he live ever in our minds!" In the longest judgment of the *questioni,* Fiammetta refutes his argument in the terms of philosophy and religion: "We wish you to know that this love is nothing but an irrational will, born of a passion which comes into the heart through a lustful pleasure appearing to the eyes and nourished in leisure by memory and by thoughts in foolish minds . . ." (IV, 46, 3). Correcting his interpretations of the classical *exempla,* she points out that Mars showed, not humility, but presumption in taking to himself the wife of another; that in Medea love led, not to generosity, but to foolish prodigality; that the acts of Paris in pursuit of Helen were not glorious, but disastrous to himself and others. Furthermore, Hercules was emasculated by his love for Iole, so that he spun wool with the women. Certainly Orpheus spoke sweetly, "but flattery is the act of a vile man." Love makes his subjects neglect their reputations, as did Aegisthus, Scylla, and Pasiphae, and causes them to break sacred oaths, as did Theseus and Tereus (IV, 46, 4–16). In short, "The beginning of this love is nothing other than fear, the middle is sin and the end grief and sorrow; therefore it is to be avoided" (IV, 46, 18–20). Love knows neither measure nor reason; only fools praise it. Even lovers wish to be free of it, but they become aware of its evils only after having been "trapped in its nets," so that they cannot escape.[52]

These, of course, are the conventional moralities on the classical myths of love, which speakers from the young Florio to Caleon himself have perverted in ways typical of lovers throughout the romance. A lady of the company puts the derailed *questioni* back on track by arguing that young people cannot avoid love, and so "I shall hold that it is permissible to fall in love, and consider this reprehensible behavior as if it were proper conduct" (IV, 47). Fiammetta herself falls back into the game, ignoring the conventional wisdom on true nobility to rule that a more wealthy, powerful, and noble lady is to be preferred to a humbler one. But the effect of this discussion on the *Filocolo* is dramatic and permanent. Florio does not at first appear to have learned much from the judgment of Fiammetta, for we are told that he returns to his hostelry inflamed by her beauty with even greater longing for Biancifiore. But shortly thereafter he has a vision, much like that of Ameto, of the three theological and four cardinal virtues in the guise of lovely ladies (IV, 73–74). At first he cannot understand the wisdom they try to communicate to him, for he can think of nothing but his longing for Biancifiore; but then, in an allegorical struggle between Christian and pagan forces, he is visited by Christ and Grace, who baptises him and clears his eyes, so that he "could both understand worldly and divine things better than before, and could love them each according to its worth" (IV, 74, 17). Finally Biancifiore (who, we should recall, was born a Christian) appears as one of the theological

52. Perella ("*Filocolo*" 331) accounts for the pervasive presence of mythology in the *Filocolo* by arguing that "Boccaccio's characters are attached to ideals that are rooted deep in this world, and to move freely they need an area from which the Christian God is absent. A universe ruled by pagan deities offers Boccaccio a subterfuge which allows for the representation of a vision of life that is at bottom incompatible with Christianity, although it is not without its own high ethics." However, Fiammetta here thoroughly and systematically demolishes the "high ethics" of love *par amours;* we are left with the theme of Christianity, which Boccaccio proceeds to develop.

virtues to lead him to heaven. His blissful vision is interrupted by his companions, and he narrates it to them, none of them (as they have never yet heard the Gospel) understanding what it means.

From the point, though, that Fiammetta exposes the Christian perspective on love and Florio experiences the Christian vision of salvation through grace, the classical lovers practically disappear from the tale. Never again—through the adventures of their reunion, marriage, and homecoming—do the couple compare themselves to them, in a book in which reference to them had been almost obsessive. The fifth and longest book of the *Filocolo*, which contains material not found in any of Boccaccio's sources, knits up the matters he has established as thematic: love, faith, and polity. The rather ambiguous tribute of the lovelorn Idalogos, imprisoned within a tree, to Biancifiore—he can scarcely believe in the existence of a faithful woman, and is sure there can be no other—definitively dissociates her from the company of the classical heroines of love, with whom she had associated herself repeatedly in the first part of the romance. Caleon cures his disordered passion for Fiammetta by bringing order to a community of savages, and Filocolo, the pilgrim, acquires the character of missionary by converting all of Spain to Christianity. These matters are clearly not extraneous to the work, but demonstrate the socially constructive subordination to the service of God of the personal passion of Florio and Biancifiore, which had been of quite a different order at its inception. The romance ends with the conversion of everyone, even including the recalcitrant old King Felix, who on his deathbed delivers to Florio an admonition to flee lust (V, 92, 16). Clearly, the love of Florio and Biancifiore has been transformed since the early days, and the indices of that transformation include both the changing aspects of Venus cited by Hollander and the changing attitude of the lovers toward the classical heroes and heroines of love.

It is to be hoped that better understanding of the role of allusions to the classical lovers within the great French and Italian poems of love may lead to a more just estimate of their literary value. Medieval works that discuss love in terms of the mythological lovers are, by definition, learned rather than popular, and thus generally proceed in accordance with a plan that depends upon literary conventions. That the plans devised by medieval writers are not always immediately accessible to us should not be taken as evidence that they do not exist. In the next chapter we will examine works whose principles of orgnization are a good deal less simple and accessible than the principle of pilgrimage; nevertheless they do exist, and an understanding of the contexts within which medieval writers may place the lovers of classical antiquity can help us to penetrate them.

4

Mythology and the Foolish Lover

Although the framework of spiritual pilgrimage is a common way in which medieval writers organize their discussions of the manner and consequences of each man's choice of spiritual allegiance, it is not the only way. They may also present protagonists *in medias res,* about to make—or having already made—a choice that will bring them misery. In such cases there is most often, somewhere within the work, an antagonist to the lover or a spokesman for reason. The advice of this person, while it goes unheeded by the protagonist, nevertheless serves to remind the reader of the alternative to the hegemony of the passions. This is the organization of Boccaccio's *Elegia di Madonna Fiammetta,* a work of such clarity that it is astonishing that anyone might ever have regarded it as the "realistic" study of a gloriously passionate love affair; yet it has been described in that way by critics from the sixteenth century to our own.[1] Fiammetta—as she tells us quite

1. Smarr, *Boccaccio and Fiammetta* 146–47, notes: "It is interesting to see how within the sixteenth century readings of the *Elegia* changed from an interpretation

plainly both at the beginning and at the end of her tale—is an *exemplum*. She hopes by detailing her sufferings in love to warn other young women away from immoderate passion: "cioé esemplo di sé donare a quelli che sono felici, acciò che essi pongano modo a loro beni, e fuggano di divenire simili a noi."[2] In her book, which takes the form of an extended monologue, she naturally makes much use of the classical *exempla* of love. Although she cites them again and again, it is not surprising that neither she nor any of her counselors seem really to understand their meaning.

The Fiammetta of the *Elegia* is a young woman of old "Partenope," happily married and famed for her beauty, who catches sight of the gallant "Panfilo" in church and falls violently in love with him. Idle and ripe for amorous diversion, they engineer a few meetings and soon become inseparable lovers. At the height of their bliss (or of Fiammetta's, at least), Panfilo announces that he must make an extended visit to his aging father to help him put his affairs in order. Though Fiammetta protests, he remains firm in his purpose, promising to return within four months. He never returns. This slender plot (we will see a similarly slight one in Machaut's *Voir Dit,* an even longer work) must sustain the weight of eight books of anticipation, lamentation, anger, guilt, and waxing and waning hope and despair. The *Fiammetta* is an exasperating work whose insistent and unrelieved psychopathology soon approaches burlesque, an effect clearly intended by Boccaccio. No one in it can think straight: not Fiammetta, crazed by passion; not her nurse, a character out of Raison by La Vieille; not her husband, a troubled and deluded bystander. Even if this were demonstrated in no other way, it would be visible in their use of the classical *exempla* of love. In her premonitory dream, in which she is stung by a serpent as she disports herself in a meadow of flowers, Fiammetta likens herself to

---

close to the one suggested above [i.e., her own, in which Fiammetta represents carnal appetite gone wild] into a more romantic one." Among others, she cites Filipopo Giunti, whose dedication to the edition of 1594 describes the love of Panfilo for Fiammetta as "amor veramente da gloriarsene" (his emphasis, however, is upon Panfilo/Boccaccio's "glorious" conquest; he does not suggest that Fiammetta herself ought to glory in it). Critics of our own time have persisted in reading the story in romantic fashion; the list of those who do so is roughly congruent with the long list of critics who treat Boccaccio's works as autobiography, provided by Smarr on p. 231n5.

2. Salinari and Sapegno, *Elegia* 157. All references to the *Elegia* are to this edition.

Proserpine (in beauty) and to Eurydice (in being attacked by the snake [6]). Unlike Eurydice, she takes up the snake and places it in her bosom, imagining its cool skin will soothe the bite already inflicted; the snake, of course, continues to bite until Fiammetta faints from loss of blood. Her real likeness to Proserpine and Eurydice, to which she nowhere alludes, is that she is soon to go to hell, the hell of irrational life in this world envisioned by commentators on the myth of Orpheus.[3] Shortly thereafter appearing in the temple, not really to worship but to display her beauty, she evokes the judgment of Paris (she appears "simile alle dèe vedute da Paris nella valle d'Ida" [7]) and then reproduces it herself, in consenting to love young Panfilo. As usual in medieval tales of love, some prominence is given to the matter of consent of the will; Fiammetta's formulation is that, "ogni considerazione all'ultimo posposta, seguitai l'appetito, e subitamente atta divenni a potere essere presa" (10). (Her nurse will later describe her as "più la volontà seguitante che la ragione.") She unambiguously characterizes the love she feels as "venerei veleni," and says, "di libera donna, divenni miserrissima serva" (11). The exhortation of the nurse, who counsels her to flee love before it takes too strong a hold, almost persuades her, but then she receives a visitation from Venus.

Appearing "ignuda, fuori solamente d'un sottilissimo drappo purpureo," (18) the goddess deploys the classical *exempla* in a conventional lover's argument on the power of love. Cupid, she says, rules over all; it is useless to resist. Even the gods are subject to his power; did not Phoebus pursue Climene, Leucothoe, and foolish Daphne? And Jupiter changed his shape for Leda, Europa, and Danae. Even I, Venus, could not defend myself from my son, as witness the tears I shed for Adonis. The strongest and most valiant men are conquered by love. Hercules, Paris, Achilles, Clytemnestra, Scylla, Ariadne, Leander, and Dido all fell victim to it: "Santo è questo fuoco, e molto potente, credimi" (19–21). Animals, too, are ruled by love; deer, boars, and lions do battle for their mates. Love penetrates even to

3. Salinari and Sapegno 6. Smarr, whose book appeared after most of this chapter had already been written, also notes (*Boccaccio and Fiammetta* 133) the impending *descensus ad inferos* of both women. Of Fiammetta's insistent reference to the classical heroines, she correctly states (143), "One of Boccaccio's frequent uses of classical allusion is to introduce a distance between the author and the narrator by evoking associations of which Fiammetta seems naively or even willfully ignorant"; such associations include those traditionally attached to Paris, Helen, Clytemnestra, Dido, Semiramis, and Cleopatra, among others.

the underworld, for Pluto's eye was caught by Proserpine. There is no shame in yielding to love, for his law is greater than the law of marriage. Pasiphae, Phaedra, Jason, Hercules, Ulysses, and I myself all had husbands or wives, yet we loved others. Why should you be the only one to resist? Overcome by this argument, Fiammetta yields to Venus, saying, revealingly, "Sia come ti piace": Thy will be done. Venus then kisses her, "quale il falso Ascanio, nella bocca a Didone alitando, accese l'occulte fiamme" (24). To the end of her story, though she reviles love again and again in her suffering, she never shows any sign of recognizing Venus's sophistry in this speech or of understanding the proper use of the classical *exempla* of love. When she uses them herself, it is to interpret her own experience in terms of theirs: she and her companions, in their beauty and dignity, resemble Semiramis, Cleopatra, Helen, Dido, Polyxena; the tardy Panfilo may be drowned at sea, like Leander; if he has fallen in love with another, he is justly caught in his own net, like Narcissus, Atalanta, and Fiammetta herself. Hearing a traveler speak of Panfilo's new love in his own country, she likens herself to Oenone, watching Paris sail home with Helen.[4] Even in her long final enumeration of the mighty brought low—which includes not only all the Ovidian heroines but Jocasta, Hecuba, Sophonisba, Cornelia, the Persian and Greek kings, and Ulysses—her point of view does not change.

Both before and after her disillusionment in love, Fiammetta altogether misconceives the moral operation of the universe. As soon as she consents to love, she determines to act "according to reason" (25) (i.e., to do nothing rash that will reveal her love). She uses all her wiles to attract Panfilo, later admits that, and still later protests that he appeared unexpectedly by night and ravished her in her bed: how could she have prevented it? (64) She is delighted when Panfilo hypocritically cultivates the friendship of her husband, but nevertheless believes all his oaths and views with astonished jealousy certain evidence that other ladies than she have reason to sorrow at his absence. When he does not appear as promised, she wishes fervently for the death of his old father (and, later, for his own and that of his mistress). She laments that

4. Salinari and Sapegno 87, 55, 66, and 103. Battaglia (*Letteratura Italiana* 246) mentions Fiammetta's resemblance to the speakers of Ovid's *Heroides*, and particularly to Phyllis (whose passion, we may recall, furnished the commonest example of *amor stultus* in the medieval *accessus*).

Fortune, which properly has nothing to do with love (!), has "put his sickle into another's corn" by bringing her such misery (83). She is the caricature of a deluded lover, who views the whole moral order upside down. Her nurse, however, is not so deluded; in fact, she has generally been regarded by students of Boccaccio as the representative of reason.[5] Certain clues within the text, however, including her use of the classical lovers, reveal that she does not really attain that status. As I have suggested, everything she says may be traced to two figures of the *Roman de la Rose,* Raison and La Vieille. The difficulty, obviously, is that the point of view of these figures is fundamentally incompatible: how, and why, does Boccaccio combine them?

The Nurse first appears before Fiammetta has fully committed herself to love, to warn her against it. Love, she says, is mad folly, which one may avoid by fleeing it in the beginning. Cupid is not a god but an infernal fury, bringing madness and despair to those who follow him. Fiammetta, whose beauty, nobility, and chastity are praised by all, should not risk losing her good name and the love of her husband in order to pursue an unknown young man to her destruction. This is indeed the counsel of reason, which the enamored Fiammetta duly rejects. The nurse, then, instead of washing her hands of the whole affair in the manner of Reason, begins to play the *amie,* actively helping to bring the love of the two to fruition and to prevent its discovery. When she sees the abandoned Fiammetta ready to succumb to despair, she first reminds her that she chose to love of her own free will:

> Amore, ancora che potentissimo signore sia, e incomparabili le sue forze, non però, te invita, ti poteva il giovine pignere nella mente; il tuo senno e gli oziosi pensieri di questo amore ti furono principio, al quale se tu vigorosamente ti fossi opposta, tutto questo non avvenia. . . . (118)

She then trots out the classical *exempla* in an attempt to remedy the situation; her use of them is revealing. Men, she says, have always deceived women, and so should you deceive them; these are the games that are taught in the court of Cupid. The gods laugh at

5. Even Smarr, who in my judgment is right about practically everything else concerning the minor works of Boccaccio, joins in this opinion (*Boccaccio and Fiammetta* 135).

the broken oaths of lovers. Jason abandoned Hypsipyle, Paris Oenone, and Theseus Ariadne, yet these women ended, not their lives, but only their loves. Medea, betrayed by Jason, took Egeus, and Ariadne Bacchus. You may find many gentlemen just as attractive as Panfilo, and indeed more faithful. Comfort yourself; Dejanira, Phyllis, and Penelope all felt more pain than you. Worldly things are shadow, not substance, and fortune changes continually. Ill fortune gives reason to hope for better; we are all tossed upon the waves of destiny. Embrace hope, and Fortune may bring you renewed joy (118–21).

We recognize in this both the cynical counsel of La Vieille and a portion—though not the critical conclusion—of the Boethian advice of Reason. The women abandoned, and the gods as lovers, teach lovers to deceive as they may expect to be deceived. The ephemeral nature of the things of the world teaches them, not to liberate themselves from the dominion of fortune by seeking the permanent goods, but to float lightly upon the waves of destiny, investing their allegiance in nothing at all. The Nurse, who well knows the old dance, has acquired some worldly wisdom, but no real spiritual enlightenment. She represents, not reason, but the Fiammetta of the future, jaded and disillusioned by a succession of foolish encounters with men whose vanity she flatters as they flatter hers. The Nurse is indeed richer in experience than Fiammetta, but like her she fails utterly to profit by the *exempla* she has learned. Not surprisingly, her advice has no effect, and Fiammetta ends her book with a whole catalogue of classical *exempla* from which she can draw, at best, only the least vicious of the moralities taught her by the Nurse: "che sola nelle miserie mie non mi veggio né prima" (143).

Another category of classical imagery—the imagery of Hades—occurs with obsessive frequency in the *Fiammetta*. In at least nine separate instances, the infernal Furies (traditionally interpreted, we may remember, as the destructive passions of men) are shown as inspiring love; in three of these instances (17, 24, 105), Cupid and Venus themselves are called Furies. Megaera, Alecto, and Tisiphone appear repeatedly to taunt Fiammetta in her misery, and once (113) she even prays to them—not to leave her in peace, but to torment Panfilo's new love on her behalf. Fiammetta compares herself, in her thirst for love, first with Tantalus and then (115–16) with Tantalus, Tityus, and Ixion together; her motive is to prove that their pain is less than hers, but the effect of her speech is to remind us of the traditional association of the infernal sufferers with the "hell" of irrational desire. Similar speeches occur in the *Voir Dit,* the *Prison Amoureuse,* the *Paradis d'Amour,* the *Book of the Duchess,* and the *Troilus;* modern scholars pause occasionally to wonder what Tisiphone has to do with love. In fact, the poets include this infernal imagery for much the same reason that they recur again and again to the classical myths of love; for the sake of the associations established by some thousand years of moralizing interpretation of these very commonplace myths.

All the narrative poems we will consider in this chapter—the *Fiammetta,* the *Voir Dit, Behaingne,* and *Navarre* of Machaut, the *Trésor Amoureux,* and the *Prison Amoureuse* and *Paradis d'Amour* of Froissart—have in common both that they purport to tell a story and that the story they tell is so slight and inconsequential in its outline as to be insignificant. Scholars have therefore deplored their threadbare conventionality and have considered them—especially the French *dits* of the later Middle Ages—to be of principally historical interest. Once having ascertained, however, that the interest of these poems does not lie mainly in narrative, we may reasonably seek it elsewhere. As we do so, we will find that the level of narrative covers over a dialectic on love that runs throughout these poems; at bottom, they are debates. The role within them of the poetic conventions—including the convention of allusion to the classical lovers—is to prosecute the argument by indirection, at the same time that they help to tell the story. Although the argument and the story take place on different levels, they may intersect with and comment upon each other; the whole is thus a *jeu d'esprit* of sufficient complexity that the poets may perhaps be pardoned for their failure to create lively and suspenseful narratives. It has often been noted that the late medieval French *dits* represent a development of the *Roman de la Rose,* but critics have not seen that, in one respect at least—in the incorporation of narrative and debate into a seamless whole—they actually improve upon it. In the *Rose,* action stops while Reason, Friend, the Old Woman, Nature, and Genius elaborate their views of love; the action, of course, such as it is, constitutes the Lover's elaboration of his own view. In the later narrative poems (not only those in French but all those influenced by the *Rose*) the conventions already established by Jean de Meun are employed in a subtler, more varied, and more economical development of the debate. This may very well be seen in the most complex of all the *dits,* the *Voir Dit* of Machaut. In this work, as in the *Fiammetta,* a lover is shown rejecting the advice of counselors who urge him to abandon his love.

The narrative of the *Voir Dit* involves the love affair of the principal speaker, an aging and ailing poet of some distinction, with a young woman of between fifteen and twenty years of age who admires his poetry and wishes to be his lover and to apprentice herself to him. They correspond; they meet several times, once perhaps consummating their love; then, after the poet conceives doubts of her fidelity based upon the reports of friends, they cease to meet, although the correspondence continues and some sort of reconciliation is effected. The most significant outcome of this rather inconclusive action is the *Voir Dit* itself, which consists of the letters supposedly written by the two, their lyrics, and the poet's reports of their meetings and of his own emotions. The poet insists repeatedly, both in the title and throughout the book, upon the truth of his account, implying that it is the narrative itself that is true, for his lady has asked him to include in it everything that took place.[6] In fact, though, just as the level of narrative masks the more significant level of debate, so the truth of the events that the poem describes is, in the end, far less important than the truth revealed through the meditations and digressions of the poet. Certain conventions establish early on that the narrator, an alter ego of Machaut who calls himself Guillaume, is suffering from the sort of love called "courtly" by modern critics and *amor stultus* by medieval

6. Lines 425–33. All references to the *Voir Dit* are to the edition of Paris, *Le Livre du Voir-Dit.* Several of the earlier critics of the poem, including Petit de Julleville, Tarbé, and Paris himself, took literally the narrator's claims to truth-telling and concluded that the *Voir Dit* "is fundamentally autobiographical and that in this quality of truth resides one of the poem's chief merits" (Calin, *Poet* 169). Although more recent scholars do not always regard the *Voir Dit* as simply autobiographical, they seem still to consider the love-narrative—rather than the mythological episodes or the lyrics—as the "main point" of the work; at least, it is to the narrative that they devote almost all discussion. Robert Sturges has seen that the focus of the *Voir Dit* is not really the narrative, but the state of mind of the narrator and his interpretations of the texts created by himself, the lady, and others ("Speculation and Interpretation in Machaut's *Voir Dit, Romance Quarterly* 33 [1986]: 23–33, pp. 24–26). G. B. Gybbon-Monypenny, "Guillaume de Machaut's Erotic Autobiography: Precedents for the Form of the *Voir Dit,*" in *Studies in Medieval Literature and Language in Memory of Frederick Whitehead,* ed. W. Rothwell et al. (New York, 1973): 133–52, regards the *Voir Dit* as one of an otherwise unrelated group of medieval narratives which he characterizes as "erotic pseudo-autobiography." I would say of the *Voir Dit* what he says of Margival's *Panthère d'Amours,* that ". . . the use of the first person is, of course, conventional and didactic rather than personal" (151).

commentators. At the beginning of their correspondence he asks her to send him her portrait; when she delays two months in responding, he falls into love-sickness, becoming melancholy, pale, and sleepless, even though he has not yet met her. Finally the portrait arrives, and he worships it as if it were an image of the goddess Venus.[7] Three times, at various points in the narrative, he compares his lady—whom he has christened "Toute-Belle"—to Helen of Troy; having met her and received her favors, he protests that if Pygmalion's image, Polyxena, Dejanira, or Helen requested his love, he would refuse (3947–54).

Throughout this time, the early, happy period of their courtship, love-debate is subordinated to narrative: the two meet at her manor, go on a pilgrimage together, attend the Lendit Fair, make love at dawn in her chamber. The terms of the debate are established, however, in several ways. The narrator, an elderly cleric/poet who finds himself writing *neuvaines* of love-verses when he should be saying novenas, knows that he cuts a ridiculous figure as a lover.[8] An *amant couart*—indeed, a *couart* in general—he trembles at inclement weather, highwaymen, his own periodic indispositions, and the potential scorn of his lady for his age and incapacity. He

7. Lines 425–33. For a more thorough summary of the poem than I will provide here, see Brownlee, *Identity* 94–156.

8. Wimsatt (*French Love Poets* 102) writes that ". . . the conventional trappings of the *dits amoureux,* the specialized diction, the classical *exempla,* the lyric set-pieces all become pointless and oppressive when made to revolve around such a lover." For "oppressive," I would substitute "amusing"; I attempt to show that the genre of the *dit amoureux* was not characteristically a sober one. Indeed, the very conventions Wimsatt cites were often employed to poke fun at lovers, or at least to cast doubt upon their enterprise. Cerquiglini (*Engin* 111–12) points out that the portrait of the lover Guillaume is not really that of the poet himself or of any individual, but the conventional portrait of a clerk: ". . . le poète est dit *apers* ou *malapers, polis* ou *desapris* non en fonction d'une jeunesse et d'une vieillesse réelles mais fondamentalement, en fonction d'une jeunesse et d'une vieillesse symboliques. Les notations sont prises au réseau analogique de la théorie des âges, des saisons, des tempéraments et des conditions, des 'estats'." The arguments of L. W. Johnson, in " 'Noviaus Dis Amoureaux Plaisans': Variation as Innovation in Guillaume de Machaut," *MFra* 5 (1979): 11–28, pp. 18–22, reinforce this view of the *Voir Dit;* noting that the emotions expressed in the lyrics cannot possibly be spontaneous and "sincere" (some of them were written before the *Voir Dit* and later included in it, and some are written by Machaut from the point of view of a woman), Johnson points to the need to understand both emotions and poetic forms as conventional in nature, thematic variations "whose shifts of emphasis and of diction combine with sound and rhythm to produce a pleasure for the reader—and listener—all the more subtle in that its elements are known in advance."

predicts that love will bring suffering (she will be cold to me, he says, then she will say it was only to test me and will give me a ring [773–808]), imagines he is foolish to think he can keep her love, and reminds himself that even the most beautiful woman is worthless unless she is faithful. These sage reflections alternate with the conventional *topoi* of infatuation: it is noble to serve Love, and he will serve him willingly till death; he, Love, and his lady are like the Trinity; her love has purified him of all vices; he will serve her like Lancelot and Tristan, will adore her as his "Dieu terrien"; indeed one should cherish women like one's right hand, for there is nothing but good in them.[9] The classical lovers are used simultaneously to praise the lady and to characterize the love itself; without mentioning the conventional (indeed inescapable) association of Semiramis with lust, Guillaume constructs an elaborate allegory in which the lady, as Semiramis, rescues Babylon (= the lover) by destroying the rebels (= Desire, Melancholy, and Doubt [4637–4736]).

This first half of the poem, in which mythology and the love-debate play a secondary role, gives way to a second half largely composed of mythological digressions, with an obsessive concern for the phenomenon of metamorphosis. Critics have imagined that Machaut, having brought the affair of the lovers to fruition, had run out of interesting material and therefore filled up the second half of the *dit* with book-learning.[10] The mythological material, however, is not really digressive, but is intended to further and finally to conclude the debate about love that is the *raison d'être* of the entire work. The debate intensifies when Guillaume, having passed two months without news of his lady, dreams that her *ymage*—which appears suddenly dressed in green, for inconstancy—turns its face away as he adores it. Appealing in his dream to the game-king, the Roi Qui Ne Ment (who takes on the *persona* of Guillaume's real lord, the Duke of Normandy), he is told that, if the changing color of a

9. 190–207, 252–55, 751–59, *lettre* X, 3014–15.

10. Whiting ("Froissart" 200) goes so far as to say that Machaut introduced the mythological material "to postpone the awful moment when his *Voir Dit* would die for lack of substance." Cerquiglini, however, in "Le Clerc et l'Écriture: Le *Voir Dit* de Guillaume de Machaut et la Définition du 'Dit'," in *Literatur in der Gesellschaft des Spätmittelalters* I, ed. H.-U. Gumbrecht (Heidelberg, 1980): 151–68, has seen that the *Voir Dit* has a roughly bipartite structure, in which the mythological material of the second part provides a commentary upon the love-narrative of the first.

dress frightens him, he would indeed be horrified by the historical metamorphoses: Lot's wife, or the victims of the Gorgons, turned to stone, and people changed to trees, marble, and many other forms. "Ovides le dit en ses fables, / En moralitez veritables" (5292–5343). The traditional "morality" of the metamorphoses was, of course, that Ovid intended to speak not of physical, but of spiritual change. Medieval *accessus* to the *Metamorphoses* explain this in various ways, but one well-known statement of the idea is that of Arnulf of Orleans:

> Intencio est de mutatione dicere, ut non intelligamus de mutacione que fit extrinsecus tantum in rebus corporeis bonis vel malis sed etiam de mutacione que fit intrinsecus ut in anima, ut reducat nos ab errore ad cognitionem veri creatoris. Duo sunt motus in anima unus rationalis alter irrationalis: rationalis est qui imitatur motum firmamenti, qui fit ab oriente in occidentem, et e contrario irrationalis est qui imitatur motum planetarum qui moventur contra firmamentum. Dedit enim deus anime rationem per quam reprimeret sensualitatem, sicut motus irrationalis VII planetarum per motum firmamenti reprimitur. Nos vero rationabilem motum more planetarum negligentes contra creatorem nostrum rapimur. Quod Ovidius videns vult nobis ostendere per fabulosam narrationem motum anime qui fit intrinsecus. Ideo dicitur Yo mutata in vaccam quia corruit in vicia, ideo pristinam formam dicitur recepisse quod emersit a viciis. Vel intencio sua est nos ab amore temporalium immoderato revocare et adhortari ad unicum cultum nostri creatoris, ostendendo stabilitatem celestium et varietatem temporalium. Ethice supponitur quia docet nos ista temporalia, que transitoria et mutabilia, contempnere, quod pertinet ad moralitatem.[11]

We saw in the first chapter that this is a very old idea; from the time of the Fathers, the metamorphoses—especially the transformations of Proteus and of the companions of Ulysses—have represented spiritual transformation by lust (in French allegorical poetry called *Desir,* a prominent personage in the *Voir Dit*). If this is what Machaut has in mind, we may expect to meet Circe or Proteus at some point in the *Voir Dit,* and indeed we do. Even at this point,

11. From the *accessus* to his *Allegoriae* (Ghisalberti 181).

though, the love of Guillaume and Toute-Belle has furnished some striking instances of the "varietatem temporalium"; having announced early in the *dit* that lovers suffer extreme emotions, Guillaume has proceeded to demonstrate the truth of that commonplace. Her letters and attentions rejuvenate him; neglected, he lapses into love-suffering and thence into real illness. He trembles when she is near, mourns when she is far away, both fears and anticipates seeing her. Aware that her interest in an aging, inept, and timorous lover is bound to fade in time, he is prey to constant anxiety. The playful reference of the Roi Qui Ne Ment to the Ovidian metamorphoses is really a thinly disguised reminder of Guillaume's "motum anime qui fit intrinsecus," his abandonment of rationality in favor of the unstable life of a lover *par amours*.[12] The king continues by treating the suppliant lover to a summary of the achievements of the Biblical inventors and the Seven Sages, with emphasis upon "him who said / That nothing was his / That could be taken away. / You should note that saying well" (5424–27). Compared to theirs, Guillaume's activities appear trivial indeed: ". . . it seems to me you're doing very little, / When you are thus surrounded / By love affairs and intrigues" (5237–39). However, the task of counseling him would be too much even for Aristotle, Seneca, Virgil, Cato, Solomon, Boethius and Plato, if they were here, for he is determined to follow Love. For each one who receives good from Love, four receive evil. At this, the king and his company laugh; even the bird dog barks, which wakes Guillaume from sleep. He goes at once to adore his *ymage,* and finding it sweetly smiling, its dress unchanged, he concludes that "mon songe / N'avoit riens de vray fors mensonge."

He no sooner arises from his knees than he is handed a letter from Toute-Belle, protesting her fidelity. When he reproaches her by return messenger for her neglect, she rewrites Ovid in an attempt to prove her innocence: neither Jason and Medea, Dido and Aeneas, Byblis and Caunus, nor Paris and Helen have loved as she loves him (5560–70). In a passage reminiscent of Paris's oath to Oenone, Toute-Belle enumerates the natural wonders that must occur before she could be false to Guillaume (mountains and valleys

12. As Cerquiglini puts it (*Engin* 87–88), "L'erreur de l'homme est de se détourner de l'amour divin, infini, pour un amour humain, failli. . . ." See her discussion of the importance of numerological allusions to Machaut's references to human and divine love in the *Voir Dit*.

would unite, the moon and stars disappear, waters run backward, stones fly through the air). Outrageously rewriting the traditional tale of Ulysses's temptation by the Sirens, she protests that they won his love by their sweet speech, whereas Guillaume will not listen to her no matter what she says. Cephalus inadvertently killed Procris as she spied upon him, but she herself could never betray Guillaume. Venus warned Adonis against hunting savage beasts, but he did not listen to her and was killed by a wild boar; Guillaume should heed her counsel to leave jealousy and love confidently without doubt (5592–5718). In fact, like other lovers we have seen, Toute-Belle is precisely reversing the traditional moralities on these myths. The names of Jason and Medea and the other classical lovers hardly constitute a sound character reference for one who seeks to demonstrate that she loves faithfully; nor does the oath of Paris, who swore to Oenone that the waters of the river Xanthus would run backward before he betrayed her. Machaut took the remaining myths from the *Ovide Moralisé,* whose moralities on them are precisely opposed to those supplied by Toute-Belle. In the terms of religious allegory, Procris represents the unbelievers, justly destroyed by God, and the wild boar of Adonis the "ordure / De luxure et de lecherie, / Qu'il demena toute sa vie."[13] We may recognize the lesson derived by Toute-Belle from the tale of Adonis as the same derived by the Lover of the *Rose:* "you should believe [your sweethearts], for their sayings are as true as history" (15755–56). It is a stock "lover's morality," by which medieval poets characterize untrustworthy speakers.[14]

Guillaume, however, is mollified, and having suffered from mistrust begins to suffer even more acutely from *desir.* Alas, he is like Tantalus, whose chin touches the water he may not drink. Considering the classical lovers—Pyramus and Thisbe, Leander and Hero, Paris and Helen—he reflects that there is little comfort in their stories, for they were all destroyed in the end (6045–6100). The gods

13. *Ovide Mor.* VII, 3513ff., and X, 3733–35 (deBoer III, 98, and IV, 100).

14. Although recent scholars of the *Voir Dit* emphasize the untrustworthiness of the speakers in the poem, they most often accept without much scrutiny the glosses offered by those speakers on the mythological material they cite. Thus Brownlee, who has made a valuable analysis of narrative voice in Machaut, seems to accept the interpretations given by Guillaume and Toute-Belle of their allusions to the classical lovers, as well as the explanation offered by the Roi Qui Ne Ment of his allusions to the Ovidian metamorphoses and that of Guillaume's secretary for his lengthy digression on the myths concerning Circe (*Identity* 139–40, 133, 143).

who loved mortals often changed their forms, becoming cows or magpies or whatever they wished, but later they changed back again. The conclusion? "J'ay les oreilles et les temples / Toutes plaines de tels exemples / Pour ce di, et si n'en doubt mie, / Sans lober et sans tricherie, / Que s'a un en voy bien cheoir, / J'en voy a douze mescheoir" (6101–6). These are not good odds, and Guillaume cannot find a single *exemple* to prove he should see his lady. Nevertheless he writes the *balade* "Je voy assez," praising his lady by comparison to the classical lovers, and protests in a letter that he would surmount as many difficulties as Pyramus, Leander, or Lancelot in order to see her.[15] But when she, having relocated nearer to him, asks him to visit her, his secretary—who to this point has abetted the affair—advises him against the journey, retelling at great length the myths of the transformations wrought by Circe. The superficial relevance of these myths to their context is very slight: insisting upon the dangers of harsh weather, highwaymen, and Guillaume's gout, the secretary says that not even Circe, with all her charms, could bring him safely on his way, nor would the giant Polyphemus treat him as badly as the highwaymen, if he fell into their hands (6914–7250). Such an elaborate development of mythological material does not seem sufficiently motivated by these very ordinary considerations; Paris calls it "tout à fait hors de propos," (286n2) and theorizes that Machaut inserted it "pour l'amusement et l'instruction de Peronne," who would not have read the *Metamorphoses*. Upon examination, however, we will see that it was intended for Machaut's well-educated contemporaries, who certainly had.

The secretary's recital is comically ill-ordered and incomplete; although he retells, or at least touches upon, several tales of the thirteenth and fourteenth books of the *Metamorphoses*, he does not seem to understand their connection with each other, and the connection he fabricates between them and Guillaume's situation is amusingly specious. He first lists the magical feats of Circe, who turned Picus to a woodpecker, the companions of Ulysses to wild boars, and Scylla to a sea monster (6984–97). Picus, he says, was transformed by Circe because he scorned her love in favor of the lovely singer Canens: but neither the charms of Circe nor the

15. *Voir Dit* 6753 [sic]–6791, and *lettre* XXXVII. The verses are wrongly numbered in the edition of Paris, going from 6103 to "6704." I have not corrected the error, but have followed the line numbers as they are given in the edition.

courage of Picus nor the song of Canens could enchant the wind, the cold, and the highwaymen that will assail Guillaume if he should attempt this journey. He then describes the horrible cyclops Polyphemus, who loved Galatea and killed her lover Acis by striking him with a rock. But even the dreadful cyclops would not treat Guillaume as badly as the highwaymen; let us write to Toute-Belle and make our excuses (7001–7250). In fact, the tales of Acis and Galatea, Scylla and Glaucus, Ulysses and Polyphemus, the companions of Ulysses transformed to swine, and Picus and Canens are all told in illustration of the power of Circe. Machaut, who did not use the *Metamorphoses* itself (so that there is no possibility that the secretary tells the tales badly because Machaut misread the Latin, as Paris supposes [287n1]), took these tales from the *Ovide Moralisé,* which repeats the well-established idea that the transformation of men into beasts by Circe represents their spiritual transformation through various vices: "vilz fornicacion," "orgueil," "ire," "haine," "glotonie," etc. Circe is the Antichrist, who offers to men the poisonous "bevrage" of worldly temptations, "qu'en eulz n'a raison ne maniere."[16] The myths told by the secretary thus have considerable relevance to the situation of the foolishly enamored Guillaume, which Machaut has already likened to that of the victims of the Gorgons (identically allegorized in the *Ovide Moralisé* as the vices "orguelz," "avarice," and "charnel delice"). The secretary, however, does not see—or pretends not to see—wherein they are relevant; in the *Voir Dit,* as in the *Rose* and much of the later European poetry of love, a part of the wit of the poem consists in the introduction of relevant myths by characters who comically misconceive their application to the situation of the lover.

The debate between Guillaume and his secretary is interrupted by the arrival of "uns sires," a person of considerable stature "loved and feared" by Guillaume, who speaks directly to the issue covertly under discussion, accrediting himself by a preliminary, pseudo-mythographic description of the "image d'Amour" as depicted by "li ancien" (7292–7399). (This description, of a young man bearing symbols of true love and disinterested friendship, is not in fact

16. Paris omits from his edition the song of Polyphemus, which Machaut took directly from the *Ovide Moralisé;* it was printed by Antoine Thomas in 1912. Both Calin (*Poet* 180–81) and Cerquiglini (*Engin* 167) note the resemblances between Polyphemus—an ugly, one-eyed poet/singer frustrated in love—and the narrator Guillaume.

classical in origin; it seems to refer to his own generous intentions toward Guillaume, rather than to the uneasy relationship between the poet and his lady.) The *sires* then says that he knows Guillaume to be so "affolez" of the lady that he is probably wasting his breath, but he must report the truth: at home, surrounded by her young suitors, Toute-Belle makes a mockery of Guillaume and his love letters; if he believes she loves him, he is deceived (7401–59). At this news, Guillaume despairs. He remembers that he once heard the same report from another friend who had been with Toute-Belle, and he decides to give up his love. His secretary confirms the reports, saying that he knew these things but feared to tell him. When Guillaume visits the court of the Duke of Normandy, where he is accustomed to receive an honorable welcome, the Duke laughs at him before all his company and says, "Friend, you're beating the bushes, / But others are catching the birds" (7586–87). Worse, he begins to be mocked on the streets. Sorrowfully, he hides his beloved *ymage* in a chest and writes the *balade* "en lieu de bleu, vous vestez vert." Toute-Belle, having heard of the *losengiers,* reproaches him in her letters; he remains carefully noncommittal.

But Love is not so easily set aside. Falling asleep one night after a week of anxious sorrow, he dreams that the *ymage* speaks to him from its prison within the chest, telling the tale of Phoebus and the crow. I have done nothing wrong, it says, weeping; why do you believe the *mesdisans?* It is a great sin to believe too quickly. I will tell you a tale. The crow was once white, and beloved by Phoebus; I will tell you how he became black. In Thessaly there was a graceful, beautiful and noble lady, whom Phoebus loved; but she loved another. The crow saw them joined by nature, and when he saw their adultery he cursed them and said he would tell Phoebus of their treachery. On his way he met the raven, who told him how she had been dismissed from Pallas's service for talebearing, and advised him to hold his peace; but he did not listen. He found Phoebus playing his harp sweetly. Oh, how foolish it is to tell one's lord a thing that will displease him, when he is enjoying himself! *Janglerie* is never in season. When the crow told Phoebus his news, he broke his harp in his rage and sorrow. Certainly it is not necessary that everything one says be the truth, nor even a quarter of the truth, so help me God. Phoebus shot Coronis through with an arrow, then repented his rash action so sorely that he rescued her unborn infant Aesculapius and changed the color of the crow to black, believing that perhaps he had lied. And he banished the crow from his court and condemned him to *jangler* forever. Have you heard this example? How can you believe reports that will cause you to lose Love and your sweetheart? May those who bear false and evil reports of lovers be changed to swine, trees, or stones (7727–8146).

Guillaume, waking, initially accepts the interpretation of the myth offered by the *ymage* and repents. Apologizing to the portrait, he reflects that one should not tell lovers unpleasant things, for they may react violently. At length, however, he decides that the tale of the *corbiaus* is not reassuring, and expends some 200 verses in a comparison of Toute-Belle with the treacherous "image de Fortune," concluding,

> Or est ma dame comparée
> A Fortune la forsenée,
> Car bien pevent aler ensemble;
> Pour ce qu'a Fortune ressemble,
> En cas de variableté
> Où il n'a point d'estableté.[17]

Presently, Toute-Belle's confessor visits Guillaume, protesting that he has certain knowledge under seal of confession that she has not been false to him; Guillaume gratefully accepts this "proof," and the lovers are reconciled. The *Voir Dit* ends with an acrostic of their names. There are troubling elements, however, in the interpretation by the *ymage* of the myth of Phoebus and Coronis. Her gloss on the myth is precisely the same as that of Cupid in the *Echecs Amoureux,* who tells the tale (along with that of the talebearer Ascalaphus) as part of his advice to the lover on how to avoid Jalousie and Male Bouche: a lover must never allow himself to be found out. Since Cupid shows himself elsewhere in this speech to be a highly unreliable glossator (for one thing, he recommends that the lover imitate

17. Lines 8381–86. In medieval literature, Fortune is traditionally associated with love *par amours*. Howard R. Patch, in *The Goddess Fortuna in Medieval Literature* (Cambridge, Mass., 1927), 53, points out that the image of Fortune with two tuns in the *Echecs Amoureux* is "practically a goddess of love"; see also the division of his book entitled "The Fortune of Love" (90–98), in which he demonstrates the connection between Fortune and love in medieval thought, and Fleming's discussion in *Roman* 124–26. Fortune has no connection with celestial love or friendship, but only with carnal love. Toute-Belle's promise in her final letter that the lovers will be outside the power of Fortune is thus without truth; see Fiammetta's similar attempt to dissociate Fortune from love (158–59).

Proteus, an infamous figure used by Jean de Meun in connection with Faus Semblant), and since his whole enterprise in the *Echecs* is characterized most invidiously by Pallas, this must give us pause. Furthermore, the crow's unpleasant news was in fact true,[18] which implies that the reports of the *losengiers* were true as well; but the argument of the *ymage* implies that both the crow and the *losengiers* were lying. The *Ovide Moralisé,* again Machaut's source for the tale, offers two interpretations of it, which it differentiates: "Ces fables espondrai briement / Par histoire, et puis autrement."[19] The interpretation "par histoire"—which in this case may probably best be translated as the "interpretation supplied by the tale"—offers the moral against jangling quoted by the *ymage:* "Nulz ne doit amer jengleour, / Ne soi croire en losengeour. / Qui s'i croit il est deceüs" (II, 2503–5). The glossator repeats this advice, apparently, because it is the moralization of the story offered within the Ovidian narrative itself; but there is nothing to suggest that he endorses it. He often distinguishes morally improving glosses on the myths from other traditional interpretations; for example, he offers three interpretations of the myth of Daphne, only one of which—the moral in praise of virginity—he identifies as a "sentence profitable" (I, 3110). In the case of Phoebus and Coronis, he continues with an "autre sentence," evidently intended to be the morally improving one. Phoebus represents God, who loves the human soul; but she is unfaithful to him. He punishes her, but when she repents he saves her child, or the good works she has done, so that she may have eternal life. The crow is Satan, who brings discord between God and the soul by causing her to act foolishly through temptation (II, 2549–2622). It is noteworthy that in this reading of the tale the talebearer becomes superfluous; discord arises through the infidelity of the soul itself, in response to temptation. The same is true in this glossator's interpretation of an even better-known myth involving a talebearer, the story of the adultery of Venus with Mars. Phoebus, who in the Ovidian narrative reveals Venus's infidelity to Vulcan, is glossed in the *Ovide Moralisé* as "sapience" (IV, 1733);

18. Guillaume even insists upon this: "Et puis je pensay longuement, / Et avoie moult grant merveille / Du Corbel et de la Corneille / Que Phebus et Pallas haïrent, / Pour ce que verité leur dirent" (8196–200). Calin (*Poet* 194) and Brownlee (*Identity* 147) also see that the *exemplum* of Phoebus and Coronis tends to prove Toute-Belle's guilt, thus subverting the argument made by the *ymage*.

19. *Ovide Mor*. II, 2455–56 (deBoer I, 224).

that is, vice is seen as being exposed by Wisdom itself, and the talebearer of the literal level disappears.

In the *Voir Dit,* the *ymage* quotes the expedient moral of the literal level; the truth to which the title of the work refers, however, exists on another plane. The exalted station of the *losengiers,* their evident good will, and the fact that the very tale chosen by the *ymage* subverts her claim that they are lying, all suggest that the lover is deceiving himself again, as he has done steadily throughout the narrative.[20] The "sentence profitable" that is within the tale, and to which the *ymage* never refers, is the recommendation that the hearer ignore the voice of temptation and detach his spiritual allegiance from the things of the world in order to serve God.[21] The truth of this tale, like the truth of the *True Story* itself, is not to be found within the narrative, which again and again presents us with the shallow and self-serving "lovers' mythography" characteristic of medieval love poetry. Our task as readers is to bring the conventional "sentence profitable" of the tales to bear against the perverse exegesis of the lovers, which itself, as we have seen, became a convention of this poetry. In the *Voir Dit,* as in the other *dits amoureux,* this is far from being a solemn task; wit is the very essence of this poetry of love. These poems are learned amusements, of which "lovers' mythography" is one of the most amusing features. The underlying issue of spiritual allegiance is, of course, a serious one, but the antics of the *fol amoureux*—his extravagant emotions, his perverse interpretations of the classical tales, his tortuous

20. Calin (*Poet* 184) also notes that the *losengiers* are "worthy, respected people, whose statements are not to be rejected out of hand." He prints (192–93) the final verses of the poem, omitted by Paris, in which Guillaume insists upon his reconciliation with Toute-Belle (Ainsi fusmes nous racordé, / Com je vous ay ci recordé, / Par tresamïable concorde . . ."). Calin concludes (202) that ". . . although the lovers do reconcile, we are never made aware of the exact relationship between them and to what extent either one loves the other or is capable of a mature relationship." The question is, I think, irrelevant; the love affair functions in the poem as an *exemplum* of unstable love *par amours,* not—by definition—a mature relationship (to the extent that that formulation would have meant anything to Machaut), and not one capable of providing us with insight into the lovers' potential for, say, disinterested friendship or a harmonious marriage.

21. Brownlee (*Identity* 106–7) and Calin (*Poet* 186) view Guillaume as a failed lover, who has not conducted himself in proper "courtly" fashion; Brownlee, however, sees also that "the role of courtly lover as such is undercut" by the irony of the *Voir Dit,* and "fin'amors as code is systematically undermined on a number of levels" (107). Cerquiglini, of course, identifies Guillaume's failure (I believe correctly) as misplaced spiritual allegiance; see note 13 above.

efforts to convince himself of what he wants to believe—were a traditional, and dependable, source of amusement for the aristocratic medieval audience of the *dits*.

The *Trésor Amoureux,* included by Scheler with the works of Froissart but probably not written by him, altogether lacks the subtlety of the *Voir Dit;* rather than circling farther and farther from the traditionally accepted moralities on the classical *exempla*, it gradually approaches nearer and nearer, finally ending in the defeat of Love by Knowledge and Reason. It begins with a traditional sort of lover's casuistry. The narrator, afflicted with love-suffering, dreams of a magnificent palace surrounded by a garden in which are two tents: one of white silk, representing the Trinity, and one of particolored velvet, representing earthly love.[22] The palace is that of Beauty, within which the lady guards the *trésor amoureux*. Congnoissance, emerging from the white tent which she inhabits with her sisters Raison, Souffisance, and Loyauté, explains these matters to the narrator and then leaves him to Cupid, warning him not to come too near the amorous flame (ll. 123–374). Cupid, who values the narrator's service all the more because he is a poet, welcomes him warmly and promises him reward if he will make a book for lovers; but he must be careful to say nothing in it against love. Dismissed by Cupid, the narrator encounters the *escuier,* another suffering lover, with whom he debates at great length certain questions: whether it is better to serve arms or love, whether both may be well served at the same time, whether knowledge is to be preferred to good fortune, whether nature or nurture is more powerful in determining character. In these debates, the narrator most often defends the point of view of Cupid, maintaining for instance that love cannot be well served by a knight who neglects his lady to fight foreign wars, that good fortune is preferable to knowledge, and that natural impulses prevail over all attempts to restrain them.

The situation is complicated, however, by the fact that both parties to the debate are lovers *par amours,* who may allude to the counsel of Reason only in order to argue against it. This requirement repeatedly leads them to maintain illogical propositions, thus paving the way for the eventual triumph of Knowledge over Love. The *escuier,* for instance, in maintaining that lovers should fight in

22. Lines 63–85 (Scheler, *Oeuvres* III). All references to the *Trésor* are to the edition of Scheler.

foreign wars for the greater glory of their ladies, is forced to argue that the ladies will remain loyal under such circumstances, while the narrator is forced to argue (against Love, as Cupid later points out) that they will not (965–79, 1126–47). Both men, having agreed that Love brings four griefs for every joy and that Reason is the way to truth, must then bring these propositions into accord with love-service, which they do (with difficulty) by concluding that a single one of love's joys more than suffices to banish four griefs, and that the truth, when determined, only brings sadness to lovers—so who would be so foolish as to follow Reason (*Bal.* I, V–XVII)? Arguing correctly that the operation of free will is essential to love-service, for Love has no power over those who do not freely assent to it, the narrator avoids the logical consequence of his argument—that one may freely decline to follow Love—in favor of the illogical conclusion that lovers ought to serve without complaint, since they chose Love (*Bal.* I, XXIX–XXXI). When Cupid arrives on the scene to ask how the narrator's *Espoir* is holding up, he offers as encouragement certain perverse glosses on the classical *exempla*. Reminding the narrator that he had promised him an explanation of the park of Love with its small, furry beasts, he conflates the *exempla* of Venus and Adonis, Atalanta and Hippomenes. Venus warned Adonis to hunt only timid animals, but then he foolishly engaged in a footrace with Atalanta, and was rescued from death only by Venus' stratagem of the golden apples (1706–1898). This fable means that the narrator, like Adonis, has chosen a lady so ferociously proud and resistant to Love that she is more dangerous than any wild beast; it is better to choose a sweet, tractable lady, "Car c'est la bichette et le dain / Agréable à deduit mondain" (1927–28).

These fables, of course, are traditionally interpreted as warnings against love *par amours;* the author's intention in putting them into the mouth of Cupid is ironic. Cupid's moralization on the tale of Venus and Adonis is in the same tradition as that of the gloss on the *Echecs Amoureux,* in which it forms a part of the commentary on Diana's advice to the lover to flee Love before it is too late.[23] Here, it occurs as one of the "Dangers that are in Love," between a discussion of the Sirens (who are said to have wings and claws because Love flies and wounds) and the *lits perilleux* of Lancelot and of Mars and Venus. In the *Ovide Moralisé,* as we have already seen, the fable is similarly interpreted as an *exemplum* against lust, while the race

23. Jones, *Chess* 637.

of Atalanta represents the chase after worldly delights.[24] At this point in the *Trésor,* Cupid and his accompanying attributes (Desir, Penser, Beau Parler, Espoir, etc.) intercede for the lover and obtain the lady's consent to his service. This favorable turn of events amazes the *escuier* and leads to the final debates of the poem. In the first of these, the narrator insists upon the value of good fortune while the *escuier* prefers "sens et entendement" (*Bal.* III, I–XIV); the observation of the *escuier* that Nature does not confer these goods leads to a debate on nature and nurture in which the *escuier* reproaches the narrator for comparing men to beasts (*Rond.* III, XV–XXII). Men possess reason, which is the only legitimate restraint upon human behavior, while beasts may be restrained only by force or the threat of force. The relevance of these arguments to the lover's happy news would have been apparent to a reader of the time, for they are the arguments of the *Roman de la Rose.* A lover *par amours* rejects *sens et entendement* in order to place his trust in Fortune, mistress of the goods of the world. In thus abandoning rationality, he lowers himself to the level of a beast, in which the promptings of nature always triumph over the restraints of civilization. This is the error of the narrator, which the *escuier,* himself a lover, falls out of character to expose.

When the *escuier* suggests that Congnoissance be called in to settle their disputes, the narrator agrees, and Congnoissance appears. Reviewing the narrator's book, she objects that, although he is "bien delité / En parler d'amours," he has neglected the permanent things:

> Qu'il [i.e., Amours] n'a gueres pourveü
> De chose qui te soit durable,
> Ne dont on puist faire absolu
> Jugement bon et raisonnable.
> (*Rond.* III, XXXI)

She and her sister Reason, however, can remedy this deficiency. The remedy she chooses takes the form of an Ovidian fable, the tale of Jupiter and Io. Jupiter, she recounts, loved Io, but his wife Juno became jealous and changed the young girl into a cow, putting Argus with his hundred eyes to guard her. Jupiter took pity on her, sent Mercury to put Argus to sleep with his flute, and changed her

24. *Ovide Mor.* X, 3733–35 and 3956–64 (deBoer IV, 100 and 105).

back into the form of a woman (*Rond.* III, XXXIII). If you do not know the *doctrine* of this fable, explains Congnoissance, I will tell it another time. As for your arguments, who can tell whether vice arises in men through nature or through nurture? But I know that my sister and I can cure it.

Here, as in other debate poems we will examine, the ostensible subject of debate is set aside and the real debate—that between love and reason—it expressed in terms of an Ovidian fable of love. The author of the *Trésor* considers the *doctrine* attached to this fable so important to the meaning of the poem that he does not expose it until the conclusion, when Love is preparing to dismiss the narrator from his service. There is evidence, though, that the narrator already knows the meaning of the fable, and that the author expected his audience to know it as well. Congnoissance moves from the tale of Jupiter and Io to a lecture on the corruption of the times, and thence to another Ovidian fable, the tale of Phoebus and Phaeton, which she never glosses at all (*Rond.* III, XXXVIII–XL). Nevertheless the narrator reacts to these two fables, neither of which has yet been explained, by thanking Congnoissance for her lesson on the order of things:

Quant Cognoissance la discrée
Par moralité et hystore
M'ot la doctrine administrée
Et rafreschie ma memoire
De verité toute notoire,
Je dis: 'Dame, par vo bonté
Et humble debonnaireté
Et par vo science parfonde
M'avez humblement remonstrée
De l'ordenance de ce monde.'
(*Rond.* III, XLI)

The "verité toute notoire" to which he refers can only be the meaning traditionally given to these two fables. The meaning he later assigns to the tale of Jupiter and Io is taken from the *Ovide Moralisé,* as we will presently see. The tale of Phoebus and Phaeton, though, conveys the central image that lies behind many debates concerning reason and the passions, that of the horses and charioteer. It was interpreted by Plato in the *Phaedrus,* and continuously after him, as representing the rebellion of the restless passions against the bridle of reason. An interpretation given by the *Ovide Moralisé* identifies Phaeton with the Antichrist, who leads the people into folly but is ultimately destroyed by the avenging fire of God.[25] That Congnoissance in fact intends such a meaning is apparent from the context within which she places the tale of Phaeton. Warning the narrator that, if he associates with men of foolish life, he is to be considered a person of no value, she advises him that it is better to leave the life of pleasure late than never. The times are evil, and even priests sin; one sees the golden chariot varying from its course in all estates of life. A foolish life will doom him in the end, but it is not too late to leave it: 'Il vaulroit mieulz tart que jamais" (*Rond.* III, XXXVII–XXXVIII). Having recounted the fable, she remarks upon Phaeton's punishment for his sin (he lies in eternal torment in Acheron, a detail not in Ovid but suggested, undoubtedly, by the gloss in the *Ovide Moralisé*), and marvels that his error has lasted so long, for even today one constantly sees the chariot misguided. But his punishment, too, will last forever.

Having received these lessons, the narrator perceives the inadequacy of his book of love-casuistry, and proposes to Congnoissance that he make a *balade* to "dire verité / De l'ordenance de ce monde" (*Rond.* III, XLI). She objects, however, that he is ill-qualified for such a task, and besides it is presumptuous to reprove in others weaknesses that one shares with them. In the example of the adulterous woman, the Bible teaches us not to blame others (*Rond.* III, XLII–XLIV). The narrator, confused, accuses her of dissimulation: surely it is not the role of Congnoissance to conceal the truth! But she continues to insist that the governing principle of a wise man must be humility, which does not inquire into the hearts of others but knows how to be patient and suffer insults, living in peace (2415–90). This discussion is surely the author's elegant *apologia* for his book, which avoids presumption by offering modest diversion and addressing the "choses durables" only by indirection. Congnoissance assures the narrator both that Cupid will find fault with his book and that he has no power to dominate those who heed her doctrine; then, upon the arrival of Cupid, she assumes a cloak of invisibility. The god of love, as she had predicted, is angry: how dare the poet claim that there are more imperfect than perfect lovers? And the *escuier* recommends flight as a remedy against love! Furthermore, it is written in the book that Reason puts out Love's fire. Has the

25. *Ovide Mor.* II, 916–93 (deBoer I, 192–93).

poet forgotten that Cupid is his king, who can punish him (2574–2656)? Beau Parler appears to defend the narrator; it is Congnoissance, he objects, who has taught him these things. Throwing off her cloak, Congnoissance receives Cupid's accusations—"j'ai perdu plus de vint cens / De mes gens par vostre langage" (2726–27)—and mounts a defense of the narrator that comically discredits him, saying that although he listened to her advice, he was too foolish and heedless to follow it; he was never really unfaithful to Cupid. She told him the tale of Jupiter and Io: what harm, she asks disingenuously, could there be in that?

It is at this point that she reveals the "verité" concealed within the fable. Io represents the human creature who seeks pleasure; she is guarded by Argus, or the world, who imprisons her in *temporalia* until God sends the Holy Spirit (= Mercury) to deliver her from the world by means of the wise words of Raison and Congnoissance (= Mercury's flute) so that she acquires knowledge of her Creator. She is then re-created as a new soul, just as she was created in the beginning (2795–2828). If the poet wishes to think of these things for his own good in the future, he must be allowed to do so; if you, Cupid, accuse him, Reason and I will help him. The author of the *Trésor* comically demonstrates the extraordinary tenaciousness of folly by showing the narrator unmoved even by this sermon, for he follows it up by attempting to convince Cupid of his loyalty. Although he has heard Congnoissance speak of Reason, he has taken no action, for he has not willed to do so; his will to serve Love remains unaltered. He has only asked Congnoissance to act as judge in the debate between him and the *escüier* (2840–84). Cupid, unconvinced, dismisses him from his service, whereupon the poor poet is so dismayed that he faints. Upon regaining consciousness, he announces resignedly his decision to follow Congnoissance and Raison, since Cupid will not have him, though he has done nothing wrong; Congnoissance reacts graciously to this rather churlish speech, summarizes the arguments between him and the *escuier,* and concludes that, in such debates, both she and Love will have their adherents—though far more, admittedly, will follow Love than Reason.[26] Awaking from his dream, the poet claims that he has

26. Lines 2957–3150. Robert Estrich, "Chaucer's Prologue to the *Legend of Good Women* and Machaut's *Le Judgment dou Roy de Navarre,*" *SP* 36 (1939): 20–39, p. 30, correctly notes that the real antagonists in the poem are Amour and Congnoissance; he believes, however, that the two are reconciled in the end. If they are, however, it is only to the extent that they agree to disagree; no middle ground is, or might be, found.

made the book "afin / Que ceulz qui aiment de cuer fin / Aient de leurs biens congnoissance / Et preignent tout en souffisance" (3197–3200). Despite this protestation the book, as we have seen, is scarcely likely to comfort lovers.

The *Fiammetta,* the *Voir Dit,* and the *Trésor* all contain expositions of the standpoint of Reason, either by the lover himself in meditations against Love, by an interlocutor, or by one or more of the personified attributes. Even in poems that do not contain such expositions, however, the doctrine of Reason may function implicitly as an essential point of reference, most often suggested by allusion to the classical lovers. This is the case in the *Paradis d'Amour,* the shortest and simplest (and probably the first) of all Froissart's narrative poems. Although it follows the general outline of the *Rose,* it lacks any explicit development of the doctrine of Reason. It cannot, however, be fully understood without reference to it. The *Paradis,* despite its brevity and relative simplicity, is not quite as easily accessible as scholars have supposed. It is ordinarily described as a poem in praise of Love, in which Froissart "achieves an effect of refined subjectivity concerning the truth and goodness of the love experience" through a dream in which "a perfect understanding is reached between the *dame* and her lover"[27]; at the same time, its indebtedness to the *Roman de la Rose* and to the *dits* of Machaut is universally recognized. In fact, it is indebted to those sources for more than just the dream-vision framework and the allegorical treatment of the love-adventure. Like them, it makes significant use of humor, and its most important messages are conveyed by indirect means.

The speaker of the *Paradis* is a lover whose love-longing keeps him awake, so that he prays to Morpheus for sleep (his lament was borrowed by Chaucer in the opening lines of the *Book of the Duchess.*)[28] In answer to his prayer, Morpheus sends him a dream in

27. Nolan, "Expropriation" 208, and Dembowski, "Tradition, Dream Literature, and Poetic Craft in *Le Paradis d'Amour* of Jean Froissart," *SLitI* 20 (1987): 99–109, p. 106.

28. Compare *Paradis* 1–4 and *BD* 1–5. All references to the *Paradis* are to the edition of Dembowski, *Jean Froissart:* Le Paradis d'Amour, L'Orloge Amoureus (Geneva, 1986). In Dembowski's view, the protagonist of the *Paradis* is a figure of "Everyman-Dreamer," and one of the principal merits of the poem is its psychological realism ("Tradition" 107–8). I shall try to show that, on the contrary, the protagonist is a conventional sort of foolish lover and the *Paradis* a Machauvian invention which is altogether un-"realistic," at least in the modern sense of the term.

which, at last, his long-unrewarded suit of his lady achieves some success. Finding himself in a *plaisance,* the narrator is moved to look back upon all his sufferings as a lover; considering how badly Love has treated him, he utters a long complaint.[29] Love, he says, you have cheated me; my lady will not hear my prayer, but acts as if she'd rather have me in my grave. If I had known when I gave heart and body to you that I would have no comfort, I would have sought another diversion. When I think of the great solaces you promised me, I believe that serving you will kill me. You're a traitor; I'll never honor you more, but displease you as much as I can, for you send me nothing but sorrow. Hope, Memory, and Sweet Thought have abandoned me, and Plaisance has betrayed me. Plaisance, I curse you; may death take me (ll. 75–202).

As he sits quietly, his head bowed, the bushes part and two ladies—who turn out to be Plaisance and Esperance—appear, shouting, "I've found him, the traitor! Get him! He deserves to be beaten!" In an attempt to appease them, the narrator comically abases himself—"I beg your pardon if I have offended; I was only speaking of the pain I have had. I see that you are very wise and noble, and it is evident that your master is a great lord. Certainly there can be nothing but good in you, dear ladies" (266–82). Agreeing to have mercy on him, they identify themselves and reproach him: surely, no one who listened to him would ever love *par amours*. Having just cursed Plaisance roundly, the narrator now attempts to flatter her—"sans vous ne poet nuls coers estre / En pensee lie et joyeuse" (364–65)—but she refuses to be distracted from his *meffait.* You have slandered us, she says, and reproached our lord, who told you that a lover must be patient, obedient, and ready to receive everything that pleases his lady. A lover who complains forgets me and has great sorrow, as you have shown today. Repentant, the narrator asks Plaisance to describe her powers, which she does with reference to the classical lovers. When young men and women achieve the age proper to love, she explains, I give them *maniere* and *atemprance,* so that they appear gracious and beautiful. Then Cupid wounds them with love, with an arrow that goes from the eye to the heart. Thus was Achilles taken with Polyxena, Neptune with Equoulenta,[30] and

29. Dembowski ("Tradition" 102) characterizes this complaint as "a formal renunciation of (the narrator's) fealty to Love." He is correct in this, but mistaken, I think, in taking seriously the subsequent chastisement of the narrator by Plaisance and Esperance, whose noisily farcical entrance into the action he nowhere notes.

30. Scheler (*Oeuvres* I, 365) notes that "Equoulenta" may be a transposition of "Leucothoe."

Leander with Hero, for whose love he perished in the sea. I could name a thousand whose sovereign I have been; as soon as lovers see each other, their hearts are pierced by that look. From that time, their nourishment is from me and my master, who loves me above all his servants. If you do not serve him with all your heart, you had better begin to do so (463–561).

Both Plaisance and the narrator, who seeks advancement in his love affair, ignore the intimations of tragedy and immorality in the tales of the three mythological couples she cites; when he asks permission to appeal personally to the God of Love, she reproaches him for wanting to have everything at once and for failing to appreciate all that Love has done for him. Then she hands him over to Esperance, who gives him the following advice on how to lead the amorous life "bellement": (1) one should give oneself entirely to love, but always maintain *mesure;* (2) one should shun jealousy, which is a great evil, but some jealousy is necessary in love; (3) one should always hope for better, no matter what happens; in this way, one can never feel discouraged; and (4) one should never reveal one's love affair (630–800).

These self-contradictory "rules of love," of course, form a witty indictment of love *par amours;* the impossible psychological balancing act required of the observant lover is a source of humor from the time of Andreas Capellanus.[31] When the narrator seeks the God of Love, who is in his garden at Narcissus' fountain, he finds him surrounded by his company of lovers: Troilus, Paris, Lancelot and others of King Arthur's court, Helen, Hero, Polyxena, Echo, Medea and Jason (957–96). Plaisance suggests that he frame his request in a *lay;* in it, he defines his plight by reference to the classical lovers. He is not Orpheus, who put the gods of Hades to sleep, but Pygmalion, or the weary Tantalus, whose chin touches the water that is denied to him. Wounded "d'uns cevelés blons / Et d'uns dois deliiés et lons / Et d'uns vers yeux a point fendus," he suffers more than Achilles, Narcissus, Paris, and Jason; only Pity can cure him, by telling the lady of his pain. She should go to the lady and say that he sees only her face, night and day, and that he lies always on a

31. Alfred Karnein has established beyond much doubt the satirical nature of Andreas's *De Amore;* see p. 275n26. On the character of Esperance, who is a deceiver wherever she appears in the *dits amoureux,* see Kibler, "Self-Delusion," and my own article " 'Lovers' Consolations of Philosophy' in Boccaccio, Machaut, and Chaucer," in *Studies in the Age of Chaucer* 11 (1989).

bed of tears, in sorrow and burning. Neither Achilles nor Paris, who in olden times were afflicted thus, felt worse. When in the lady's presence, he is often so overcome by her attractions, as was Hippomenes by those of Atalanta, that he loses the power of speech; so does ardent desire affect him. Such a life is too painful; will Pity not intercede? (1079–1354)

Unfortunately, what is principally memorable about this particular group of classical lovers is not the amorous pain they suffered, but their extraordinarily strong association with the social destruction and personal disaster occasioned by love. The love affairs of Troilus, Paris and Helen, Lancelot, Achilles and Polyxena are all connected with the fall of kingdoms, and those of Orpheus, Hero, Echo, and Medea with death and betrayal. Pygmalion, of course, suggests idolatrous carnal love, and Tantalus disordered passion. The narrator is correct in associating these figures with suffering, but he fails to perceive that any likeness of their unlucky love affairs to his own augurs ill for his chances of success. Cupid, pleased by the *lay,* charges Plaisance and Esperance to ease the lover's pain (1394–98). They guide him to the lady, whose reception of his suit pleases him greatly; it is, however, incidentally amusing that she does not really receive him very warmly. When he asks her to "donner grasce et confort," she laughs at him and asks, "Compains, que volés vous avoir?" (1503). Before agreeing to anything, she warns him she won't go "hors d'ordenance"; humbly, he asks if she would do him the honor of speaking to him. What, she replies, would he like her to say? Is she not honoring him enough just in looking kindly upon him (1506–31)? When he asks her to accept his service, she again responds with a question: "Is that what you would like?" He takes her silence for agreement, whereupon she reproaches him for rejoicing prematurely; if he shows unseemly haste, he will lose her favor through *outrecuidance.* He must be obedient and persevering, and must never ask for anything that may displease her (1561–82). The interview ends pleasantly enough, with lover, lady, and the personified attributes enjoying a new *balade* together; the lady, approving the *balade,* crowns her poet/lover with a garland of flowers.

At this point, the narrator wakes, thankful that Morpheus has distracted him from his sorrow by granting him a vision of the Paradise of Love.[32] The real purpose of the narrative is very likely

32. Lovers in the *dits* are much given to praying to, and praising, Morpheus;

to serve as a frame for a number of accomplished *lays* and *balades* of love,[33] but it has, incidentally, a double-edged irony. First of all, its outline—in which a suffering protagonist first utters a complaint and then finds relief in a "celestial" vision—parodies that of the *Consolation of Philosophy.* This device, which we will see again in the *Fonteinne Amoureuse* and *Remede de Fortune* of Machaut, is a common one in French love-vision poetry from the time of the *Roman de la Rose.* In the *Rose,* of course, humor proceeds from the Lover's un-Boethian resistance to the philosophical lecture of Reason, whereas in the later love-visions it proceeds from the substitution of the lover for Boethius, the love-attributes for Lady Philosophy, and confirmation in the irrational life of love-service for deliverance from another sort of irrational servitude to Fortune. This learned joke on the lover and love-service becomes a convention of the *dits,* as we will see. Second, the Paradise must appear, to anyone but a hopelessly infatuated lover, a good deal less than paradisal; the narrator is accosted, accused, reproached, admonished, and finally, after heroic exertions and protestations, granted a brief interval of *esbatement* with his acid-tongued lady. Further, even this modest (and entirely imaginary) gratification is interrupted when he awakens, to take up again the life of a frustrated suitor. His real condition demonstrates the truth of the ironic subtext contained in the "rules of love" and the lover's own mythological allusions, but what is funniest in the poem is that the *paradis* demonstrates it as well. The poem, an early production of Froissart which is a good deal less complex and accomplished than the later *dits,* attempts some of the same ironic effects as the *Roman de la Rose,* in which the vision itself exposes the deficiencies of love *par amours* and the lover awakes to find that his conquest is imaginary. Although no character in the *Paradis* speaks for Reason, the lover's folly is exposed by his own farcical speech and behavior and that of the personified "virtues" of love, as well as by his

---

however, he is in fact a shape-shifter in the same mold as Proteus, a master of illusion who sends visions that deceptively mirror the fondest delusions of lovers (see Margaret J. Ehrhart, "Machaut's *Dit de la fonteinne amoureuse,* the Choice of Paris and the Duties of Rulers," *PQ* 59 [1980]: 119–39, p. 134). I suspect that the speech Chaucer gives to his narrator in the *Book of the Duchess* (". . . I had never herd speke, or tho, / Of noo goddes that koude make / Men to slepe, ne for to wake; For I ne knew never god but oon" [ll. 234–37]) is a sly dig at the well-known character of Morpheus.

33. Dembowski ("Tradition" 108) well notes that the *Paradis* incorporates an art of poetry.

identification with the classical figures conventionally associated with *amor stultus*.

The much more complex *Jugement dou Roy de Navarre* of Machaut also lacks any development of the doctrine of Reason; it depends, however, upon the earlier *Jugement dou Roy de Behaingne,* in which that doctrine is thoroughly developed. In the *Navarre* the narrator, a cleric/poet, is accused of having defamed ladies by his judgment in the *Behaingne*. Because Machaut's fundamental concerns in the two poems are really the same, it is desirable to begin by looking briefly at the *Behaingne,* in which the classical lovers do not appear. This *jugement* has a superficial conceptual symmetry, which critics have most often taken to be real: a lady describes her grief at the death of her lover, a knight describes his grief at the infidelity of his lady, and each claims to be the more aggrieved, whereupon the narrator intervenes to bring them to the King of Bohemia, who rules in favor of the knight. Ostensibly, the poem is "about" the question whether death or betrayal is the greater misfortune for a lover. Its formal proportions, however, are odd; the lady's speech evoking the circumstances of her love and explaining her feelings occupies only 80 lines of the text, whereas the corresponding speech of the knight occupies 620.[34] Clearly, the poem is really "about" whatever issues are raised in the speech of the knight. His speech is organized as follows:

- ll. 261–301—his determination to follow Love, his prayers to Love, and his choice of the lady
- ll. 302–408—a minute description of the lady's appearance, from *cheveus, front, oeuil, nes,* and *bouche* to *hanches, cuisses, jambes,* and the unseen *seurplus* ("dont je ne vueil maintenant dire plus")
- ll. 409–52—the effect of her appearance upon him (he loses, among other things, "scens, vigour, et maniere")
- ll. 453–572—his uncertainty whether to reveal his love, the revelation, and his rejection by the lady
- ll. 573–611—his long service without reward, and her eventual declaration of love

34. Lines 125–205, 261–880. All references to the *Behaingne* are to the edition and translation of Palmer, *Judgment.* The edition of James I. Wimsatt and William W. Kibler, *Guillaume de Machaut: Le Jugement du Roy de Behaigne and Remede de Fortune* (Athens, Ga., 1988), appeared too late for my use here.

ll. 612–83—his great happiness and his pledge to serve her faithfully
ll. 684–721—his overthrow by Fortune, who awards the lady to another, and his sorrow
ll. 722–860—his attempt to find someone to blame for his sorrow, in which he exonerates Fortune, the lady, and Love and blames himself, God, and Nature
ll. 861–80—conclusion and assertion that he suffers more than the bereaved lady

Judging from the length and comprehensiveness of the knight's speech, it is the history and situation of this lover, and not the *demande d'amour* itself, that most interest Machaut. In his recital of his history, the knight—like Boccaccio's Fiammetta of the *Elegia*—reveals both considerable confusion about love and a smattering of Boethian wisdom, which, however, he is never able to mobilize in order to extricate himself from the "crueus maus d'amer." The speech of the knight is reminiscent of the *De Amore* of Andreas Capellanus: he falls in love through a process of sight and meditation, love makes him timid and fearful, he delivers an elaborate protestation of vassalage, and the lady replies with a speech as drily noncommittal as those of the women in Andreas' third and fourth dialogues ("Il n'est nuls biens qui ne soit remeris, / N'il n'est aussi maus qui ne soit punis. / Si que, s'Amours vous a d'amer espris, / Son guerredon / Vous en rendra en temps et en saison . . ." [529–33]). For those who remain unconvinced that Andreas sufficiently exposes the misguidedness (or, in come cases, the manipulativeness) of his lovers *par amours,* it can certainly be shown that Machaut does. He gives us a knight who means to praise Love in his speech, but whose emphases fall suggestively upon Boethian and Augustinian *topoi* that force us to evaluate this love by the criteria of reason. He chooses his lady, he says, by Fortune ("qui de mentir a tous est trop commune"); the sum of all goods and all knowledge could not compare to her love; he makes her his "dieus terriens."[35] The lady at first suggests cryptically that she herself is not the cause of his suffering, then grants her love, and finally withdraws it. Attempting to understand these events, the knight reflects that he should not blame Fortune, who merely acted according to her nature in withdrawing her favor; worldly goods are ephemeral: "Si bien ne sont

35. *Beh.* 284–85, 409–27, 663.

fors que droite aventure; / Ce n'est qu'uns vens, une fausse estature. / . . . C'est fols s'i fie!" (741–44). Nor should he blame the lady, who acted according to the dictates of Love in leaving him to love another (746–63). In a virtuoso exhibition of lover's sophistry, he decides that he cannot blame Love, either, because it was with him in good fortune and even now, in bereavement, does not abandon him, for he still loves. He ultimately places the blame upon God and Nature, for failing to put faithfulness in his lady, and upon himself for allowing her beauty to lead him into "servitute" and "mortel peril" (764–860).

His speech is ruefully funny, not only because he misses the logical conclusion of the Augustinian and Boethian arguments that his terms suggest, but because he continually recurs, with evident delectation, to the physical attractions of the lady. Her moist complexion, her blond hair, her "sein pognant," her body "si bel, si gent, si dous" furnish material for some one hundred fifty lines of initial exposition and numerous agonized exclamations thereafter.[36] In several locations, the knight states plainly that the lady's beauty, and not any attractions of a higher order that she may have possessed, was the cause of his love and now causes his despair. When the narrator escorts him and the bereaved lady to the court of Behaingne for judgment, and the king has assembled his counselors Reason, Love, Loyalty, and Youth, Reason seizes right away upon this aspect of the knight's attachment to his lady. Love *par amours,* she says, is fleshly by nature, "And its desire and its nature / Are completely inclined toward enjoyment."[37] As for the lady whose lover has died, she will forget him in time, for it is not within the power of Love to continue to love what it cannot see: "As far as love which is earthly / Is concerned, experiencing it is having it." Such lovers "[love] the body much more than the soul" (1707). Reason diagnoses the pathology of the knight, who cannot withdraw from love:

36. Lines 300–452, 476, 494, 575–82, 698, etc.

37. Lines 1710–11. Calin (*Poet* 45) correctly states that "*Raison* reigns supreme in King John's court, mistress over all other allegorical figures, including *Amour*. . . . Love's supremacy in the courtly world is undermined." He concludes from this, however, that "The *JRB* reflects late medieval interest in a more naturalistic, noncourtly erotic, the most illustrious example being Jean de Meun's portion of *Le Roman de la Rose*" (45–46). In my opinion, there is nothing new, and certainly nothing "naturalistic," going on in the *Behaingne;* it is simply a debate between Reason and Love in which Love is defeated. That defeat occurs because the arena of the debate is not the psyche of the lover, but the objective, external world represented by the court of King Jean.

> . . . Compaingnie, / Amour, Biauté, et Juenesse la lie,
> Et Loiauté, qu'oublier ne vueil mie,
> En grant folie,
> En rage, en deuil, et en forcenerie
> Le font languir, et en grant jalousie,
> Et en peril de l'ame et de la vie.
>
> (1733–39)

If, she adds, the knight had followed her counsel, he would have ceased to love the lady when she took another lover; but Beauty, Love, and Youth ". . . le norrist / Avec folour / En ce meschief, en celle fole errour, / Car il en pert le sens et la vigour." Even if he regained the love of the lady, he could not enjoy it, for he could never trust her again. His situation, therefore, is entirely hopeless, so long as he cannot withdraw his affection from the lady; he thus suffers more than his companion bereaved by death (1755–84).

The remaining personifications—Love, Loyalty, and Youth—speak according to their natures, Love and Youth urging the knight to continue to serve the faithless lady, and Loyalty confessing that he would not offend against her if he now left the lady to serve another (1785–1920). But the speech of the knight and the comment upon it of Reason, head of the king's council, contain the real *matière* of the poem. The situation of the sorrowing lovers does not change significantly within the poem; the gracious king, in an attempt to allay their suffering, keeps them eight days and regales them with gifts, and they return home praising his generosity. Machaut's emphasis is not really upon them or upon the *jugement,* which merely furnishes the witty pretext for a discussion of the causes and consequences of misplaced spiritual allegiance. The poem is not "courtly," if by "courtly" is meant "frivolous"; a poem lacking in moral seriousness would hardly be a fitting tribute to the real Roi de Behaingne, Machaut's patron Jean of Bohemia, whose court is (as the poet gracefully pretends) ruled by Reason. Like Fiammetta in the *questioni d'amore* of the *Filocolo,* Reason derails the original love-debate and substitutes for it another, more serious one. It is characteristic of Machaut's wit that the real *demande d'amour* of the poem is named by the king in a statement apparently reproaching his counselors for wandering from the subject at hand: "Nous ne sommes pas assemblé ici / Pour desputer / S'il doit amer sa dame ou non amer, / Mais pour savoir li quels a plus d'amer, / Et qui plus sent crueus les maus d'amer . . ." (1923–27). By the time he delivers it, however, the horse is out of the barn, for the subject has been both debated and resolved.[38]

In a poetry in which narratives conceal debates, it should not be surprising to find that "debate" poems conceal debates other than the ostensible ones. This is true as well of the *Jugement dou Roy de Navarre,* a far longer and more complex work than the *Behaingne.* The *Navarre* is one of the cleverest productions in all literature, in which practically every line has several sorts of comic or ironic resonance;[39] it deserves much closer study than I will be able to give it here. It has received general attention for its vivid introductory lines on the plague, which seem to have little relevance to the later *demande d'amour.* The poet, alone in his room, muses upon the perfidy of mankind; everyone seeks to cheat others, and covetousness rules. In his youth, things were different, but the world, after all, is vanity. One can only live happily and try to do well (ll. 37–136). Then he has an even more melancholy thought, this time of the plague and the disasters that accompanied it. Death was loosed upon the world; estates lay fallow, domestic animals wandered unclaimed. At length, when the plague ends, he goes rabbit hunting—in the figurative sense, it would seem, for he soon encounters a noble lady with a considerable retinue (like the bereaved lady of the *Behaingne,* the poet does not at first notice the presence of the stranger, and is reproached for his inattention).[40] She denounces the judgment of *Behaingne* as unjust to ladies and proposes that he visit her at her manor, where the King of Navarre will judge the case anew.[41]

38. Kemp Malone's criticism of the *Behaingne*—that it contains "not a spark of genuine feeling . . . from beginning to end" (*Chapters* 37)—is unfair. The charms of this poetry of love (beginning with the *Roman de la Rose*) are all intellectual; even the relations between the personages are described in the vocabulary of philosophical debate, and ultimately they are altogether subordinated to the relations between ideas. I view these relations as fundamentally clear and traditional, and cannot agree with Palmer ("The Metafictional Machaut: Self Reflexivity and Self-Mediation in the Two Judgment Poems," *SLitI* 20 [1987]: 23–39, p. 33) that the real debate of the *Behaingne* remains unresolved.

39. Estrich ("Navarre" 38) and Calin (*Poet* 117) are among the few scholars to have perceived that the *Navarre* is a very funny poem. David Lanoue, in "History of Apocalypse: the 'Prologue' of Machaut's *Jugement dou Roy de Navarre,*" *PQ* 60 (1981): 1–12, p. 1, makes the excellent point that the *Navarre* parodies the structure of the *Behaingne.* All references to the *Navarre* are to the edition of Hoepffner, *Oeuvres* vol. 1.

40. Lines 760–801. Estrich ("Navarre" 27) quotes Sypherd's finding that ignorance of a guide or companion is a convention of love-vision.

41. There is no evidence for the notion—defended by early critics of the *Navarre*

When he arrives, he finds that the lady's council consists of twelve other ladies—Congnoissance, Raisons, Attemprance, Pais, Foy, Charité, Honnestez, Franchise, Prudence, Largesse, Doubtance de meffaire, and Souffisance. (The lady herself, though we do not discover it until later, is the personified attribute Bonneürté.) Each is asked to defend the proposition that the lady whose lover died rightly felt greater pain than the betrayed knight. Because they must all adhere to this conclusion, the speeches of the personifications do not reflect their proper natures. Most of them are not, in fact, the usual personified attributes of love, but a combination of philosophical and theological virtues who are here illogically impressed into the service of Love.[42] Such a technique is not, in itself, unusual; Attemprance, Franchise, Souffisance, Honnestez, and even Prudence traditionally have one meaning in the language of philosophy and religion and another in the language of love. Raisons, Foy, and Charité, however, do not; they are exclusively philosophical and religious virtues, here presented as partisans of Love. Machaut employs this strategy for the sake of the comedy (and, *sub integumentum,* the moral instruction) to be derived from the perversion of these virtues as they argue against the judgment of Reason in the

---

and, more recently, by Calin (*Poet* 41) that Machaut was forced to reverse the judgment of the *Behaingne* by a real public outcry or a "minor literary furor" created by outraged ladies. The evidence, on the contrary, is that such judgments, and their reversal, were purely a matter of literary convention. Certainly the ladies who, in the poems themselves, reproach the poets for their literary offenses are fictional, nor can they be convincingly identified with real persons; Machaut's Bonneürté is a personification, and Chaucer's Alceste a mythological character. In making, and reversing, such judgments the poets are simply engaging in a *jeu d'esprit,* moving counters in the ongoing debate between Love and Reason, a debate which ultimately reflects an internal psychological conflict within every human being. Palmer ("Metafictional Machaut" 37) has well said that Guillaume "is called to account only because such a matter makes interesting poetry, affords the real Guillaume the opportunity once again to please the court and advance his own reputation."

42. Margaret Ehrhart, in "Guillaume de Machaut's *Jugement dou Roy de Navarre* and Medieval Treatments of the Virtues," *AnM* 19 (1979): 46–67, rightly points to the ultimate origin of certain of these twelve virtues as cardinal virtues and gifts of the Holy Spirit; however, by attempting to fit them all into one of those categories, she neglects the importance of the tradition of love-allegory in the *Navarre.* Surely "doubtance de meffaire" does not have its proximate origin in *timor domini.* Lanoue ("Apocalypse" 8) believes that the twelve ladies evoke the signs of the Zodiac and the idea of cosmic order, and suggests that they represent virtues lacking in the world of 1349. However, it is necessary to account for the fact that, in Machaut's scheme, the "virtues" do not behave virtuously.

Behaingne. That judgment, as we have seen, was correct, not because it gave the victory to the knight, but because it proceeded from the morally correct view of carnal love enunciated by Reason. The point of view of Bonneürté, that ladies are truer lovers than men, is both morally irrelevant and indefensible; it is incidentally amusing that she herself, though here portrayed as the partisan of love *par amours*, properly signifies the *summum bonum*.[43] The arguments of the virtues, which make copious use of the classical *exempla* of love, are amusing for a number of reasons: they most often do not address the question at hand (which of the lovers of the *Behaingne* suffered more), but another (whether men or women show greater loyalty and sacrifice in love); they often argue in opposition to their supposed natures (Foy threatens Guillaume, for instance, and Franchise seems to approve of Medea's dismembering her brother [2315–76, 2780–90]); they go off on tangents, shout each other down, and finally abandon all pretense of forensic decorum. Guillaume appears equally foolish, as he tries to "top" their classical *exempla* with ever more sanguinary and pointless contemporary or legendary ones. At length the king convicts Guillaume—apparently for lèse-majesté rather than for the deficiencies of his argument, which was no sillier than the others—and sentences him to write a *lay*, a *chanson*, and a *balade*.

In the *Navarre*, then, an "assigned" debate (whether the bereaved lady or the betrayed knight suffers more) gives way to a debate upon the relative merits of men and women as lovers, which in turn masks a debate upon the two loves. In such a context, it should not be surprising that the personifications moralize the classical *exempla* perversely. The discussion begins in orderly fashion, as Bonneürté offers the example of the subdued behavior of bereaved female turtledoves in proof that a lady who loses her lover through death feels a hundred times the grief of a betrayed lover. Guillaume objects that, if there is no remedy for death, there is equally no remedy for betrayal, which is a kind of death: "qui languist, il ne

43. There is general agreement on this; although Palmer ("Editor's Comment," *SLitI* 20 [1987]: 1–7, p. 4) believes that Bonneürté represents "not only the poet's traditional beloved, but also the patron and, to a large degree, literary tradition itself," Lanoue, Douglas Kelly, and Ehrhart all view her as, in Kelly's words, a "Boethian principle of universal order and felicity"; Calin ("A Reading of Machaut's *Jugement dou Roy de Navarre*," *MLR* 66 [1971]: 294–97, p. 294) translates her name literally as "happiness or good fortune." Most scholars do not, however, acknowledge that Machaut has parodied even this principle in the *Navarre*.

vit mie" (1762). Attemprance, who holds Souffrance by the hand as she boasts of her ability to sustain the right, then recounts with relish the story of a young woman who languishes and finally dies after hearing of the death of her lover in a tournament: no man ever died so of grief! (Guillaume replies that betrayal is harder to endure than death [1863–2076].) Pais, in her turn, offers the violent example of Dido as one that "sert bien a mon propos," though of course it does not at all, tending rather to prove betrayal worse than bereavement through death (2094–2132). Guillaume counters with the story of a "clerc a Orliens" who, hearing through secret letters of the marriage and pregnancy of his lady, became mad and bestial; clearly, this man experienced more grief and pain than might a hundred ladies in seeing their lovers die (2215–2314). Foy, with stunning irrelevance, then accuses Guillaume, in clotted legal language, of basing his argument upon secret documents that perhaps contained unfounded reports: how can one be sure that the clerk's lady had married? (2315–76)

The speech of Charité, who does not address the assigned topic any more effectively than the other speakers, is a little masterpiece of subtle wit. Beginning with an appeal to "Bonne Amour" and to "the Power who gave me the name Charity," it then moves to a long-winded tale of a gardener who rejoiced at the development of a graft into a full-grown tree, with flowers, leaves, and fruit. Charity seems to be making the theologically legitimate point that the "clerc a Orliens," if he loved his lady with genuine "Bonne Amour," would rejoice in her honorable marriage, which offers her the opportunity for fulfillment and maturity. She concludes, though, by pointing out that a married woman, with her greater prosperity and social prestige, is even more desirable as a lover: "Cest raison bon cuer enflame / D'amer mieus assez que devant" (2524–25) Guillaume protests that she has not answered his argument: the clerk, whether rightly or not, suffered greatly. If she can show that any woman has ever felt such grief as that clerk, he'll acknowledge himself bested. Honnestez then argues that the clerk was not grief-stricken, but simply demented, a madman who slept on dungheaps; what he felt was only "le cuer entalenté / Des grans soties qu'il faisoit" (2575–2624). Surely he descended quickly from grief to madness and thus did not feel grief for very long; the lady grieved much longer. Guillaume's response, which develops the general topic of madness with a long disquisition on the cause and cure of rabies in dogs, debases the discourse irretrievably.

The original debate, hopelessly mired in irrelevancies and obscurities, is finally lost forever when Franchise, who speaks next, proposes to show that women are more loyal in love than men. Ariadne abandoned her country, father, friends, and brother Androgeus for Theseus, but he betrayed her for Phaedra. Medea, too, left her father and country, killed Peleus, and hacked her dear brother to pieces, all to make Jason king, but he left her for Creusa. Thus, Guillaume, one doesn't find in men as great loyalty as in women.[44] And, adds Franchise—apparently recalling the original topic of debate—where there is less love, there is less pain. To attempt to account for all the grim comedy of this speech is probably to destroy it, but it is obvious that the bloody tales of betrayal and murder told by one "virtue" in illustration of another make quite a different point about "love" from that intended by Franchise, whose interpretation inverts the traditional "sentence profitable" of the classical *exempla* of love. The fact that the sort of love under discussion regularly gives rise to such unreason is Machaut's fundamental assumption in the *Navarre*. To demonstrate it he escalates the war of *exempla,* so that they become ever bloodier and more senseless. Guillaume correctly observes that the treason of Theseus or Jason doesn't help anyone's argument, for these are not the first or the last betrayals in love, as much by women as by men. Then, however, he counters these *exempla* by reference to the loyal lover of the Chatelaine de Vergi, Lancelot, and Tristan; and he cites another tale, of a married woman who gives a ring to her lover, exacting a promise that it will never leave his finger unless she remove it. Seeing the ring on the knight's hand and recognizing it, her husband comes raging home, demanding that she produce it. Pretending to seek the ring, the lady sends an urgent message to the lover

44. Lines 2699–2822. Calin (*Poet* 120) attacks the whole procedure of argumentation by *exempla,* claiming that it is absurd to attempt "to prove universal psychological and moral judgments based upon a few contemporary or historical anecdotes," and that in the *Navarre* "book-learning and authority are called into question" (121). Certainly Calin is correct in maintaining that we cannot take the trial seriously, but that is not because it proceeds through argumentation by *exempla.* That procedure was an honored and customary one in the Middle Ages—the evidence adduced throughout this study for medieval use, and misuse, of the classical *exempla* should be sufficient proof of that—and we may recall that Machaut imself, in the *Confort d'Ami,* explicitly invokes and defends it. The trial is a burlesque because of the perverse use made by both sides of the traditional *exempla*—and also, of course, because of the vulgarity and absurdity of the folktale of the severed finger, misused by the narrator as an *exemplum.*

that he must return it right away; so he cuts off his finger and sends it back along with the ring. Could anyone, demands Guillaume, ever make a more loyal or loving gesture? "Certes, nennil!" (2851–2901). Calin suggests that the lover's reaction arises from despair at being betrayed by the lady;[45] but there is no evidence at all that he fails to understand the situation or that, upon receiving her message, he feels any emotion whatever besides chivalrous anxiety ("A po li cuers ne li fendi / Car il ot päour que sa dame / Honte pour li n'eüst ou blasme"). His gesture is gratuitously foolish and destructive, and serves to characterize the "love" and "loyalty" espoused by lovers *par amours*.

This *exemplum* is so outrageous that Prudence immediately objects to it, but without seeing that Franchise's use of the classical *exempla* suffered from the same defect. All parties to the debate are now mired in the exposition and defense of *exempla,* which they conduct with notable illogic. Prudence tries to establish that the Chatelaine de Vergi suffered more than her lover, for she died undeservedly whereas he merited death for revealing their love (indeed, he should have been pulled apart by wild horses); as for Lancelot and Tristan, they had far more honor from their exploits than their ladies had benefit (2928–90). Guillaume suggests that the debate be ended, for in any case it is certain that women are inferior to men: they forget quickly, and laugh and cry over little things, whereas the hearts of men are wise, mature, stable, virtuous, and humble (3009–70). Largesse is outraged but refuses to comment upon the matter, as ". . . on ne puet bon argüement / Faire seur mauvais fondement" (3091–92). Doubtance de meffaire, of course, is aghast at such a spectacular *meffait,* but Guillaume only makes matters worse by asserting that not one good woman could be found among half a million (3093–3108). Souffisance reproaches him: no one should speak ill of women, in whom is all good. At this point the ladies all begin to speak at once, and when Doubtance can be heard over the din she returns to the battle of *exempla.* Thisbe, she says, made the ultimate sacrifice for Pyramus; nothing can be harder to endure than death (3171–3212). Souffisance chimes in: Hero drowned in the sea out of sorrow for Leander. Aha! objects Guillaume; here is an example that works in my favor, for it was Leander who braved the tempest to reach Hero (3213–3364). When

45. *Poet* 112–13.

a judgment is requested, Mesure effectively demonstrates that the *exempla* alleged by Guillaume might equally well be alleged against him (the reader is left to supply the corollary, that the same may be said of the *exempla* alleged by the ladies). Raison scolds Guillaume, not for arguing foolishly but for failing to conform to the usages of Love: having been accused of slandering ladies, he should have apologized instead of litigating against so great a lady as Bonneürté. Conscious of his guilt at last, Guillaume writes the *Navarre* to acknowledge it, and agrees to compose the three other poems required by the king.[46]

The poem's wit, of course, resides in the fact that none of the conclusions that are reached, or that might possibly have been reached within the terms of the debate, are valid: it is impossible, as well as unnecessary, to determine whether the bereaved lady suffers more than the betrayed knight or whether men or women are better lovers. Raison, uncharacteristically obliged to defend Love, delivers a speech on the nature of Bonneürté that hints at her proper identity—she offers security from Fortune, appears in all good things, and disposes men to the contemplative life—but ultimately recurs to the silly debate. How dare Guillaume contradict so great a lady? He stands convicted of discourtesy—and besides, he

46. Lines 3767–3832. Kelly, in an ingenious but, I think, altogether mistaken argument, claims (*Imagination* 138–41) that the judgment of the *Behaingne* had to be reversed as a result of Machaut's gradual development of a "new poetic" in which Hope and Souffisance replace Desir, thus sublimating the love and rendering the lover independent of the decisions of his lady and of Fortune itself (an independence indeed proclaimed by Esperance in the *Remede*). Kelly cites the change in allegorical characters from the *Behaingne* to the *Navarre,* pointing out that those of the *Navarre* show the influence of the *Remede.* I believe, however, that Kelly mistakes the manipulation of certain comic and ironic devices for a real change in Machaut's notion of love *par amours.* In the next chapter, I will try to show that Hope—not only in the *Remede,* but in all the love-visions beginning with the *Roman de la Rose*—is a deceiver whose assertion that a lover *par amours* can be independent of Fortune is a lie (indeed it is shown to be a lie by the conclusion of the *Remede,* in which the lover is peremptorily rejected by the lady and is much affected by that rejection; though he chooses in the end to continue to hope against reason, he is very far from achieving *souffisance*). Machaut's choice of allegorical personages depends upon his particular strategy in each poem. In the *Behaingne,* it is to oppose Love, accompanied by its conventional attributes, to Reason; in the *Navarre,* it is to show certain virtues which may be associated either with religion or with love—as well as the theological virtues themselves, which do not usually appear in the *dits*—as they are perverted through their association with love. The strategy of the *Bahaingne* is straightforward, that of the *Navarre* subtler and more ironic.

has not proved his case. The decision of Raison is, perhaps, as reasonable as possible under the circumstances; that Guillaume has behaved unchivalrously is really the only fact that might be concluded from the evidence presented. The presence of the classical *exempla* of love reminds us that their proper meaning, the central truth about love, has remained undeveloped, not only by the erring cleric Guillaume, but by the entire consistory of the personified virtues. That, in turn, demonstrates that—as the introduction to the poem suggested—the times are still out of joint.[47] Guillaume, fictional alter ego of Machaut himself, finds riotous irrationality wherever he goes, from the morally and physically diseased community at large to the comically perverse court of love.[48] In conflict with it, he is himself unavoidably infected by it, resorting to bizarre *exempla* and lapsing into gross misogyny. In the end he reasserts the claims of reason by feigned submission to its opposite, yielding gracefully to the judgment of the lovers' tribunal even as he writes the double-edged *Navarre* in mock-penance for his nonconformity. The clearsighted, clerkish wit of the poet behind the *persona* appears as the only organizing force in a world gone mad.

The work of Froissart which most closely corresponds to the *Navarre,* both in its degree of subtlety and in its use of perverse mythographic exegesis, is the *Prison Amoureuse,* ostensibly written to lighten the actual imprisonment of Froissart's patron Wenceslas of Brabant after his defeat at Bastweiler in 1371.[49] Like the *Navarre,*

47. Lanoue and Ehrhart have well seen the connection between Machaut's introductory evocation of the Last Judgment and the theme of judgment in the *Navarre;* Ehrhart's suggestion, in "Machaut's *Jugement dou Roy de Navarre* and the Book of Ecclesiastes," *NM* 81 (1980): 318–25, that both the form and the content of the introduction are indebted to commentaries on the book of Ecclesiastes is acute and intriguing. I cannot agree, however, that the second part of the *Navarre* presents a remedy for the disorders described in the introduction. Dahlberg ("Love and the *Roman de la Rose,*" *Speculum* 44 [1969]: 568–84) notes that, in the discussion of justice in the *Rose* (5459–92), we are reminded that justice is based upon love. It seems to me that this connection between justice and love underlies the burlesque trial of the *Navarre;* certainly the *names* of the virtues suggest a solution to the problems Machaut explores, but the solution is never dramatized.

48. The usual view of the relationship between the terrors of the introduction and the comedy of the love-court is that of Charles Muscatine, who argues (*Chaucer and the French Tradition* [Berkeley, 1957], 100) that "the plague scenery will set off the beauty of the palaces and pleasances to come." Even Calin, who perceives the irony of the *Navarre,* believes that the court is therein presented as "beneficial to social order" ("*Navarre*" 297).

49. Kibler, in "Poet and Patron: Froissart's *Prison Amoureuse,*" *L'Esprit Createur*

too, the *Prison* lacks any genuine spokesman for Reason. Although it contains more historical material than Froissart's other poems of love—reference to the courage shown by Charles of Behaingne at Crécy, to the visit of Prince Lionel of England to Savoy in 1368, and to the logistics of battle in a mock war between armies of personified attibutes[50]—its central concern is still the activities and state of mind of the lovers. One of these is the narrator, a poet determined to serve Love but discouraged by the lighthearted callousness of his lady; the other is "Rose" (in terms of the fiction, a code name for Wenceslas), a correspondent who wishes to exchange poems and letters about love without identifying himself. The condition of the lovers is sufficiently characterized by the first letter of "Rose" to the narrator, in which he requests friendship and counsel. He suffers, he says, from a "maladie," conceived by thinking intently about his lady and by looking upon her lovely face; he loves, but fears to speak. What should he do? He encloses a *balade* of love-suffering. The narrator, who adopts the device "Flos" and the sign of a daisy, replies warmly with an encouraging letter (noting, however, that ladies cannot be trusted to reveal their feelings, for they are inclined by nature to seek mastery over their suitors [Lettre II, 51–56]) and a *balade* expressing his own love-melancholy. He is not surprised that Rose's love has grown through association with his lady, for the nearer one is to the fire the more one burns; however, he sees no remedy for either of them but to serve in patience.

The correspondence continues, Rose's lady at length accepts his service, and the *balades* and *virelays* exchanged by the two are so highly prized by the court circle that the poet's lady and her friends playfully steal them from him.[51] The bulk of the *Prison,* though, is

---

18 (1978): 32–46, p. 33, notes that some parts of the *Prison* were probably composed before, and some after, Wenceslas's actual imprisonment, but that Froissart and Wenceslas were apparently not in touch during it. Kibler does, however, believe (unlike Fourrier, *Prison* 27) that the letters reproduced in the *Prison* were actually exchanged between the two.

50. Lines 65–100, 363–83, 2528–2846. All references to the *Prison* are to the edition of Fourrier.

51. Lines 1133–57. The fact that Shears (Froissart 210) cites this scene, in which the playful young aristocrats chase each other round a courtyard, as illustrative of Froissart's highest artistry sufficiently demonstrates the need for a better understanding of the love-visions as a poetry of ideas. Even Fourrier appreciates the *Prison* mainly for "les moments où, sans voile de la mythologie, de la personnification, du symbole, le poète s'offre à nous tel qu'il est et nous montre la réalité tout bonnement comme il l'a vécue et comme il la vit" (*Prison* 28). Surely Froissart, who must have taken the greatest pride in the intellectual exercise offered by his poetry, would have considered such appreciations inadequate.

taken up with a *dit* sent by Flos to Rose, and a dream described by Rose to Flos, together with elaborate and carefully arranged commentary on both. Flos is moved to compose the *dit* when Rose's lady, who has assured him of her loyalty, gives to another a ring he had hoped to receive from her. In his melancholy, Rose asks Flos to divert him with "un petit dittié amoureus" on some new matter never before put into rhyme, such as the tale of Pyramus and Thisbe, Aeneas and Dido, or Tristan and Yseult (Lettre V, 40–48). Flos responds with the pseudo-mythological tale of Pynoteüs and Neptisphelé, saying that he found it in Ovid. Although Flos claims initially that Ovid records the story and ends by insisting that it must be true, since he translates it word for word as "Ovides le met en son livre," the tale does not in fact appear in quite the same form in the *Metamorphoses*. In composing it, he has conflated three tales that do appear in the *Metamorphoses*—those of Pyramus and Thisbe, Pygmalion and Galatea, and Phoebus and Phaeton—into one, altering them slightly and giving new names to the lovers. His conspicuous insistence that the tale is from Ovid has puzzled critics, since Froissart's courtly audience would have recognized immediately both the Ovidian fables and the changes made in them by Flos.[52] In Flos's version, the lovers Pynoteüs and Neptisphelé are accustomed to meet in a garden, near a fountain. One day, arriving at the garden and finding Pynoteüs absent, Neptisphelé is attacked and carried away by a lion. Pynoteüs, arriving later, finds her belt, bloodied by the lion, and laments extravagantly, cursing all beasts. He seeks out the lion and takes vengeance upon him, but can find no remedy for his grief; he loses his appetite, neglects his health, and contemplates death and a future of suffering in the underworld (1316–1657). At length he determines to make an image of Neptisphelé and pray to Phoebus that he will give it life. He constructs the image with great care, reproducing Neptisphelé's appearance in every detail, then utters a long and oddly circuitous prayer to Phoebus, ostensibly praising the miracles he has performed—making the laurel evergreen, slaying the Python, correcting the errone-

52. Whiting, however, is not puzzled, since he (with others of the older critics) considers the tale of Pynoteüs and Neptisphelé merely a filler. More recent scholars have seen that the mythological episodes have a function; Fourrier accurately notes that they "déterminent et illustrent en images l'analyse psychologique que donnent les lettres en prose . . ." (*Prison* 15), and Claude Thiry ("Allégorie et Histoire dans la *Prison amoureuse* de Froissart," *SFr* 61–62 [1977]: 15–29, p. 26) detects historical allegory in the tale of Pynoteüs and Neptisphelé, as well as in Rose's dream.

ous course of Phaeton—but in fact devoting 140 of the 175 lines of the prayer to a retelling of the episode of Phaeton (1767–1907). Phoebus grants the prayer of Pynoteüs and animates the image, and the lovers are restored to each other.

Having finished his *dit,* Flos says of it:

> Chi n'an mençongne ne errour,
> Car pour otel je le vous livre
> Qu'Ovides le met en son livre,
> Qui fu sages et grans assés,
> Et croi qu'il n'euïst jà passés
> Tel recors ne mis en memore,
> Se vraie ne tenist l'ystore.
> Et pour ce que ceste matere
> Me sambla de tres grant mystere
> Et moult tres amoureuse ossi,
> En le maniere l'escripsi,
> Que devant moi le vi en lettre,
> Ensi que me sceus entremettre
> Dou dittier et del ordonner.
> (1989–2002)

It is apparent enough both that the tale is neither new or "vraie" in the usual sense of these words and that he did not set down the *matere* quite as he found it. Where, then, are we to look for the "tres grant mystere" hidden within the story of love? Froissart does not tell us, but instead has Flos enclose his *dit* in a letter to Rose advising him on his love affair. He receives no word from Rose for an extended period, during which he writes three *balades* of his frustration in love, comparing himself to Tantalus and protesting "Ne je n'i voi ores nul avantage / Au bien amer; fols est qui s'i ahert" (2054–55). At length he receives from Rose a letter and a chest containing a book which Rose has written about a dream he has had. In the dream, he sets out to war to defend the ladies Justice, Pité, and Raison against the army of Orgueis, but because he is abandoned by Avis and Atemprance he is finally captured and imprisoned.[53] Avis, Atemprance, Souvenirs and Esperance attend

53. Lines 2318–2857. It is important to note, as does Dembowski ("Position" 135n11), that the dream of Rose has another level of meaning, apart from those I will discuss: "Le songe raconte d'une façon voilée et avec force figures allégoriques . . .

him in his prison, where he is tormented by thoughts of his lady; Souvenirs brings him a compassionate message from her (2847–3306). Imagining himself as a lion imprisoned by lesser beasts, he appeals for help to the eagle, who sets out with firebrands to rescue him. Terrified, his jailer and counselor Atemprance begs him to deliver her from the fiery eagle (3349–92); at this point, Rose awakens.

Rose's dream is notable for its conversion of the conventional language of serious moral discourse to the purposes of a love-vision. When Justice, Pity and Reason first appear to him, they complain that they were honored of old, but now their land is taken away and they are altogether "hors de saison": "On n'use que de rançonner, / De desrober et de pillier / Et li fors le foible essillier" (2377–79). An army of vices, led by Pride, is arrayed against them, and they do not know where to turn unless Rose will help them. This first part of the vision is apparently Froissart's compliment to Wenceslas, imprisoned for fighting in a virtuous cause; it is witty as well, for we soon see "Justice," "Pity," and "Reason" converted to "virtues" of the lady favorable to her lover, and "Pride" to her resistance against Love. The first hint of this is the treason of Avis, who goes over to join his mother Atemprance in the ranks of the enemy;[54] at the battle, each of the attributes fights, not his opposite as in a conventional battle of vices and virtues, but his counterpart in the hostile forces: "Hardement contre Hardement / S'encontrerent premierement, / Et Jonece dessus Jonece. / Emprise, Renom et Proëce / Cascuns son compagnon encontre" (2706–10). In sending the book of his dream to Flos, Rose requests a commentary on it, which Flos duly provides; it confirms that the war represents the "vie amoureuse," with the attributes allied to Rose as the qualities of spirit which move him to undertake the life of love, the three virtues as

l'histoire de son bienfaiteur (i.e., Froissart's), Wenceslas de Luxembourg, duc de Brabant, qui fut captif du duc de Gueldre après la bataille de Baesweiler, en 1371, et pour qui son frère l'empereur Charles IV dut intercéder." For detailed (and somewhat conjectural) analyses of the allegorical correspondences between the dream and actual historical events, see Thiry, "Allégorie et Histoire"; Fourrier (*Prison* 21–27) gives a good historical summary.

54. As Thiry points out ("Allégorie et Histoire" 22) the defection of Avis and Atemprance appears odd on the level of historical allegory; can Froissart be saying that Wenceslas took actions in battle that showed a lack of these qualities? But Thiry also notes that the correspondences between the historical and amorous allegories are not perfect (24; I would say they are very loose indeed), and the defection of these qualities makes good sense as love-allegory.

the *bonté, beauté,* and *maniere* of his lady, and the opposing forces as her resistance. The lover is defeated by the lady's beauty, which imprisons him in *langueur* or jealousy. The eagle represents Franchise, who will come to soften the lady's resistance (Lettre IX).[55]

In the same letter, Flos provides for the first time a commentary on the tale of Pynoteüs and Neptisphelé. The two lovers, he says, represent Desir and Plaisance; the lion is Envie, which slays love. The act of Phoebus, God of Love, in bringing the statue to life represents the renewal of joy between lovers that occurs when a lover filled with desire prays to the God of Love and receives mercy. Rose may keep that joy forever if he serves his lady loyally, which pleases the God of Love, and if he refuses to believe in dreams and visions, "car che ne sont que toutes coses vainnes et nulles" (Lettre IX, 157–58). Both this gloss and the gloss on the dream are odd in several respects. First of all, neither the dream nor the Ovidian stories take the expected form; the dream, having begun as a conflict between Reason and Justice on one side and Pride on the other, degenerates into an allegory of the *vie amoureuse,* and the Ovidian stories appear subtly altered and conflated. Second, Flos's gloss on the tale of Pynoteüs identifies Phoebus, conventionally interpreted as the principle of rationality, as the God of Love, and omits any mention of the lengthy and crucial episode of Phaeton. Finally, Flos concludes his commentaries on the dream and the *dit* in a startling fashion, by warning Rose that his continued joy in love depends upon his refusal to believe in visions.[56] Since, as we have seen, truth was ordinarily believed to reside in correct understanding both of the classical tales and of visions, Flos is saying that Rose can continue to enjoy love only if he rejects the truth. This proposition should not surprise us, for it is a venerable one in the literature of love; we have encountered it most recently in the *Trésor*.[57]

55. Thiry ("Allégorie et Historie" 24) views the love-allegory as awkward and imposed, and Kibler ("Poet and Patron" 45) believes that the *Prison* is "really" about the battle, and Rose's "lady" is actually Justice. However, the love-allegory is carefully worked out and generally consistent, which cannot be said of the historical level of the narrative. There is indeed a rude descent from the genuine virtues of Justice, Pity, and Reason to the love-virtues of the lady, but surely that is a part of Froissart's meaning.

56. Kibler ("Poet and Patron" 45–46) has detected the inadequacy of Flos's commentary, but believes that Froissart may have wished to avoid offending his patron with more pointed commentary. It seems to me probable that both Froissart and his patron recognized, and were vastly amused by, the fictional Flos's inadequacies as an interpreter of classical tales and dreams.

57. See page 175.

Such a reading is consistent, however, only if Flos fails to locate the truth in his commentary on the story of Pynoteüs and Neptisphelé. The tales that furnish the material of this *dit* are among the best-known of all the Ovidian tales, and the one Froissart places in central position—that of Phoebus and Phaeton—contains the central truth about the disaster that results from failure to govern the passions. We have already seen that Alanus, Jean de Hauteville, John of Garland, Petrarch and many others moralize the tale of Pyramus and Thisbe as an *exemplum* against the dangers of love *par amours,* and that Jean de Meun expends much time and care in comparing the love of Pygmalion for his image to the love of *Amans* for the Rose.[58] The close conjunction of the two tales in the *dit* of Flos, however, may be illuminated by their conjunction in the speech of Diana to the lover in the *Echecs Amoureux,* where they serve as warnings against the perils of the Garden of Deduit.[59] The fruit of the mulberry tree, Diana explains, grew dark upon the death of the lovers in token of the bitterness that is in love. Ovid tells that Pyramus and Thisbe had much sorrow in love, which was at first sweet to them and then became bitter, like the fruit of the trees in Love's garden. In speaking of other dangers of the garden, Diana alludes to Circe, the Sirens, and the "lit perilleux" of Mars and Venus, then to the tale of Pygmalion. The example of this clever craftsman should indeed warn men to keep away from the Garden of Deduit, for he fashioned an image so lifelike that he became mad with love for it and behaved as if it were alive.

The gloss on the *Echecs* repeats this conventional interpretation of the tales, adding certain psychological insights of patristic origin. Of the tale of Pyramus and Thisbe, the glossator writes:

> And he who wished to consider the life of love carefully would find that there is incomparably more evil than good in it, as was said earlier. And Ovid expressly testifies to this. And however one sees it, the end of love is most commonly sad and

58. See pages 62, 75, and 114–16. Claire Nouvet ("Pour une Économie de la Délimitation: La *Prison Amoureuse* de Jean Froissart," *Neophil.* 70 [1986]: 341–56, pp. 347–351) points out that Froissart's rendition of the tale of Pygmalion in the *Prison* was evidently influenced by the version of Jean de Meun in the *Roman de la Rose.* On Jean's intention in telling the tale, see the excellent discussion of Fleming, *Roman* 228ff.

59. The *Echecs* glossator lists the *exempla* cited by Diana; see Jones, *Chess* 659. All references to the gloss on the *Echecs* are to this translation.

> painful. And the history of Pyramus and Thisbe his mistress, of whose love Diana reminded us, shows this to us well. (653)

After retelling the story, he adds a "Confirmation of the Evils in Love":

> This history enough confirms that in the life of love joy and grief, good and evil are always intermingled, that, however the beginning may be, the end of love is easily painful. And therefore the fable pretends that this mulberry tree that used to bear white mulberries always bore black ones after the death of the lovers. The trees whose shade is fatal also show and signify that it is not good to enter where trees are this way, i.e., the garden of Mirth. But one should flee and separate himself and completely withdraw from the crazy company of the games, idleness and great vanities that are found there. For these are contrary things, contagious and full of great danger. . . . Diana reminded him of all the things above the better to explain the great dangers of the garden of Mirth, to the end that he might protect himself and draw back in the way that Ulysses protected himself from the potions of Circe and the dangerous songs of the Sirens. (655–56).

In the *Echecs,* Diana's allusion to Pyramus and Thisbe is only the first in a whole battery of allusions to the classical tales of love; Narcissus, Pygmalion, Myrrha, Phaedra, Philomela, Scylla, Medea, Phyllis, and Dido all illustrate the dangers of love (641–85). Addressing the tale of Pygmalion, the *Echecs* glossator begins: "Now let us see what truth can be in this fable, for there was never any doubt that it should not be understood literally" (661). Having suggested a possible historical explanation for the tale (Pygmalion loved a real maiden, who was still as an image in that she at first showed him no sign of love), he then uses it to explain the psychological phenomenon of idolatrous love:

> One could also very well say more generally that a man who has chosen a lady or a girl from among the others, whom he loves with true, perfect love, willingly has her beauty and form portrayed in his imagination so that they cannot leave his memory. And according to this, one can properly enough say that he loves his image. (662)

That the words "true" and "perfect" imply no endorsement of the love of Pygmalion may be seen from his conclusion: "However one sees it, still, according to the writings, this kind of love has been seen more than once and this explanation serves well to the purpose of Diana" (664).

It is clear, then—not only from the evidence of the *Echecs,* but from a great many similar moralizations of these tales by contemporaries and near-contemporaries of Froissart—that the lovers have uttered both perverse fables (for neither Rose's dream nor Flos's *dit* takes the form suggested by its terms) and perverse commentaries on them. The dream, in which Rose is never really rescued from his prison, implies in fact that a lover *par amours* is likely to lose his head (i.e., to be abandoned by Avis and Atemprance) and to remain imprisoned indefinitely by jealousy and frustration. Flos, seeing this, first glosses the dream as hopefully as possible and then tells Rose to ignore it. Rose seems not to detect the deficiencies in the commentary offered by Flos on the dream or on the tale of Pynoteüs and Neptisphelé, but his lady does, for—having read and copied the correspondence between the two men—she asks for a gloss on the prayer of Pynoteüs to Phoebus, which Flos had omitted from his commentary (Lettre XI, 31–39). In his reply, Flos asks pardon for "forgetting" this part of the tale—"il ne me puet pas de toutes coses souvenir, quant on a le corage espars en pluiseurs pensees" (Lettre XII, 61–63)—and then gives a substantially traditional gloss, which he cleverly converts to the terms of love-service. The golden chariot, he says, represents *Fole Plaisance,* and the horses *Jonece, Lie Pensée, Wiseuse,* and *Fole Emprise.* Phaeton, who represents Desire, believes that he can govern himself wisely in the life of love, but Phoebus, or Love, warns him that "voirement ne scet il mie qu'il emprent." Although Phoebus advises Phaeton to follow the path of Reason, using the bridle of Avis, the crop of Atemprance, and the reins of Congnoissance, Phaeton gives the horses their heads and ends in disaster, which Flos interprets as "la fole et ignorans gouvrenance d'un amant et le fortune qui li sourvient par mesdisans envieus, qui li desrompent et descirent sa joie et genglent et espardent parolles par le monde, dont toute sa bonne aventure est morte et perie . . ." (Lettre XII, 139–43). In a neat reversal of the meaning conventionally assigned to the tale, Flos then glosses the ending, in which Phoebus reassumes control over the horses (= Reason reassuming control over the passions) as a return to the life of love, assuring Rose that "often, when *pité* and *francise* see the lover in such a plight and deprived of all joy, they purchase his peace with his lady and still the gossip and envy of the *mesdisans* and renew his joy; and if he receives this grace, then he may count himself happy, and from that day forward rule and moderate his behavior so that he governs himself more wisely in the life of love than he had done theretofore."[60] The *Prison* ends with this gloss.

Flos thus manages to interpret the dream, the *dit,* and—in a final *tour de force* of perverse "lover's mythography"—the tale of Phaeton in a way calculated to encourage Rose in the life of love, though the materials of which these fictions are composed suggest the opposite interpretation.[61] Froissart adds the witty touch that, by the end of the poem, Rose enjoys the favor of his lady, while Flos languishes unrewarded in the *prison.* He notes, though, that there are two *prisons:* that of the lady's favor and that of *refus.* In either one, the lover is in bondage. The initial, transparently false claim of Flos (it is not Froissart's own, but that of his fictional alter ego, the lover) that he has taken the *dit* of Pynoteüs and Neptisphelé *verbatim* from Ovid is the first advertisement to the reader that Flos's rendering of the wisdom of the ancients is not to be trusted; it is confirmed by his unconventional moralization of the easily recognizable Ovidian tales. The *Prison Amoureuse* is not, of course, really intended either to praise Love or to warn King Wenceslas away from it; had the king not already known the traditional moralizations of the Ovidian tales of love, he could not have read the poem intelligently in any case. Rather, the poem is a complex *jeu d'esprit,* a witty diversion based upon the medieval custom of seeking truth through commentary on classical tales and visions.[62] Seeming to

60. Modern exegetes continue to offer new and ingenious interpretations of the tale of Phaeton: Douglas Kelly ("Inventions" 89) believes that the foolish love of Phaeton is contrasted with the "noble" love of Pynoteüs, and in "The Genius of the Patron: the Prince, the Poet, and Fourteenth Century Invention," *SLitI* 20 (1987): 77–98, p. 96, sees in Phoebus a figure of the patron, without whose guidance the poet (Phaeton) is doomed to disaster; Nouvet ("Économie" 346) sees in the death of Phaeton an allegory of the death of amorous desire in Flos.

61. Fourrier (*Prison* 20) and Thiry ("Allégorie et Histoire" 25–26) suggest correspondences between the dream and the *dit;* Thiry even claims that they both describe, *sub integumentum,* the same historical events. In any case, he is correct in pointing to the three levels of the *Prison:* contemporary history, poetic rendering of that history, and allegorization of the poetry in the sense of love-psychology.

62. Kelly (*Imagination* 163) compares the expositions of the *dit* and dream to the interpretations of the hermits in the *Queste del Saint Graal:* "In both cases there is an attempt to express the ineffable: the mystery of the grail, the mystery of royalty,

praise Love, it covertly undermines it through learned allusions, in a subtler development of the tradition begun by the *Roman de la Rose*.

Although I will not here consider them in detail, the lyrics of the fourteenth century follow the same conventions as the narrative poems of love in their treatment of the lovers of classical antiquity. Poets speak with two voices, both of them conventional rather than confessional in the modern sense. When a poet speaks with the voice of an infatuated lover, he may express admiration or envy of the classical lovers, or compare himself (or his lady) to them; when he speaks with the voice of reason, he will reject the love they represent. Medieval lyrics are not spontaneous, heartfelt effusions of poets overcome with passion, but highly ordered rhetorical exercises in which, as L. W. Johnson has seen, both the poetic forms and the emotions expressed are traditional in nature.[63] In their formal aspect, the lyrics achieve variety through the subtle play of invention within established structures. In the matter of content, they achieve it in the same way, through the inventive reorganization of established *topoi:* praise of love (the joy of love, the beauty of the lady or of springtime landscapes), love-lament (unrequital, fickleness, separation), meditation upon Fortune, desire, the consequences of possession or of loss. Ultimately, those *topoi* emerge from an Augustinian model of the struggle between earthly and heavenly loves. The emotions characteristic of "courtly" love were not considered to be of a privileged nature, somehow outside the scope of the

---

the mystery of love. In the final analysis, the exposition is simply another means, like narrative or dream vision, of converging on the Ineffable that forms the images and concatenations of discursive explanations." I doubt, however, that Froissart's approach here is to the Ineffable; instead, the poem constitutes an elaboration of a tradition of love-vision whose philosophical foundation is Boethian/Augustinian and whose development is dialectical, conventional and not especially profound.

63. As Johnson writes of the lyrics of Machaut, "Conditioned by the ways we have thought about poetry for two hundred years, one is tempted to object that surely the *emotions* expressed can be real, even if the first person of the poem and the circumstances surrounding it are a fiction. This, however, is precisely what surely is not the case in the fourteenth and fifteenth centuries. The emotions expressed in love poems, as well as the sentiments, moral or otherwise, set forth in ethical or even satiric poetry . . . may themselves be as conventional as the forms and the *topoi* which translate them. They are meant to be—once more, I cannot insist too strongly—and labelling them 'conventional' simply misses the point. To Machaut such a criticism would doubtless have seemed a kind of surface compliment; of course he is conventional, deliberately so—but that says nothing of the skill with which he uses the conventions" ("Noviaus Dis" 19).

religio-philosophical debate between reason and sensuality; on the contrary, they were defined in the same terms as those expressed, analyzed, and debated in the more discursive narrative poems.

This is demonstrated by moralizing poems with intercalated lyrics, like the *Trésor Amoureux,* but there could be no clearer evidence of it than the commentary of Dino del Garbo on Cavalcanti's lyric "Donna mi priega."[64] Written, as Cavalcanti pretends, in response to a lady's request for a definition of love, this highly condensed lyric of five fourteen-line stanzas consists of cryptic allusions to Scholastic commonplaces on the nature of love *par amours*. Love, he says, is an accident, a habit of the soul and will, proceeding from a seen form and unrelated to the operations of the intellect (II, 157). Its judgment is unsound, for it conquers reason and turns man away from the perfect good. Love is changeable, and brings neither joy nor wisdom (158). Dino explains that "love is a passion following upon the will in the sensitive appetite, which is in the heart"; it arises not only from a natural inclination, but from purpose and choice, functions of the will (191). The sort of love involved in the lyric is a corporeal passion, which thus cannot be located in the intellect, since the nature of intellect is incorporeal and incorruptible (199). Love corrupts reason and judgment, since as Aristotle says "the sensitive appetite is not regulated by reason but rather runs away from it" (III, 122); the good perceived by the lover may be only apparent, not real. Consequently, "[love] turns man away from his perfect good inasmuch as it keeps man from the use of his reason, which is the proper *differentia* of man, so that he can no longer judge concerning the universal and ultimate good but is held to the particular good apprehended by the sensitive appetite" (126).

Dino further distinguishes between *amor amicitiae,* by which a person is loved for himself, and *amor concupiscentiae,* by which he is loved for the good or advantage one may get from him (130). The love between men and women of which Guido speaks is, of course, a type of *amor concupiscentiae*. Guido advises against such love ("Et non si muova perche allui sitiri; / et non si giri per trovarvi gioco" [II, 156]) because "it makes a complete slave out of the lover so that no liberty remains to him" (III, 136). From this lyric and Dino's commentary on it we may see that, like every other medieval poet of

64. Otto Bird, "The Commentary of Dino del Garbo on Cavalcanti's Canzone d'Amore," *MS* 2 (1940): 155–203, and 3 (1941): 117–60. References to the commentary, cited in the text, are to this edition.

love, Guido has two voices, the voice of the lover and that of reason. In most of his lyrics he speaks with the voice of the lover, but in this one he speaks with the voice of reason. Although he elsewhere celebrates love *par amours,* Guido here locates it within the moral universe, and Dino is correct to relate his discussion to philosophical insights into the dynamics of concupiscent desire. These considerations, whether expressed or not, are relevant not only to the lyrics of Guido, but to those of the Italian and French poets of the fourteenth century. Of course they also form the intellectual background of the traditional medieval moralizations of the classical lovers, who often appear in those lyrics.

Let us take, for example, Petrarch, whose intellectual judgment upon his early love for Laura we have already seen.[65] The leading mythological metaphor of his *rime* is of course the love of Apollo for Daphne and her transformation into the laurel, a myth traditionally interpreted (in a manner most inimical to lovers) as a glorification of virginity.[66] In addition, Petrarch in the *rime* compares the obdurate Laura to Narcissus, protests that she is lovelier than Polyxena or Hypsipyle, and yearns to enjoy just once what Pygmalion enjoyed "mille volte" with his statue.[67] As Sara Sturm-Maddox has noted, this Ovidian material is consistently associated (as is the metaphor of metamorphosis) with the experience of a love fatal to the soul.[68] All of Petrarch's praise of Laura in the *rime* is placed within the framework of a debate, the struggle within the lover's soul between earthly and heavenly allegiances.[69] The voice that compares Laura

65. See pages 77–78.

66. See pages 134–35.

67. *Rime* XLV, CCLX, LXXVIII.

68. *Petrarch's Metamorphoses: Text and Subtext in the* Rime Sparse (Columbia, Mo., 1985). See her chapter "The Ovidian Subtext," pp. 9–38. In her view, Petrarch attempts to translate his feelings for Laura from Ovidian to Dantean terms, but never entirely succeeds; thus Laura does not become a "gloriosa donna," nor is love finally interpreted in the *Rime* as a transfiguring experience.

69. In my view, Sturm-Maddox's discussion is indispensable to an understanding of the *Rime,* which (although carefully organized, as we know, by Petrarch) may appear to oscillate unpredictably between what she calls the "Ovidian" and the stilnovist perspectives. Petrarch thus dramatizes the internal conflict of allegiances experienced by the poet-lover (as Sturm-Maddox points out, "the poet in whose voice the story of the *Rime sparse* is told . . . is of course a persona to be distinguished from the author of the collection, just as the pilgrim Dante is to be distinguished from the author of the *Commedia,* and the coherence of the first-person story that emerges from the final ordering of the poem is independent of its possible and occasional coincidence with events in the life of the historical Petrarch" [2]).

to the classical heroines of love is not that of the poet/philosopher Petrarch, but that of a conventional *persona,* the foolish lover. Dante employs the same voice when, in the *rime petrose,* he protests that Love will kill him "con quella spada ond'elli ancise Dido";[70] certainly any similarities between Dante and Dido must be purely formal and rhetorical in origin. This speaker is not in any sense Dante himself, but his creation; more accurately, the creation of his place and time, the archetypal foolish lover.

These conventions persist substantially unchanged in the lyric poetry of fourteenth-century France. In the love lyrics of Machaut, Froissart, and Deschamps, the speaker may protest that he loves his lady more than Paris loved Helen; that she is more beautiful than Helen, or more impassive than Pygmalion's image; that he suffers more, or would willingly suffer more, than Paris, Jason, Narcissus, Leander, or Achilles did for their loves. This is the voice of the foolish lover, a perfectly conventional and unindividuated voice whose utterances were to be judged, not on their reason—for they are thoroughly irrational—but on their artfulness and melodiousness as verse. When the poets speak with the voice of reason, they acknowledge the meaning traditionally assigned to the tales of the classical lovers. In Machaut's "Balade d'Amant Recreü," a disillusioned lover recognizes his error; the classical *exempla* do not, after all, teach the joys of love *par amours:*

Ceulx dient qui ont amé
Que vie est de joie plaine;
Mès quant j'y ay bien pensé
C'est de tristour la fontaine.
Je l'aperçoy par Helaine,
Par Tisbé et Piramus
A qui mort en vint soudaine.
Pour ce n'ameray je plus.[71]

He could name more, he says, who died painfully for love; he, for his part, would like to live a long time, and therefore he will renounce love.

70. *Rime* 80, 36, ed. K. Foster and P. Boyde, *Dante's Lyric Poetry,* 2 vols. (Oxford, 1967), I, 172.

71. Lines 1–8, ed. Vladimir Chichmaref, *Guillaume de Machaut: Poésies Lyriques* (Paris, 1909), 638.

Deschamps—who in many lyrics celebrates the beauty and virtue of the classical heroines—writes a *balade* of warning against marriage in which they appear conventionally moralized as *exempla* of destructive vice:

Les hystoires puet l'en noter
De Dalida, Semiramis,
D'Elayne qui se fist embler,
S'en furent destruis mains pays.
Par Dyannira fut trahis
Hercules et sa char bruslée
Par la chemise envenimée;
Dydo fut royne de Cartaige,
Qui corrompit son mariaige;
Helas! que fist Clythemetra
A son seigneur? Qui sent tel raige,
Lors se marie qui vourra![72]

Again, the voice that—in lyrics of longing, pleading, and parting—describes Dido and Helen as infinitely desirable, like the admired lady, is the voice of the foolish lover. Even in the absence of other indicia, this conventional voice may be recognized by its attitude toward the classical heroines of love, which precisely opposes the traditional moralizations of their tales. We have heard the voice of the lover in the French narrative poems that are Chaucer's sources, and we will continue to hear it in the works of Chaucer himself.

72. MCCX, 13–24, quoted from Queux de St.-Hilaire, *Oeuvres Complètes* VI, 216–17.

5

Classical Lovers in Chaucer

In the poetry of Chaucer, the classical heroes and heroines of love naturally appear most prominently in the dream-vision poems strongly influenced by the French tradition: the *Book of the Duchess,* the *Hous of Fame,* the *Parlement of Foules,* and the *Legend of Good Women.* Although Chaucer uses them in conventional fashion—like the French poets, he surely intended his allusions to them to serve as clues to the meaning of the poems in which they appear—there has been no critical agreement on the meaning of the allusions or the poems themselves. In the *Book of the Duchess,* for instance, Chaucer's narrator reminds the despairing knight that his soul will be lost if he allows himself to die of sorrow as did Medea, Phyllis, Dido, Echo, Samson, and "many another" (ll. 723–35). John McCall believes that this sensible advice emphasizes the poor judgment and self-indulgent, unnatural sorrow of the knight; Earle Birney writes that the dreamer must be a great bourgeois to blame Dido for dying of love; Julia Ebel thinks that the dreamer's citing the classical lovers shows his misunderstanding of the knight's situation; and Marc Pelen dismisses the list of heroines as "casual antifeminist exempla."[1] Surely such radical critical disagreement would not be possible if Chaucer's French and Italian sources had not been so persistently misread. As long as we believe that Machaut and Froissart were naive, frivolous poets "chiefly concerned to teach the rules to be followed by courtly lovers in their love affairs,"[2] whose mythological "digressions" reveal a deficient sense of structure, we will fail to understand both their use of mythology and Chaucer's. Fully half of the *Book of the Duchess* is translated directly from the *Behaingne,* the *Remede de Fortune,* the *Dit de la Fonteinne Amoureuse,* the *Paradis d'Amour* of Froissart, and the *Roman de la Rose*. Scholars have evidently assumed that Chaucer borrowed the diction of Machaut and Froissart without borrowing, or even respecting, the ideas or structural characteristics of their poetry. I believe that is as unlikely as it sounds.

The questions most often asked about the *Book of the Duchess* concern the character of the dreamer, the function of the introductory mythological digression on Ceyx and Alcyone, the proper interpretation of the knight's sorrow, the meaning of his description of Blanche, and the nature of his whole exchange with the dreamer. Clearly, it will not be possible to address the matter of Chaucer's intention in listing the classical heroines without first addressing, at least briefly, these larger questions. The varying opinions of McCall, Birney, Ebel, Pelen, and other critics about the function of the classical heroines within the poem are based upon differing opinions about the larger questions the poem raises. A growing number of critics believe that the Chaucerian dream-visions are governed by a "secular esthetic"[3] that makes speculation on their moral significance irrelevant; we are not, therefore, called upon to determine the moral valence of the knight's sorrow or the lady's character, but only to absorb the cumulative impressions conveyed by the three parallel tales of grief (the narrator's, Alcyone's, and the knight's).[4] There is good reason, however, why readers of the

1. McCall, *Chaucer Among the Gods: The Poetics of Classical Myth* (University Park, Pa. 1979), 21; Birney, "The Beginnings of Chaucer's Irony," *PMLA* 54 (1939): 637–55, p. 645; Ebel, "Chaucer's *The Book of the Duchess:* A Study in Medieval Iconography and Literary Structure," *CE* 29 (1967): 197–206, p. 204; Pelen, "Machaut's Court of Love Narratives and Chaucer's *Book of the Duchess,*" *ChauR* 11 (1976): 128–55, p. 146.

2. Malone, *Chapters* 42.

3. The term is Ebel's, *"Book of the Duchess"* 205.

4. Ebel writes (*"Book of the Duchess"* 206), "The three planes of Chaucer's poem

poem have not, for the most part, been content to do this; it is the same reason why they should not have been content to regard the *dits amoureux* of Froissart and Machaut as simply "courtly" (often used as a synonym for "secular"). Beginning with the *Roman de la Rose,* French (and Italian, and English) poets of love constructed their narrative poems according to a recipe that deliberately combined moral and religious considerations with "courtly" elements. In my discussions of French and Italian love poetry, I have tried to suggest that they did this in order to bring the perspective of (Christian) religion and (Boethian) philosophy to bear upon the behavior of the lovers they portrayed. It will be worthwhile to take a moment to consider the principal ingredients of the recipe for the medieval *dit amoureux.*

Every narrative poem of love we have considered thus far has as its center the tale of a lover who pursues a lady who (1) ultimately rejects him, (2) ultimately accepts him, after an initial rejection, or (3) ultimately rejects him, after an initial period of acceptance. That this outline, *tout court,* suffices for a modern tale of love may be seen by hundreds of nineteenth- and twentieth-century romances; but medieval *dits* also typically contain the following additional ingredients: (1) one or more classical "digressions," most often from Ovid; (2) examination of, or allusion to, the problems of Fortune, free will, and the election of a way of life; (3) some development of the *topoi* of reason, sensuality, and Nature; and (4) conventionally foolish talk by the lover in which he systematically states the opposite of the received wisdom on the above topics. Now, a serious love poem can certainly do without these things; Keats's "Isabella," though based upon a tale of Boccaccio, does very well without them (they are still to be found, however, in the *Don Juan* of Byron, who uses them to poke fun at his lovers indirectly).[5] They do not advance the narra-

---

have no paraphrasable—or moral—impact. They merely enhance and refine our awareness of the poem's central figure. . . . The poem's three parallel tales of love and loss elucidate each other; the pivotal dialogue which is the most compelling of the three emblems of grief has no ulterior point or theological motive."

5. And who even links Ovid to moral instruction: "When amatory poets sing their loves / In liquid lines mellifluously bland, / And pair their rhymes as Venus yokes her doves, / They little think what mischief is in hand. / The greater their success the worse it proves, / As Ovid's verse may give to understand" (V, 1, and VI, 87–88, ed. T. G. Steffan et al., *Lord Byron:* Don Juan [New Haven, 1982], 219). Byron writes that the moral of his tale is that passion leads to woe: "The nightingale that sings with the deep thorn, / Which fable places in her breast of wail, / Is lighter far of heart and voice than those / Whose headlong passions form their proper woes. / And that's

tive, and they would have no place in a purely "secular" composition; their function is to stimulate the reader to consider the lover's feelings and behavior in the light of religion and philosophy. In the light of religion and philosophy, the behavior of lovers *par amours* is ridiculous; humor is therefore a very significant element in the French, Italian, and English narrative poems of love (*pace* John Lowes).[6] That the dream-visions of Chaucer, as well as those of Machaut, Froissart, and Boccaccio, all contain the above ingredients suggests that they have more in common than some borrowed phrases. Consideration of what, exactly, they have in common may help to resolve certain questions concerning the early poetry of Chaucer, as well as throwing light upon the function of the mythological material within the overall scheme of the love-visions. I will suggest, as I have done for Machaut, Froissart, and Boccaccio, that Chaucer's use of mythology is closely related to his use of the other extra-narrational ingredients of the *dit amoureux*.

In composing the *Book of the Duchess,* Chaucer took the introductory passage on the narrator's love-sickness from the *Paradis d'Amour;* its eight years' duration probably derives from the *Behaingne,* in which the bereaved lady cites "sept ans ou huit entiers" as the duration of her love-service (l. 125). Critics who argue that the narrator's melancholy derives from some other cause must deal, not only with the conventional love-imagery of the lady as physician (if the physician is God, Christ, or death, why does the speaker say resignedly, "that wil not be mot nede be left"?) and of the melancholy as against nature, but also with the well-established association of sleeplessness with love-longing. None of Severs's examples of medieval states of melancholy not due to love-sickness really resemble the first forty-three lines of the *Duchess.*[7] In Machaut's *Fonteinne*

the moral of this composition, / If people would but see its real drift" (VI, 87–88, ed. Steffan et al. 285–86).

6. Who found only "two mild essays at humour" in all of Machaut! (*Geoffrey Chaucer and the Development of His Genius* [Boston, 1934], 120.) Malone, for his part (*Chapters* 43), finds humor positively "alien" to Chaucer's French sources. See also Wimsatt's protest against this view (*French Love Poets* 98).

7. Severs, in "Chaucer's Self-Portrait in the *Book of the Duchess," PQ* 43 (1964): 27–39, summarizes critical opinion to 1964 on the nature of the narrator's melancholy, acknowledging (though his own theory is different) that most scholars have identified it as love-sickness. More recent conjectures include *accidia* (Pelen), madness (Rose Zimbardo, "The *Book of the Duchess* and the Dream of Folly," *ChauR* 18 [1984]: 329–46) and Burtonian "head-melancholy" (John M. Hill, "The *Book of the Duchess,* Melancholy, and that Eight-Year Sickness," *ChauR* 9 [1974]: 36–50).

Amoureuse, recognized as Chaucer's main source for the tale of Ceyx and Alcyone,[8] the narrator begins with praise of a lady and later mentions his own melancholy, but does not explicitly connect the two; like Chaucer's narrator, he finds his condition relieved ("Lors fui je tantost hors d'esmay")[9] when he hears the complaint of the lover. In fact the love-sickness of the narrator in the *Duchess* is not, as Lawlor would have it,[10] especially significant for the rest of the poem, for the dream-state immediately relieves it and he does not again speak as a lover.

The *Fonteinne Amoureuse,* which I have not discussed, is laden with mythological "digressions." Its melancholy narrator, as he is preparing for sleep, overhears through his open window the eloquent love-complaint of an anonymous gentleman in a chamber nearby. This lover mourns because he must go abroad and leave his lady, who does not even know of his love. He compares himself to Paris and Pygmalion, and makes use of the suggestive phrase that in leaving his lady he is "taking the straw and leaving behind the grain" (ll. 235–420). The greater part of his lament is devoted to a retelling of the story of Ceyx and Alcyone, with both comic and pathetic touches, concluding with a prayer that Morpheus might appear to his lady in the lover's own form—"a moitié morte" as it is—to beg mercy. If Morpheus would agree to do so, he would give him a sleeping-cap and a new feather bed. Truly, he would rejoice more than Pygmalion if the god of sleep would grant his prayer.[11] As he utters this lament, the poet/narrator, in his separate chamber, is busily transcribing it *verbatim.* He admires it so much that, at daybreak, he presents himself at the *hostel* of the lover in order to meet him.

The lover, it develops, is a duke of noble appearance; he welcomes

8. Calin, in "Machaut's Legacy: The Chaucerian Inheritance Reconsidered," *SLitI* 20 (1987): 9–22, p. 10, identifies the *Fonteinne* as the most important single source of the *Book of the Duchess;* see his discussion of narrative elements common to the two poems. Palmer ("Comment" 2) points out that the *Book of the Duchess* derives its structure from the *Fonteinne,* although its details are drawn from other sources.

9. Line 221. All references to the *Fonteinne* are to the edition of Hoepffner, *Oeuvres* III.

10. "The Pattern of Consolation in *The Book of the Duchess,*" *Speculum* 31 (1956): 626–48, p. 643.

11. Lines 539–970. Douglas Kelly (*Imagination* 129) believes that "The idolatry of Pygmalion that Jean de Meun castigates with such wit . . . becomes, in Machaut's conception of love, an acceptable idolatry." He thus confuses Machaut with his creation, the lover who makes the appeal to Morpheus.

the poet and takes him to a *plaisance* containing the fountain of Narcissus, on which is carved the story of Troy: Venus the "maquerelle" (procuress), Paris, and Helen, with all their adventures, as well as the tale of Troilus and Briseyda.[12] The duke tells the poet that this was once the garden of Cupid, where Venus and Jupiter [*sic*] came often to kiss, embrace, and enjoy "le deduit ou nature /Mist plus son entente et sa cure" (1035–1388), and that the carvings were wrought by Pygmalion himself. Explaining that the *fonteinne amoureuse* has made many lovers "amer si / Que pluseurs en ont esté mort," he invites the poet to drink from it. He refuses, protesting that no power could increase the love which is already in his heart, and in turn invites the duke himself to drink. He, too, refuses, saying that "il en avoit tant beü / Qu'il s'en tenoit pour deceü" (1423–38). The two then fall asleep in the garden, and the poet dreams a "songe . . . veritable / Et bon." In the dream, Venus appears to retell the story of the marriage of Peleus and Thetis disrupted by Discord, who casts the golden apple before the three goddesses, and of the ensuing judgment of Paris. She interprets the story as a demonstration of her great power: ". . . le sage fais foloier / Et le plus riche humelier" (1817–18). Finally, Venus reproaches the sleeping duke for mistrusting her and brings about "Le Confort de l'Amant et de la Dame," in which the lady appears to assure the duke of her affection and to defend Venus, who after all successfully aided the affair of Jupiter and Danae.[13] She leaves him with a ring,

12. It is significant that, as Brownlee (*Identity* 197) remarks, "motifs (even verbal reminiscences) from the *Rose* form, as it were, the visible building blocks of the description" (of the pleasance).

13. Lines 1569–2382. Calin (*Poet* 163) correctly observes that Venus is a richly comic character; the comedy is not, however, a "tribute of loving intimacy," unless we understand the intimacy in question as Machaut's familiarity with the tradition of Venus as misguided and misguiding. Her comic attributes, identified by Calin as "pride, quick temper, and sensuality," are amusing indeed, but they are also warnings which in this case the lover chooses not to heed. Pelen (*Book of the Duchess* 136–39) is right to emphasize the importance of the mythographic tradition of Troy to the narrative of the *Fonteinne;* one must not, however, take seriously Venus's claim that "devotion to herself solves all the discord caused by the golden apple of Eris." This is "lovers' mythography," appropriate to such a speaker; the opposite is true.

Brownlee (*Identity* 202) astutely notes that, in the speech of Venus, ". . . narrative bereft of any interpretive discourse is thus presented as a gloss, as a sufficient explication of the 'signefiance' (v. 1605), the 'substance' (v. 1606) of a given text. This point is all the more striking since Machaut's source for the Ovidian matière of Venus's speech (and he goes out of his way to call attention to the fact that he is working from a written source) is the *Ovide Moralisé,* in which narrative discourse is

which he discovers on his finger upon awakening; he discovers also that he and the poet have had the same dream.

In its general outline, the *Fonteinne* is, as Michael Cherniss has said,[14] a "vision poem written in the Boethian tradition." Like the *Paradis d'Amour*—and like the *Remede de Fortune,* which I shall discuss shortly—it begins with the complaint of the protagonist and proceeds to a comforting vision granted him by a divine or allegorical *persona.* Machaut does not, however, use this Boethian outline in a serious attempt to adapt the resources of the *Consolation* to the service of love *par amours,* as Douglas Kelly and others have suggested;[15] instead, he uses it as part of a witty parody in which

---

regularly interrupted by interpretive discourse." He adds that the context is one in which "an implicit thematization of the process of glossing and interpreting invests such a transformation with a particular significance." He concludes, however, that Machaut's purpose is to "demoralize" the source. I believe, on the contrary, that the well-known moralization of the choice of Paris as the choice of the sensual life acts as an implicit commentary upon the speech of Venus and upon the state of mind of the lovers who are persuaded by it.

The "Confort" itself, as Ehrhart (*"Fonteinne"* 134) points out (and Kibler ["Self-Delusion" 93] says the same of the "Confort" in Froissart's *Espinette Amoureuse*) is an illusion of the lover, a worshipper of Venus and Morpheus who believes dreams to be true in the literal sense but does not look beneath the surface for the instruction implicit in the classical tales to which Venus alludes. Laurence de Looze, "Guillaume de Machaut and the Writerly Process," *FrF* 9 (1984): 145–61, p. 148, notes that there are no fewer than seventeen sub-texts, or "mini-narratives," included in the *Fonteinne* in the form of dreams, tales, poems, and myths. He concludes that "the superabundance of narratives and poems is indicative of the *Fonteinne amoureuse's* narcissistic, metaliterary concern with its own existence as narrative poetry" (150). I believe, however, that the "mini-narratives" are included because they are meaningful both as allusion and as the subject of self-revealing commentary by the characters of the *dit.*

14. *Boethian Apocalypse: Studies in Middle English Vision Poetry* (Norman, Okla., 1987), 169–70.

15. See Kelly, "Patron" 79, and Palmer, "Vision and Experience in Machaut's *Fonteinne Amoureuse,*" *JRMMRA* 2 (1981): 79–86, p. 79. Jean Rychner, "La Flèche et l'Anneau," *RSH* 183 (1981): 55–69, p. 59, similarly believes that "l'aventure de ces dits constitue une sorte de rélais ou l'amant reprend contact avec les sources idéales de l'amour pour continuer ensuite sa carrière amoureuse comme s'il était retrempé." Since Hoepffner reported his discovery of an anagram in the *Fonteinne* containing the names of Machaut and the Duc de Berry, the lover of the *Fonteinne* has been almost universally identified with the duke himself. However, Ehrhart (*"Fonteinne"* 121, 130) points out both that the existence of the anagram is open to question (only one manuscript gives the required reading, and Hoepffner found it necessary to make certain changes even in that one) and that the behavior of the nobleman in the *Fonteinne* is not portrayed as praiseworthy. I believe, with Rychner (68), that the

expectations conditioned by the *Consolation* are systematically overturned. In place of Boethius, whose misfortunes are serious and overwhelming, we are offered a sleepless lover; in place of Lady Philosophy, spokesperson for Reason, Machaut gives us Venus, her opposite. Where Lady Philosophy leads Boethius upward, out of bondage to misfortune, Venus leads the lover to ratify the judgment of Paris, symbolically confirming him in his error.[16] The parody is, of course, an urbane joke of a conventional sort on the lover and on Love itself.

It is not surprising, then, that the "idealistic" elements of the *Fonteinne* are more than balanced by its elaborate development of certain mythological *topoi* which, from the time of the *Rose,* suggested the deceptions and disasters attendant upon love *par amours.*[17] Nor is that theme altogether subterranean, for there are also the frank epithet applied to Venus, the lover's admission that the waters of the fountain can cause death, and the refusal—comically diplomatic in the case of the narrator, perfectly explicit in that of the lover—of both men to drink from it. Machaut took his mythology from the *Ovide Moralisé,* where the shipwreck of Ceyx is interpreted as the drowning of the souls of men in earthly delights, and the marriage of Peleus and Thetis as a type of ideal marriage, in contrast to the disastrous affair of Paris and Helen.[18] Certainly the *Fonteinne* is no sermon, but a learned diversion based upon the convention of love-service; it would not qualify as learned, however, or as worthy of the attention of its courtly audience, if Machaut did

---

portraits of poet and nobleman in the *Fonteinne* are—as is usual in the *dits*—"estate portraits" with pseudoautobiographical coloration.

16. Palmer (*"Book of the Duchess"* 383) interprets the choice of Paris as representing "the dominion of love over other worldly experiences as it teaches what rewards are to be gained through proper submission [to love]." Certainly this is the interpretation given to the tale by Venus and by the lover of the *Fonteinne,* but it must be carefully distinguished from the interpretation Machaut would have given to it, or would have wished his reader to give to it. On the meaning traditionally assigned to the choice of Paris, see Ehrhart, *"Fonteinne"* 128ff. Robertson, who knows the pervasiveness of the traditional interpretation of the choice of Paris, believes that the tale was included in the *Fonteinne* as a warning to the Duc de Berry (a young married man about to go into exile) to avoid the error of Paris (*Preface* 234); however, the nobleman of the *Fonteinne* is in fact identified with Paris, portrayed, like him, as a worshipper of Venus.

17. Ehrhart has understood this; see her discussions of Machaut's allusions to Ceyx and Alcyone and the myths of the garden and fountain (*"Fonteinne"* 124ff).

18. *Ovide Mor.* XI, 3788ff. and 2401ff. (deBoer IV, 210ff. and 175ff.).

not follow the established practice of defining through carefully chosen mythological allusions the love of which he speaks. That word "diversion" is important, for he does not do this solemnly, but as a witty, gentle joke on the lover, offered in the same spirit that the lover himself has offered the jokes on Morpheus's cap and feather bed in the midst of an otherwise direful love-complaint. It is essential to recognize that, contrary to prevailing (and entirely unaccountable) critical opinion, the genre of the narrative poem of love was never, at any time or in any language, a solemn one.[19] All of the poems we have examined—the *Roman de la Rose,* the *Amorosa Visione* and *Ameto* of Boccaccio, the *Espinette, Buisson,* and *Paradis* of Froissart, the *Trésor,* and the *Behaingne* and *Navarre* of Machaut—contain significant elements of humor and burlesque. Of these, more than half are specifically love-visions. The tradition Chaucer inherited, then—the one, at least, that he chose to use in composing the elegy of the duchess Blanche—was one in which a conventionally light, witty surface supplied the entertainment expected by the court at the same time that mythological and Boethian digressions, together with the comical blunders, irrational persistence, and chronic incomprehension of an infatuated lover or doltish narrator, constructed the dimension of moral seriousness that the aristocratic audience also expected.

The lover of the *Fonteinne* misinterprets, in characteristic lover's fashion, all of the mythological material he cites. From the tale of Ceyx and Alcyone, interpreted by the *Ovide Moralisé* as a warning against overdedication to temporalia, he derives only the idea that Morpheus might intercede for him with the lady (708–14). He admires extravagantly the garden of love with its fountain decorated with the love-disasters of Troy. In his dream, he symbolically reenacts and ratifies the judgment of Paris; the meaning he derives from the dream is that Venus is, after all, to be trusted (1341–42, 2699–2744). Chaucer uses the same convention of mis-glossing in the *Duchess,* except that—since he puts the tale of Ceyx into the mouth of the narrator, who mocks his own love-suffering from the

19. The *Fonteinne* itself contains more elements of comedy than I have suggested in this brief discussion. See Ehrhart's reference (*"Fonteinne"* 123) to the humorous traits of the narrator. It is partly because of the *Fonteinne*'s general lightness of tone that I cannot, finally, agree with her that it was intended as a negative *exemplum* for rulers, a warning against neglecting the common good to pursue *fin'amors.* Certainly there is the conventional light mockery of lovers here, but political issues are not much emphasized.

beginning—the fashion in which it is misapplied is comical rather than specifically amorous. Unlike Machaut's lover, Chaucer's narrator emphasizes the application of the tale to its context:

> My first matere I wil yow telle,
> Wherefore I have told this thyng
> Of Alcione and Seys the king.
> For thus moche dar I saye wel,
> I had be dolven everydel,
> And ded, ryght thurgh defaute of slep
> Yif I ne had red and take kep
> Of this tale next before.
> And I wol telle yow wherfore;
> For I ne myghte, for bote ne bale,
> Slepe, or I had red thys tale
> Of this dreynte Seys the kyng,
> And of the goddes of slepyng.
> (218–30)

It is an even sillier application than that of Machaut's lover: instead of bribing Morpheus to intercede for him with his lady, Chaucer's narrator will bribe him to get some sleep. The emphasis upon love remains; like Machaut, Chaucer depicts a narrator who begins in a love-melancholy from which he soon recovers, then offers a frivolous application of the tale of Ceyx and Alcyone. In both poems, this juxtaposition of *topoi* seems intended to suggest that what follows will be a less than entirely solemn work about love *par amours*.

Much of Chaucer's humor in the *Duchess* is elaborated from suggestions in Machaut. The detail of Morpheus's comically opening one eye, as well as the bribe of the feather bed, comes from the *Fonteinne* (632, 808–10); the apparently uncomprehending narrator, who seems at times to understand more than he reveals, is a character we have already met in the *Navarre*. Like the French and Italian poets of love, however, Chaucer insists too much upon Augustinian and Boethian *topoi* for the reader to view the poem's humor as an indication that it "lacks high seriousness." Chaucer's insistence, comical as it is, upon the marvelous nature of his dream, which no one could be wise enough to interpret (276–89), amounts to insistence upon its real meaningfulness; he, like Machaut, went back to the *Ovide Moralisé* for the tale of Ceyx and Alcyone,[20] and Ceyx early introduces the Boethian concern for the impermanence of *temporalia* in his parting pronouncement, "To lytel while oure blysse lasteth." The mythological etchings upon the windows of the dream-chamber ("al the story of Troye . . . / Of Ector and of kyng Priamus, / Of Achilles and Lamedon, / And eke of Medea and of Jason, / Of Paris, Eleyne, and of Lavyne . . . / Of al the Romaunce of the Rose") recall the carvings upon the fountain of Narcissus in the *Fonteinne,* but Chaucer may also have taken the idea from the *Roman de la Rose,* the *Teseida,* or even the *Guigemar* of Marie de France. As we will see, lists of the classical lovers occur three times in the *Duchess;* wherever they occur, they point to the betrayal, suffering and death associated with love *par amours.*

It has been said that Blanche is a stock character;[21] I believe, however, that this is true only of the knight. Chaucer makes it as easy as possible for us to recognize the stock from which he comes. His complaint and his personal history are drawn largely from the *Behaingne* and from the *Remede de Fortune* of Machaut (though Chaucer adds the revealing lines—589 and 709—in which the knight compares himself to Tantalus and Sisyphus).[22] In the *Behaingne,* as we have seen, the formal *demande d'amour* masks a debate between Reason and Love. I have not yet addressed the *Remede,* which has been so widely misread that it is fair to say that criticism has rendered it incoherent.[23] It begins with the narrator's

20. Noted by Wimsatt, "The Sources of Chaucer's 'Seys and Alcyone'," *MAE* 36 (1967): 231–41, pp. 238–40.

21. John Manly, in "Chaucer and the Rhetoricians," *PBA* 12 (1926): 95–113, characterized the portrait of Blanche as an exercise in the rhetorical art of *descriptio,* and Stephen Manning ("Chaucer's Good Fair White: Woman and Symbol," *CL* 10 [1958]: 97–105) sees Blanche as the personification of the virtues of courtly love. This seems to me rather more true of the knight. Benjamin Harrison, "Medieval Rhetoric in the *Book of the Duchess, PMLA* 49 (1934): 428–42, pointed out that the rhetorical devices Chaucer is generally thought to have derived from the Latin manuals of rhetoric more likely derive from Machaut.

22. See B. A. Windeatt, ed. and trans., *Chaucer's Dream Poetry: Sources and Analogues* (Cambridge, 1982), 167–68, and Wimsatt *French Love Poets* 155–62 for a line-by-line list of parallels between the *Book of the Duchess* and its French sources. Wimsatt (92) notes Kittredge's similar research.

23. Hoepffner, in his introduction to the *Remede,* characterizes it as an "Art of Love" in which Machaut seeks to teach the sort of "courtly" love that "fait naître dans l'homme toutes les vertus sans lesquelles il ne saurait mériter l'amour de celle qu'il adore" (xvi, xiii; all references to the *Remede* are to this edition). Wimsatt (*French Love Poets* 109) seems to think that Esperance fulfills her promises, and

extravagant praise of his lady, culminating in a lay expressing the hope that she may learn of his love for her. At length the lady sees the lay and asks him who wrote it; he cannot reply for shame, and instead retires to the Parc de Hesdin, where he utters a long lament on Fortune and Desire (841–1480). At length he is visited by the lady Esperance, who delivers what has been called a Boethian lecture on Fortune.[24] In summary, she says:

> The ancients depict Fortune with two faces; she is not to be trusted. Surely the best goods are those which cannot be lost. The sovereign good is a gift of Nature, who uses reason; such a good cannot be lost, and is incomparably superior to the gifts of Fortune. There is no security in Fortune. I will tell you what you must do to be happy: achieve governance over

---

Pelen writes that "the poem concludes with an ideal wooing scene and a love-celebration" (*"Book of the Duchess"* 136), whereas in fact it concludes with the lady's apparent rejection of the lover and his desperate and sophistical attempts to reassure himself. I shall not here attempt to deal with every detail of previous scholarship on the *Remede,* which I believe has never had justice done to it; I shall address only the most prominent points of difficulty.

24. Critics of the poem have noted certain difficulties and incongruities in Esperance's adaptation of Boethius. Douglas Kelly writes (*Imagination* 130), ". . . the controversy over the value of idealized love must have become very acute for Machaut to have had to resort to the unlikely resources of Boethius to support his idealization. . . ."; Calin (*Poet* 61) notes the paradoxical fact that Esperance seems to be preaching "a remedy against Fortune and, at the same time, how one can attain one's ends through Fortune"; and Brownlee (*Identity* 51) sees that "The arguments of Books 2 and 3 of the *Consolatio* when utilized in the *Remede* do not lead to the elevated metaphysical and ethical conclusions of the original. Rather they are used to affirm the value of courtly love service by a character who personifies belief in its value." Although all these statements tend irresistibly to the conclusion that the speech of Esperance doesn't work, no one reaches that conclusion. Instead, Kelly claims that Machaut took the speech "very seriously" as recommending a sort of *amor purus* (the allusion is Kelly's) involving "the separation of hope and desire" which "gives ideal love a preeminence that is meant to capture its purity and realize its essential nobility" (*Imagination* 122). Calin concludes that the speech is a serious attempt to "resolve conflicts exposed in *Le Roman de la Rose* between the Boethian and courtly philosophies" by promoting an "ecstatic, mystical relationship" with the lady (instead of with God) (*Poet* 61–62). Brownlee seems to agree with Kelly that the effect of the speech is indeed to free the lover from the power of Fortune, "since his love does not depend on external events (e.g., his success or failure with a particular dame) but is, rather, a purely internal experience" in which "the condition of hope becomes emotionally and imaginatively self-sufficient and fin'amors a kind of sublime solipsism" (*Identity* 6). I will suggest that Machaut is about something far less sublime and more traditional.

> yourself, be ruled by Reason, and keep the virtues of Pacience and Souffissance. Happiness comes from enduring all in patience. Fortune has in fact been your friend, for she lent you her goods. When you undertook to love, you embarked on the perilous sea of Fortune, and as Fortune's servant you had to obey her laws. Having taken away her goods, she has left you the most valuable things: your life and your sense. Since Fortune is changeable, ill fortune should give you hope of better. Do not value the goods of Fortune, but keep Pacience and Souffissance, for they will set you on the road to the *summum bonum*. But do not think you should leave Love; on the contrary, I wish you to love loyally. True lovers are under the dominion, not of Fortune, but of virtue. You should go to your lady now, but don't be dismayed by love-suffering; remember me. (1608–3180)

This lecture is a witty *tour de force* of Machaut, a "lover's *Consolation of Philosophy*." Its internal inconsistencies, intended by the poet to be obvious and amusing, proceed from his conversion of the language of philosophy to the service of love, which resembles his similar conversion of the theological virtues in the *Navarre*. The patience recommended by Boethius—a branch of the cardinal virtue of Fortitude—does not consist in unremitting service to a lady; lovers of ladies are, by definition, under the dominion of Fortune. Esperance is lying. This should not be surprising, for we have seen lovers deceived and abandoned by Hope in practically every one of the poems of love, beginning with the *Roman de la Rose* (in which the Lover himself declares that ". . . he who draws too near to Hope is a fool . . . many have been deceived by her" [4083, 4088]). We may recall that Boccaccio characterizes the Fiammetta of the *Elegia* by putting into her mouth the same foolish statement that Fortune rightly has nothing to do with love *par amours,* and that her old nurse recommends that she should take from ill fortune hope of better fortune to come[25] (in fact, Boethius recommends indifference to fortune both good and ill). *Esperance* is not, then, "a courteous Boethian queen of love who . . . offers [the lover] Boethian inspiration and a marriage ring by which he may be restored to his lady with a better kind of love," but a dangerous deceiver.[26] If the *Remede*

25. See pages 158–59 and 160.

26. Pelen 143. The consistently deceptive character of Esperance has been noted by Kibler, who writes ("Self-Delusion" 95), "Of all the allegorical figures which populate the poetry of the late Middle Ages, *Esperance* is the most delusory."

displays any consistency, the lover will be disappointed in his expectations; and indeed he is. After a brief interval of improved relations with his lady, during which she apparently accepts his service, he suddenly finds himself rejected.[27] Although the lady protests that she treats him coldly only to keep their love secret, he fears that she loves another; but he cannot believe that, with all her good qualities, she could lie. Like the lover of the *Roman de la Rose,* he reflects that one should always believe whatever ladies say. He concludes the poem with praise of Love, which gives him Hope.

We have seen this same movement—from rejection to brief acceptance, and back again—in the *Espinette,* the *Voir Dit,* and the *Trésor;* in a more general sense, it is the movement of all the love-visions in which a melancholy dreamer awakes to find that his fantasy of acceptance and gratification has evaporated. This movement itself constitutes an ironic commentary on love. I consider the *dits* in such detail because I wish to establish that none of Chaucer's sources, which have been repeatedly characterized as "idealistic" and "didactic" works inculcating the principles of courtly love, really seeks to praise or redeem love *par amours;* instead, they do quite the opposite. These sources, the best-known *dits* of the most celebrated French poets of Chaucer's time, were before Chaucer's eyes as he wrote—and would have been fresh in the minds of his courtly audience. And, although Chaucer makes changes in tone and emphasis which have been well described by scholars, he borrows all of the essential ingredients of the *dit amoureux.* The ingredients of the *Duchess* are, quite simply, the ingredients of the *dits.* An

27. Lines 4139–54. In plain defiance of Machaut's actual conclusion, scholars of the poem wax rapturous about the psychological development of the lover as a result of the speech of Esperance. Douglas Kelly writes that "The first meeting between the poet and the lady illustrates the wrong kind of love, based on fear, uncertainty as to the lady's feelings towards him, and the possibility of the lover's failure to realize his desire. The second meeting illustrates the right kind of love. It rests on the certainty that the lady knows his sentiments and cannot but respond to a love purified and sublimated as hope" (*Imagination* 150). Calin believes that, after the speech of Esperance, "an inept, narcissistic, cowardly adolescent has been transformed into a relatively mature member of society" (*Poet* 63). Brownlee rejoices in the liberation of the lover from the power of Fortune, but is puzzled by the "elaborate attempt on the part of Amant to convince himself to believe his lady. His arguments seem doctrinaire and abstract . . . ," and finally "The authenticity of the poet-protagonist's love experience within the context of the story line seems to be put into doubt, or at the very least, rendered problematic" (*Identity* 59). He does not, however, pursue that insight to its logical conclusion.

examination of Chaucer's use of those ingredients reveals that, if literary convention means anything at all, the knight in black is a lover *par amours*.

The knight's situation, and Chaucer's description of his condition, are taken from Machaut's depiction of the bereaved lady in the *Behaingne*. They both long for death, fall in a swoon, fail to respond when spoken to, and protest that there can be no help for their sorrow. The knight's lament in terms of contraries ("Myn hele is turned into seknesse, / In drede ys al my sykernesse; / To derke ys turned al my lyght . . .") is indebted to the lament of that lady (177–86), which is based in turn upon Reason's invidious recital of the oxymorons of love in the *Roman de la Rose* (4293ff.).[28] Although the situation of the lady in the *Behaingne* is the same as that of Chaucer's knight—she has lost her lover through death—Machaut clearly characterizes her love as carnal and her sorrow as inordinate. In the hearing before the king's council, Reason points out that "Amour vient de charnel affection, / Et si desir et sa condition / Sont tuit enclin a delectation" (1709–11); lovers *par amours* care much more for the body than for the soul. In such love there is always sin, and the soul sorrows over this. Three things—Love, lover, and beloved—are necessary to the maintenance of a love affair, and an affair in which one of these is missing is not worth a rotten apple (1694–99). The lady will suffer, but as her love diminishes her suffering will diminish as well. The implication of the poem's conclusion is that Reason is correct, for the bereaved lady does not die but feasts for a week at the castle and departs laden with gifts. I do not, of course, wish to imply that the condition of Chaucer's knight is exactly the same as that of Machaut's lady, or that the tone of the *Duchess* is the same as that of the *Behaingne*. Students of Chaucer's sources have always acknowledged that what he changed is as important as what he borrowed, and I will presently suggest that there are certain critical differences between the *Duchess* and the *dits amoureux*. The similarities, however, are essential to our understanding of Chaucer's meaning.

The knight's complaint against Fortune is drawn from the *Remede* and from the *Roman de la Rose,* in both of which the discussion of Fortune is specifically related to the condition of a lover *par amours*.

28. Bossuat (*Le Moyen Âge: Histoire de la Littérature Française,* vol. 1 [Paris, 1931], 237) makes the penetrating comment that all of Machaut's narrative work is a commentary on the *Roman de la Rose*.

Like the lover of the *Remede,* the knight complains of the ugliness and deceitfulness of Fortune, who laughs with one eye and weeps with the other; both call Fortune "envyouse charite," although in the *Remede* that is only one among a string of colorful oxymorons (1128–76). The real solution to the problem of Machaut's lover is to leave the service of Fortune by abandoning his love-service; however, he ends by succumbing to the blandishments of Esperance, who assures him that he can have *Bonneürté* and his lady at the same time. From the *Roman de la Rose* Chaucer took the analogy of the chess game, traditionally suggestive of the operation of Fortune (6669–88). Here, it forms a part of the speech of Reason in which she undertakes to dissuade the Lover from continuing to serve Love. In likening love-service to other sorts of enslavement to Fortune, she digresses into a sort of *De Casibus,* telling how kings confident in their power—Manfred, king of Sicily; Conradin, his nephew; and Henry, brother to the king of Spain—lost their chess games with Fortune and were overthrown. Why should the lover, who has kissed the rose and therefore foolishly believes that he must always live in comfort and delight, imagine that he can defeat Fortune, who has overcome such great men? "By my head," says Reason, "you are foolish and stupid" (6752). She concludes her discourse on chess with a lecture on the *integumentum,* reminding the lover that he must cherish the wisdom of ancient books as insurance against the vicissitudes of Fortune: "What is the value of whatever you study when its sense fails you, through your fault alone, at the very time that you need it?" If the lover had not dedicated himself entirely to his disordinate love, he would understand her words. Wise Socrates "did not fear the God of Love in any way, nor did he budge on account of Fortune" (6777–6888).

The details of the knight's personal history—his idleness in youth, his decision to serve Love, his introduction to his lady under the auspices of Fortune—are taken from the *Behaingne* and the *Remede,* in which their significance is unequivocal. Like Chaucer's knight, the knight of the *Behaingne* began to serve Love even before he found himself attracted to a particular lady (265–71); the lover of the *Remede,* whose history is similar, says that his condition as a youth was like that of a blank tablet, able to receive whatever impression anyone wished to make upon it (26–30). He might have done better than to serve Love, but Love was the first art to make an impression upon his mind, since he was governed by Youth in idleness, and his heart and behavior were flighty and unstable (45–

50). Chaucer uses all these details, translating closely, and adds the detail from the *Behaingne* that it was Fortune ("the false trayteresse pervers!") who brought the knight and his lady together. In both the *Behaingne* and the *Remede,* the love of the knights for their ladies is in every respect unfortunate. The lover of the *Remede* manages to deceive himself through trust in Hope, even in the face of his lady's indifference, but in the *Behaingne* the treachery of the lady is apparent to all. The knight's tragedy is that he cannot withdraw his love from the unfaithful lady, so that Reason concludes he is even more to be pitied than his companion bereaved by death.

The knight's description of the lady is, again, a conflation of details from the *Behaingne* and the *Remede.* Most of his description of the lady's physical appearance is taken from the *Behaingne,* in which, as we have seen, the knight dwells so minutely and enthusiastically upon the physical characteristics of the lady as to make it obvious that he "aimme miex assez le corps que l'ame" (*Beh.* 1707); indeed he says hardly anything about her character. Certain of Chaucer's remarks about the character of the Duchess Blanche—her moderation, reasonableness, friendliness, benevolence, trustworthiness—derive from the description of the lady in the *Remede* (167ff.). Unfortunately, they do little to redeem the knight's passion, since the lover of the *Remede* deceives himself about the characteristics of the real lady, and is quite obviously describing his lady only as he imagines her to be. It is significant, however, that Chaucer adds to the description of the lady material from the Song of Songs and the Book of Wisdom that suggests her imperishable spiritual qualities.[29] In the *Roman de la Rose,* too, he finds the striking analogy of the phoenix, cited by Nature as an example of defiance of Death through ceaseless regeneration (15977–16004). The knight knows of his phoenix only that it is unique—"ther livyth never but oon"—and now it is gone; but to an audience acquainted both with the commonplaces of Biblical exegesis and with the *Rose,* it would have suggested the Resurrection. To these matters, which are altogether outside the tradition of amorous *descriptio* in the *dits,* I shall return presently.

All of the details I have so far reviewed have tended to liken the

29. In his line-by-line analysis of the sources of the *Book of the Duchess* (*French Love Poets* 155–62), Wimsatt mentions biblical sources for ll. 905, 946, 961–85, and 972. See also his article, "The Apotheosis of Blanche in *The Book of the Duchess,*" *JEGP* 66 (1967): 26–44.

love of Chaucer's knight to the misguided love *par amours* of the protagonists in the French *dits* which were Chaucer's sources. A further likeness may be seen in the knight's story of his advances to the lady—his timidity, her initial refusal and final acceptance, his joy—all of which also derives mainly from the *Behaingne.* I shall soon discuss Chaucer's use of the classical lovers, which I believe casts additional light upon the nature of the knight's passion. One detail within the poem, however, appears decisive. At the point when the narrator suggests to the knight that he (like the lover of the *Remede* from which much of his description is taken) is describing not the lady herself but only his *idolum*—"I leve yow wel, that trewely / Yow thoghte that she was the beste, / And to beholde the alderfayreste, / Whoso had loked hir with your eyen"—the knight protests vigorously (as generations of critics have done after him). Even if he had been a great hero, he argues, he would still have loved his lady, and he would never stop loving her for all the world! At this point, the narrator makes a revealing remark, which has been repeatedly noted and variously explained by scholars—none of whom, however, has discussed its relationship to its source. He says, "Me thynketh ye have such a chaunce / As shryfte wythoute repentaunce." Repentance! says the knight; why, I would be a traitor indeed if I repented of loving my lady. These lines are taken verbatim from the *Roman de la Rose,* indeed from the same part of the speech of Reason in which she likens the operation of Fortune to the game of chess and warns the lover to heed the wisdom of old books. After reminding the lover that Socrates placed no value upon Love or Fortune, Reason asks him to abandon Love and serve her alone. The lover replies that he cannot change, that he must follow Love even if it led him to hell. His heart is not his own:

> . . . ja n'est il pas a moi.
> Onques encore n'entamoi,
> Ne ne bee a entamer,
> Mon testament pour autre amer.
> A Bel Acuel tout le lessai,
> Car tretout par cuer mon laiz sai,
> Et oi par grant impacience
> Confession sans repentance;
> Si ne vodroie pas la rose
> Changier a vous par nulle chose. . . .
> (6917–26)

Just as the lover told all his love to Fair Welcoming, the knight has told his to the narrator: they have confessed, but neither wishes to repent. For the lover of the *Rose,* to leave Love and follow Reason would be treason; so would it be for the knight, who describes his allegiance to the lady in precisely the same terms.

In such a context, the dreamer's suggestion that the knight's soul will be lost if he allows himself to die of despair makes perfect sense. Here, as in the French and Italian poems of love we have examined, the folly of the classical heroines adumbrates that of the lover himself. And, like the lovers in those poems, the knight rejects the traditional wisdom derived from the classical tales: "Thou wost ful lytel what thou menest; / I have lost more than thow wenest." In fact, the narrator certainly knows that the knight's lady is dead, though he pretends not to; in quoting the lyric of mourning he emphasizes that he heard it in full ("ten vers or twelve") and that he remembers it precisely (". . . ful wel I kan / Reherse hyt; ryght thus hyt began:"). The earthly lady, however, is a "fers"—a chess piece, a gift of Fortune—for which it is inappropriate to "make this woo." The narrator has discerned, from the knight's words and attitude, that like the lady of the *Behaingne* he can find no comfort in his mourning for the earthly part of his dead lover. In the terms of the Boethian philosophy of the *dits,* his difficulty does not lie in the death of his lady, but in himself. The only philosophical comfort in such a case is to abandon his attachment to Fortune and to the earthly part of his lady, as Reason recommends to the lover of the *Rose* when she urges that he, too, "Remembre . . . Socrates, / For he ne counted nat thre strees / Of noght that Fortune koude doo" (717–19). Like that lover, the knight answers, "I kan nat soo." If that is to be the last word in the matter, he will indeed end in the same way as the foolish classical lovers Medea, Phyllis, Dido, and Echo; the narrator therefore leads him through the process of "shryfte," apparently in the hope that by defining his condition he will come to recognize it.

His condition, however, has not changed by the time of the narrator's suggestion that "Yow thoghte that she was the beste," for the knight replies by comparing himself with another list of classical figures—Alcibiades, Hercules, Alexander, Hector, and Achilles—with emphasis upon the death of Achilles for love:

> . . . I wolde thoo
> Have loved best my lady free,

Thogh I had had al the beaute
That ever had Alcipyades,
And al the strengthe of Ercules,
And therto had the worthynesse
Of Alysaunder, and al the rychesse
That ever was in Babyloyne,
In Cartage, or in Macedoyne,
Or in Rome, or in Nynyve;
And therto also hardy be
As was Ector, so have I joye,
That Achilles slough at Troye—
And therfore was he slayn alsoo
In a temple, for bothe twoo
Were slayne, he and Antylegyus,
And so seyth Dares Frygius,
For love of Polixena—
Or ben as wis as Mynerva,
I wolde ever, withoute drede,
Have loved hir, for I moste nede.
(1054–74)

Robert Jordan has noted the objections of Root, Tatlock, Brewer and others to such "gratuitous, half-comic digression(s)," which seem to demonstrate Chaucer's willingness to "disrupt . . . the tone of elegy" that should dominate the poem.[30] In fact, though, the function of this "digression" is the same as that of the first and second lists of classical lovers: to suggest that the knight loves Blanche with an earthly love that can find no expression now that her earthly part is gone. The tone is indeed "half-comic," for the sufferings of such lovers were never portrayed with complete seriousness in any of the *dits amoureux,* and Chaucer has chosen the form of the love-vision for his tribute to the memory of Blanche. The introductory tale of Ceyx and Alcyone, though certainly not untouched by humor, furnishes an instance of the destructiveness of despair; for those acquainted with the tale in the *Ovide Moralisé* (as both Machaut and Chaucer certainly were), it furnished a more explicit reminder of the danger of investing one's allegiance in earthly things. The lists of classical lovers in the dream-chamber and in the narrator's

30. "The Compositional Structure of *The Book of the Duchess,*" *ChauR* 9 (1974): 99–117, p. 113.

reproach to the knight function in the same way; the knight, however, both misunderstands and rejects the traditional meaning of the tales.

He shows himself no wiser in this passage, in which he means to choose classical figures famed for their virtue, but concludes by recalling the unworthy death of Achilles. These verses are based upon the *Remede,* in which the lover uses the heroes in substantially the same way, except that he says nothing to evoke their traditional association with Love (108–34). Chaucer deliberately has his knight "digress," in order to suggest the customary rhetorical use of this list of heroes as "the great conquered by love" in arguments that Love Conquers All. The knight does not, of course, mean to make that point; to insist upon the foolish behavior in love of even the greatest men is inimical to his argument that any man, no matter how great or virtuous, would rightly love his lady. But the point is made despite him, not that he was justified in loving, but that the great men he cites were not. The knight follows up this speech with the assertion that his lady ". . . was as good, so have I reste, / As ever was Penelopee of Grece, / Or as the noble wif Lucrece." If she was, she would not have been a suitable partner for a lover *par amours.*

And indeed it seems that she was not. Many of Blanche's attributes are imported from the *dits amoureux,* but others are Scriptural. Chaucer's emphasis upon her purity—as symbolized by her name ("goode, faire White"), her throat like a tower of ivory, and her character as the resting place of Trouthe—tends to liken her to the Virgin.[31] The Scriptural origins of the long passage comparing her to a torch from whom all may take light, a "chef myrour" of brightness, and a crown of precious stones have been discussed by Robertson and Huppé in their study of the poem. Chaucer probably took his comparison of her to "the soleyn fenix of Arabye" from the *Roman de la Rose,* where the terms in which Nature describes it clearly suggest the Resurrection;[32] the association, however, was a

31. On these matters, see D. W. Robertson and Bernard Huppé, *Fruyt and Chaf: Studies in Chaucer's Allegories* (Princeton, 1963), 76–78, and the more detailed analysis of Wimsatt, "Apotheosis of Blanche."

32. Lines 15977–95. "There is always a single phoenix that lives, up until its end, for five hundred years. At the last it makes a large, full fire of spices where it sits down and is burned. Thus it brings about the destruction of its body; but because it keeps its form, another phoenix returns from its ashes, no matter how it was burned. It may possibly be the very same phoenix that Nature thus brings back to life. Nature

commonplace. Blanche, then, is not a "stock character" of romance. The situation is not quite that of the *Behaingne,* but that of the *Amorosa Visione* (or even of the *Divina Commedia*), in which the lover must learn to surrender his inappropriate carnal love for a lady whose nature is celestial. Like the lover of the *Visione,* the knight does not appear to do that within the course of the poem; whether one believes that he does or not depends, of course, upon one's interpretation of the symbolism of the hunt, a matter about which it may not be possible to achieve certainty.[33] I would like to suggest, at least, that in addition to the two alternatives most often proposed (i.e. that the knight's "heart" is "caught," or relieved, and that it is not) there exists the third possibility that the hunt does not resolve that question any more definitively than the dialogue it parallels.

The identity of the knight does not, perhaps, matter a great deal. Critics have seen in his apparently exclusive love relationship with Blanche strong evidence that he must represent John of Gaunt, but on the other hand the relationship clearly is not marriage (the knight is not the same age as John, and he professes ignorance of certain of the lady's physical features). Chaucer may have used the

is so fecund for her species that she would lose her entire being if she did not cause the phoenix to be reborn. Thus, if Death devours the phoenix, the phoenix still remains alive; if she had devoured a thousand, the phoenix would remain" (Dahlberg 271).

33. There is wide critical disagreement over the meaning of the hunt. Robertson and Huppé regard it as a figure of Christ's "hunt" for the human soul, and the escape of the hart as an indication that "the will of the speaker is too overwhelmed to accept at once the formal consolation of the Church" (*Fruyt and Chaf* 97); Georgia Crampton believes that the hunt represents the "public, social world" that the knight must eventually rejoin ("Transitions and Meaning in *The Book of the Duchess," JEGP* 62 [1963]: 486–500, p. 491); Joseph Grennen sees the unsuccessful hunt as "both verbally and conceptually an analogue to the psychosomatic process of the Black Knight's capitulation to grief" (" 'Hert-Huntyng' in *The Book of the Duchess," MLQ* 25 [1964]: 131–39, p. 132); M. Angela Carson concludes that the escape of the *hart* indicates that the knight's *heart* has been eased by the remembrance of past happiness with Blanche ("Easing of the 'Hert' in the *Book of the Duchess," ChauR* 1 [1966]: 157–60, p. 159); Helen Phillips views the hunt, like the knight's remembrance of Blanche, as "the seeking after a desired object which is discovered at the end to be lost" ("Structure and Consolation in the *Book of the Duchess," ChauR* 16 [1981]: 107–18, p. 111); and R. A. Shoaf, in an interesting article on medieval penitential lore, characterizes the hunt as "an allegorical image of the process of confession" ("Stalking the Sorrowful H(e)art: Penitential Lore and the Hunt Scene in Chaucer's *The Book of the Duchess," JEGP* 78 [1979]: 313–24, p. 315).

form of the love-vision, and the convention of love *par amours,* as an accustomed and forcible way of portraying the despair of loss, as it might be felt by anyone suddenly bereft of the presence of a great and virtuous lady. If the knight were, indeed, intended to represent John of Gaunt, the duke would not likely have been offended; Froissart, after all, represented King Wenceslas as a lover, in a poem that, although witty and diverting, is not ultimately flattering to that species, and Machaut preached against love-sickness to Charles of Navarre.[34] All the poets of love placed themselves in the position of the lover by creating self-deprecating alter egos who both represented and did not represent themselves; at bottom, they represented themselves under the influence of irrational, and somewhat ridiculous, infatuation. The evidence is that overvaluation of temporalia, most commonly in the form of love *par amours,* was considered a practically universal (though, ideally, temporary) aristocratic failing, and it is with real resentment that Pierre Col accuses Gerson of never having fallen prey to it.[35] Certainly, too, there are essential distinctions, as well as essential resemblances, between the lover of the *Roman de la Rose,* who is gratuitously and incorrigibly foolish for over 17,000 lines, and the knight of the *Duchess,* whose love is tested by grief and found wanting. My point is finally that, in the matter of his use of the classical lovers, Chaucer follows traditional practice; that is, he consistently associates them with the theme of overvaluation of temporalia, which is central to their appearances in literature from patristic times to the fourteenth century and beyond.

Unlike the *Duchess,* the *Hous of Fame* borrows very little of the diction of the *dits amoureux,* but it nevertheless, as Sypherd accurately remarks, takes the form of a love-vision. It contains the traditional elements of love-vision: apparently extraneous classical material juxtaposed to the narrative, meditation upon Fortune, reason and sensuality, and nature, and some of the commonplace pronouncements of foolish lovers. It strains the boundaries of the form, however, by filling in this outline with material from Dante, Alanus, Macrobius, and the Scriptures. The form of the love-vision in its French manifestations was not capacious enough to accommodate Chaucer's concerns, and eventually he would abandon it. It is, however, the form whose history best illuminates his use of the

34. See pages 196–206 and 87–89.
35. See page 139.

classical lovers in the *Hous of Fame.* The list of classical lovers in the poem grows out of the introductory tale of Dido and Aeneas, which like the tale of Ceyx and Alcyone in the *Duchess* has often been said to have little relevance to what follows.[36] From the tale of Dido and Aeneas, the narrator progresses to a meditation upon the propensity of men to betray women, using as *exempla* the ladies of the *Heroides:* Phyllis, Oenone, Hypsipyle, Medea, Dejanira, Ariadne. Since Dodd recommended in 1913 that we accept the point of view here expressed as Chaucer's own,[37] critics have generally done so; to doubt Chaucer's sincerity in this passage, after all, would seem to be to convict him of indifference to the plight of ladies betrayed in love. We must, however—to borrow a phrase of Mark Twain—gird our loins to doubt it, if we are to preserve what coherence may be discerned in the *Hous of Fame* in its unfinished state.

Chaucer's narrator begins the *Hous of Fame* with a reflection upon the nature and causes of dreams, concluding that he cannot tell the nature of his own dream, or interpret it with certainty. There follows an invocation to Morpheus, god of sleep (who dwells upon Lethe, "a flood of helle unswete"), containing three requests: that Morpheus give the narrator the power to recount his dream accurately; that God grant his hearers favor in love and protect them from mishaps; and that Christ himself curse those who maliciously misinterpret the dream (1–110). Either the narrator is a bit of a fool, who comically overestimates the significance of his dream, or the dream is to be a veritable *oraculum.* Chaucer's following adaptation of the *Aeneid* casts light upon this question. Finding himself, in his dream,

36. Paul Ruggiers, in "The Unity of Chaucer's *Hous of Fame,*" *SP* 50 (1953): 16–29, p. 16n2, notes that Coghill, Legouis, Curry, Percy Van Dyke Shelly, Marchette Chute, and J. S. P. Tatlock all find that the *Hous of Fame* lacks unity. Manly ("Rhetoricians" 8) characterizes the *exemplum* of Dido and Aeneas as "entirely unnecessary." More recently, the poem has been critizied on the same score by James Winny: "There seems no compelling reason why . . . Dido should occupy so conspicuous a place in this opening phase of a dream which then ignores love" (*Chaucer's Dream-Poems* [London, 1973], 111). The most scathing criticism is of course that of Muscatine, who spoke of the "elaborateness and pointlessness" of the poem, and said that it belongs to the "decadence of late Gothic art" (*French Tradition* 246).

37. William Dodd, *Courtly Love in Chaucer and Gower* (Gloucester, Mass. 1959), 121: "We need not hesitate to accept such utterances [as ll. 383–87] as sincerely expressive of Chaucer's own feelings. Indeed, that sense of the sadness of human life which so often manifests itself in his writings could find no more compelling cause for expression than man's faithlessness and woman's sorrow."

within the temple of Venus, he retells the tale of Troy that he sees engraved upon a brass tablet. He begins in the epic manner of Virgil—"I wol now singen, yif I kan, / The armes, and also the man / That first cam, thurgh his destinee / Fugityf of Troy contree, / In Itayle . . ." (143–47)—then quickly summarizes the history of Aeneas in Troy and upon the sea, and finally comes to rest upon the episode of Dido. Upon his arrival in Carthage, Aeneas tells the queen of his adventures upon the sea, whereupon she makes him "hyr lyf, hir love, hir lust, hir lord," regales him with gifts, and believes everything he says. Alas, what harm is done by false appearances! What a mistake women make when they give their love to strangers! Some men show a fair front, until they have got what they want; then they complain of their ladies and betray them. Truly, Dido too quickly loved a guest (239–88). But let us tell how Aeneas "lefte hir ful unkyndely": when she saw that he was determined to go to Italy, she wrung her hands and exclaimed against the falseness of men; implored him to have pity on her; insisted that she would die without him; reminded him that she had always been loyal to him; lamented that men have no *trouthe,* that hers is the fate of every woman, that her reputation would be lost (315–60). None of this availed in the least, for finally he "was forth unto his shippes goon." Seeing this, she impaled herself upon his sword; anyone who wishes to know the whole story may read it in Virgil or in the *Heroides* of Ovid. But oh, the damage that has been done by such disloyalty! One may read of it and see it everywhere. Think of how Demophon betrayed Phyllis, whereupon she hanged herself; was this not a pity? And Achilles was false to Briseida, Paris to Oenone, Jason to Hypsipyle and Medea, Hercules to Dejanira, and Theseus to Ariadne, who had saved him from death (362–426). But to excuse Aeneas of his fault, the book says that he was ordered by Mercury to go to Italy.

Passing quickly over the subsequent adventures of Aeneas—the voyage to Italy, the loss of Palinurus, the journey to the underworld, the arrival in Italy and marriage to Lavinia—the narrator prays that Venus may save us all and lighten our sorrows, as she did for Aeneas. He expresses his admiration for the decor of the temple ("Yet sawgh I never such noblesse / Of ymages, ne such richesse" [471–72]), then passes outdoors into a fearful desert, where he is soon seized by the eagle. The narrator's point of view, and the events he describes, make sense only in the light of the literary tradition governing the use of the *exemplum* of Dido and Aeneas, his leading instance of the "untrouthe" of men. It is well known that commentators on the *Aeneid* and the *Metamorphoses*—Fulgentius, John of Salisbury, Bernardus Silvestris, the third Vatican Mythographer, Boccaccio in the *De Genealogia,* and the author of the *Ovide Moralisé,* to name a few—saw in the adventures of Aeneas a paradigm of the spiritual journey of every man on earth, and in his detention by Dido an *exemplum* of the soul's temptation by lust. Bernardus writes:

> Tempestatibus et pluviis ad cavernam compellitur, id est commotionibus carnis et affluentia humoris ex ciborum et potuum superfluitate provenientis ad immundiciam carnis ducitur et libidinis. . . . Itaque ducunt pluvie Eneam ad caveam iungiturque Didoni et diu cum ea moratur. Non revocant eum turpia preconia fame quia iuventus libidine irretita nescit "quid pulchrum, quid turpe, quid utile, quid non." Tandem post longam monetur hiemem a Mercurio ut discedat.[38]

And Boccaccio:

> Secundo, quod sub velamento latet poetico, intendit Virgilius per totum opus ostendere quibus passionibus humana fragilitas infestetur, et quibus viribus a constanti viro superentur. Et cum iam non nullas ostendisset, volens demonstrare, quibus ex causis ab appetitu concupiscibili in lasciviam rapiamur. . . . Et sic intendit pro Dydone concupiscibilem et attractivam potentiam, oportunitatibus omnibus armatam. Eneam autem pro quocunque ad lubricum apto et demum capto. Tandem ostenso, quo trahamur in scelus ludibrio, qua via in virtutem revehamur, ostendit, inducens Mercurium, deorum interpretem, Eneam ab illecebra increpantem atque ad gloriosa exhortantem.[39]

This interpretation of the episode is not, however, confined to the mythographers. Augustine repented his youthful "foolish tears" for

38. IV, 1, ed. Julian Ward Jones and Elizabeth Frances Jones, *The Commentary on the First Six Books of Virgil's* Aeneid *Commonly Attributed to Bernardus Silvestris* (Lincoln, Neb., 1977), 24–25.

39. XIV, 13, ed. Romano, *Genealogie* II, 722–23.

Dido, and we may recall that Petrarch, in the *Secretum,* puts the *exemplum* of Dido into the mouth of Augustine as an illustration of the poet's own foolish choice of the sensual life in youth.[40] Alanus, in the *De Planctu,* includes Aeneas among those infected by the madness of Cupid.[41] Dante, like Virgil, locates Dido in the underworld, among the "peccator carnali / che la ragion sommettono al talento"; he describes her, unsympathetically, as "colei che s'ancise amorosa, / e ruppe fede al cener di Sicheo."[42] The author of the *Echecs Amoureux* names Dido as one of the monitory *exempla* of love cited by Diana to the lover in her speech warning him away from the Garden of Deduit, and the commentator on the *Echecs* remarks that "the goddess Diana reminded the author in his youth, as he pretends, of the loves described above (that is, those of Pygmalion, Myrrha, Phaedra, Philomela, Scylla, Phyllis, Dido, and Hero and Leander) so that he might take an example from them and be aware of the danger that lies in such loves."[43] Boccaccio in his commentary on the *Commedia* makes the same use of Dido that Chaucer makes of Aeneas in the *Hous of Fame:*

> "La infelice Didone, secondo Virgilio, per un forestiero affabile, mai più non veduto, subitamente dimenticò il lungamente e molto amato Siccheo; assai bene verificando quello che l'autore nel *Purgatorio* delle femine dice:
>
> Per lei di la assai vi si comprende
> quanto in femina fuoco d'amor dura,
> se l'occhio o 'l tatto spesso nol raccende.[44]

Boccaccio's final word in the passage, however, is against "disonesto appetito" itself.

In medieval terms, then, the tale of Dido and Aeneas represents an *exemplum* against lust. As we have seen, when a character in a learned medieval work speaks with approval of the passion of Dido

40. See page 76.
41. *De Planctu* Mtr. 5, 21–28. I have preferred the construction of Douglas Moffatt, *The Complaint of Nature* (New York, 1908)—which makes a Nero out of the lovestruck Aeneas—to that of Sheridan, which makes an Aeneas out of a presumably lovestruck Nero.
42. *Inf.* V, 61–62.
43. Jones 686.
44. I, 2, 98 (ed. Padoan, *Esposizioni* 75).

(or of any of the other Ovidian heroines except Penelope), it is because the author of the work wishes to establish the point of view of that character as irrational. The Old Whore of the *Roman de la Rose* uses the tale of Dido in precisely the same way as Chaucer's narrator in the *Hous of Fame,* as a demonstration of the perfidy of men. She even remarks, as does Dido in *Fame,* that all women come to a bad end in love, and like Chaucer's narrator she calls the manner of Dido's death "a great pity." She concludes foolishly that women should "deceive men in turn, not fix our hearts on one" (13173–13268). Jean's purpose in this speech is certainly not to "make wommen to men lasse triste" (to paraphrase the *Legend of Good Women*), but to establish the shortsighted and carnal perspective of the Old Whore; the proper morality upon the classical *exempla* of love is that one should flee love *par amours,* not that one should unite corrupt intention to corrupt practice. When Boccaccio's Florio and Ameto compare themselves or their ladies to the classical lovers they point up their own moral error, as the nymph Fiammetta explains in her lyric in praise of the heavenly crown of Ariadne, symbolic of persistence against evil: "And if, when Aeneas left her without farewell, Dido had turned her desire to this crown, she would have found a remedy for her iniquitous life while alive, and perhaps in a better fashion than history tells; nor would Byblis have been sorrowfully parted from the world; rather, in waiting, the soul would have conquered the flesh" (36, 34–42). The Fiammetta of the *Elegia* defines for the reader her foolish and self-destructive nature partly by her constant identification of herself with the classical heroines of love, including Dido.[45] The lover of the *Amorosa Visione,* who has certain affinities with Chaucer's narrator in *Fame,* also sees the story of Dido portrayed within the Temple of Love, and weeps with pity at her betrayal (XXVIII, 1–3). Like Chaucer's speaker, Boccaccio's concludes that he has never seen anything so magnificent as the decor of this temple, only to be rebuked by his celestial guide, who admonishes him that ". . . these things are fallacious and without truth." We have seen the same convention operating in the *Voir Dit,* where Toute-Belle, having been accused by Guillaume of indifference, attempts to reaccredit herself as a faithful mistress by reference to Medea, Dido, Byblis, and Helen; truly none of them loved as she does![46] To the alert reader the

45. See pages 143 and 155–61.
46. See pages 166–67.

comparison is humorous, but it also serves as a sort of moral locator for the character of Toute-Belle, whose love is quintessentially worldly and changeable.

Geffrey's enthusiastic sponsorship of Dido and the other classical heroines, then, tells us certain things about him. It tells us, first of all, that he is a lover *par amours* or a partisan of such lovers, despite his protestation that he "kan not of that faculte." He is, indeed, established as a disappointed lover by the long speech of the eagle explaining why Jupiter has vouchsafed him the vision—"That thou so longe trewely / Hast served so ententyfly / His blynde nevew Cupido / And faire Venus also / Withoute guerdon ever yit . . ." (615–19)—as well as by his prayers to Venus and his desire for "love-tydynges." It tells us, too, that this speaker who can neither gloss the classical tales correctly nor raise his eyes to celestial things without being blinded is probably wrong about other matters as well. He is probably wrong about his dream, in which we should not, after all, expect to find *hy sentence;* and indeed it turns out to be a parody of *hy sentence,* into which a good deal of wisdom has nevertheless found its way by indirection. Anyone who believes that, because Chaucer in conventional fashion identifies love's fools by their effusive sympathy for the classical heroines, he therefore feels no compassion for those ladies, is guilty of an undistributed middle (and probably has not read the *Troilus*). Like other medieval writers, Chaucer wishes to construct an implied comparison between the traditionally accepted moralization of the classical tales and the (by his time almost equally well-established and recognizable) "lover's morality," in order to identify his speaker as a lover and to set the tone of humorous, indirect self-disparagement, and urbane mockery of love *par amours,* that was a convention of the *dits.* Although it is not possible to establish definitely that *Fame* was influenced by the *Amorosa Visione,* the journey of Chaucer's narrator closely parallels that of Boccaccio's lover; they both witness the pageants of Love and Fame and are filled with wonder at them, and they both end their journeys without experiencing any real enlightenment. In both works, Love and Fame are discredited—Boccaccio's guide lectures against them, and Chaucer's narrator finds that the temple of Love stands in an arid waste and the judgments of Fame are irrational—but nothing is set in their place.

It is not, however, correct to conclude that therefore neither the *Amorosa Visione* nor the *Hous of Fame* teaches anything. Teaching by indirection is itself a convention of many of the works in which the classical lovers appear as *exempla,* and much indirect instruction is offered in both works, more cleverly by Chaucer than by Boccaccio. Boccaccio's lover (as well as his reader) is instructed by recurring allusions to the strait path which he refuses to take; it is, his guide promises (and we may readily believe) the way to true happiness. Unfortunately, the lover (and even, alas, the reader) regards it until the very end as a sort of boring school exercise, a piece of drudgery he will attack on Sunday evening after he has enjoyed his weekend. Chaucer's narrator fares a good deal better, for he is given specific hints as to the way out of his entrapment in the blind inequities of Love and Fortune's sister, Fame. It seems unlikely that the eagle—who is far too droll and prosaic to represent anything like Contemplation, Philosophy, or Poetic Inspiration—understands any better than his passenger the doctrines implied by the scientific wisdom he so enthusiastically imparts; his job, after all, is to convey to Geffrey his dubious "reward" of the sight of the houses of Fame and Tydynges. Under the guise of explaining the operation of these houses, he nevertheless implies the orthodox philosophical way out of the kind of servitude to Fortune represented by Venus and Fame.

For instance, the eagle's doctrine of the *kyndely stede* or natural resting place of all things is ostensibly presented in answer to Geffrey's question how every sound can find its way to the Hous of Fame (729–56); at the same time, however, that it answers that question, it suggests the Boethian and Augustinian doctrine of the natural home of the soul. The eagle's subsequent question ("Have I not preved thus symply, / Without any subtilite / Of speche, or gret prolixite / Of termes of philosophie . . . ?" [854–57]) seems intended to establish that he does not understand the implications of what he has said, and Geffrey's comically elaborate reply ("A good persuasion / . . . hyt is; and lyk to be / Ryght so as thou hast preved me") suggests that he has not understood it, either. The detail that they flew so high that "al the world . . . / No more semed than a prikke" (906–7) suggests passages of the *De Consolatione,* the *Paradiso* and the commentary of Macrobius on the *Somnium Scipionis* all of which refer to the philosophical detachment and spiritual sufficiency achieved by those who liberate themselves from servitude to Fortune; but the eagle shows interest only in the features of the landscape below. Worse, he compares their flight, in the same breath, to the legendary flights of both the wise Scipio and the foolish, presumptuous Icarus (911–24); apparently, he knows no better than Geffrey which sort of flight they are making. When Geffrey looks down upon the "ayerissh bestes" and begins to "wexen in a were," perhaps preparing to receive "clere entendement" at last, the eagle breaks in noisily to offer him instruction concerning the stars, which Geffrey laconically declines. That Geffrey learns nothing of any use from his extraordinary flight is Chaucer's best joke in the *Hous of Fame*.

The inefficacy of Geffrey's vision of the Temple of Venus as a vehicle of moral instruction had been established by his simple-minded admiration of the temple itself and of the classical heroines; that of the *Hous of Fame* is established by its nature (as the offspring of Ovid's House of Rumor and the Houses of Fortune in the *Anticlaudianus* and the *Roman de la Rose*) and by the extravagantly capricious nature of Fame's judgments. As in the Temple of Venus, Geffrey is overcome by the "grete craft" and 'beaute" of the architectural ornaments of the Hous and by the spectacle afforded by its musicians, *tregetours,* and celebrities, as well as by the appearance of Fame herself. Chaucer's humor is both playful and pointedly erudite: Fame's shifting size, for instance, wittily parodies Boethius's Lady Philosophy, and Geffrey's principal recollection of Hercules (that he "with a sherte hys lyf les" [1414]) reminds us of the love-disasters of the first book. Geffrey, however, gives no sign of ability to interpret accurately the things he observes; even as Fame delivers her perverse judgments, he is simply lost in wonder. If we grant that Chaucer wished to suggest certain moral conclusions upon the tableaux he presents, and at the same time grant that he evidently did not wish to do so by means of a moralizing narrator, the proportions of the *Hous of Fame*—which have been much criticized—become more understandable. The cumulative impact of the *comédie larmoyante* that is Geffrey's version of the *Aeneid,* of the eagle's lengthy and suggestive, but literally quite pointless lectures, and of the frustrating irrationality of Fame's judgments, would not have been great enough to lend moral seriousness to the poem if Chaucer had made them neater and "better proportioned." Ultimately, Geffrey's persistent bewilderment and innocent admiration of all he sees suggest precisely what Chaucer probably wished to suggest: that the operations of Fortune, as manifested in the two arenas of Love and Fame, are bewildering and may indeed stimulate admiration and allegiance in unreflecting persons. The matters one ought to reflect upon in order to avoid subjection to Fortune are suggested in the speeches of Geffrey and his eagle. Those two, however, are so unrelentingly (and comically) attentive to the literal level—both as speakers and as auditors—that they never gain any access to the meaning Chaucer communicates through them.

Such an understanding of the poem does not, alas, serve to eliminate many of the conjectures advanced by scholars as to its probable ending. Literary propriety requires only that the promised *love-tydyinges* advance Geffrey's real understanding of the nature of Fortune no further than the instruction he has thus far received. It is necessary to take note of the apparently genuine suggestion (2131–40) that there are particular *tydynges* that he wishes, or expects, to hear, and about which he remains coyly uncommunicative. The appearance of Christ, or even of Boethius, in a context as riotously irrational as this last book would surely violate the propriety established by Chaucer;[47] and it is inconceivable that he might ever have shown himself so indiscreet, or so uncharitable, as to reprove John of Gaunt publicly for his relationship with Katherine Swynford by means of some fictional "man of auctorite."[48] Geffrey's unwillingness to divulge the *tydynges* in question makes it unlikely that the "man" would have divulged them, either. Perhaps there were genuine news (of a royal engagement?) of which everyone was aware already, so that Chaucer might safely continue his pattern of frustrating poor Geffrey by introducing a man of no real authority bearing tidings of no real import. It remains possible that he never finished the poem or that, in the social context within which it was originally presented, he might have made his point without continuing it. Surely one point he wished to make, as did Boccaccio in the *Amorosa Visione,* is the lesson of the classical *exempla* of love: that servitude to Fortune leads to frustration.

There is practically unanimous critical agreement upon the function of the list of classical lovers presented as part of the decor of Venus's temple in the *Parlement of Foules.* To the four lovers named by Boccaccio in the *Teseida,* his principal source, Chaucer adds

47. Koonce (*Fame* 264) and F. X. Newman, "Somnium: Medieval Theories of Dreaming and the Form of Vision Poetry," Princeton dissertation 1962, 381, believe that the "man of authority" is Christ; Ruggiers ("Unity" 28) suggest Boethius.

48. This is the hypothesis of Frederick C. Reidel, "The Meaning of Chaucer's *Hous of Fame,*" *JEGP* 27 (1928): 441–69. Bertrand Bronson ("Chaucer's *Hous of Fame:* Another Hypothesis," *University of California Publications in English* 3 [1934]: 171–92) also believes that the "man" will announce a scandal, but is not so bold as to specify it.

eleven more from Dante's *Inferno,* with the intention (as J. A. W. Bennett and others have seen) of emphasizing the instability and tragic potential of love *par amours.*[49] There is considerable disagreement, however, upon the place of this portrayal of "likerous" love within the poem as a whole. The *Parlement* is composed of three main divisions: the summary of the *Somnium Scipionis,* the description of the garden of love, and the parliament itself. Early critics of the poem deplored its lack of unity: Tatlock, Wells, Sypherd, Dodd, Root, and others questioned the relevance of the *Somnium,* and the long description of the garden, to the bird-parliament.[50] Later critics have suggested various unifying principles: the topic of Love itself, in its earthly and heavenly manifestations; the paired oppositions that recur within the poem, like the contrast between the welcoming and forbidding aspects of the garden or the common and aristocratic birds; or even the overarching concern with the processes of reading and writing.[51] The concern, however, with which the poem opens

49. Bennett, *The* Parlement of Foules: *An Interpretation* (Oxford, 1957), 101–5. Others who have made substantially the same point include Robert W. Frank, "Structure and Meaning in the *Parlement of Foules,*" *PMLA* 71 (1956): 530–39, p. 536; Rhoda Selvin, "Shades of Love in the *Parlement of Foules,*" *SN* 37 (1965): 146–60; pp. 152–53; Winny, *Dream-Poems* 124–25; and George Kane, *Chaucer* (New York, 1984), 59. Lowes ("Chaucer and Dante," *MP* 14 [1917]: 129–59, pp. 130–32) was the first to note that Chaucer augumented Boccaccio's list of lovers in the *Teseida* with others from *Inferno* V, 58–69.

50. R. M. Lumiansky ("Chaucer's *Parlement of Foules:* A Philosophical Interpretation," *RES* 24 [1948]: 81–89, pp. 81–82) lists most of the older scholars who criticized the *Parlement* for a lack of unity. J. S. P. Tatlock, in *The Mind and Art of Chaucer* (Syracuse, N.Y., 1950), 66, claims that "the classic narrative is used as introduction not because of any bearing on the contents of the rest of the poem but for its own splendor, also perhaps to lend dignity. . . ." R. K. Root (*The Poetry of Chaucer* [New York, 1906], 66) writes that "the real action of the piece does not begin till nearly three hundred lines have rolled melodiously by," and according to W. Owen Sypherd (*Studies in Chaucer's* Hous of Fame [New York, 1965], 23) "the guide African leaves [the narrator] at the entrance to the Park, and after that there is never a suspicion of any influence from the *Somnium Scipionis.*" R. C. Goffin, "Heaven and Earth in the *Parlement of Foules,*" *MLR* 31 (1936): 493–99, notes the similar views of Wells and Dodd.

51. Most critics of the poem acknowledge that love is a central theme; an especially strong statement of the case is made by Selvin, "Shades of Love." For paired oppositions as the principle of unity, see Charles O. McDonald, "An Interpretation of Chaucer's *Parlement of Foules,*" *Speculum* 30 (1955): 444–57, and Michael Kelly, "Antithesis as the principle of Design in the *Parlement of Foules,*" *ChauR* 14 (1979): 61–73; for the view that Chaucer is mainly concerned with the processes of reading and writing, see Robert W. Uphaus, "Chaucer's *Parlement of Foules:* Aesthetic Order and Individual Experience," *TSLL* 10 (1968): 349–58, and Kathleen Dubs and Stoddard Malarkey, "The Frame of Chaucer's *Parlement,*" *ChauR* 13 (1978): 16–24.

and closes, and the one topic that runs all the way through it, is the predicament of the narrator.

Chaucer's narrator in the *Parlement* is the same sort he constructed for the *Hous of Fame:* a droll, bookish fellow who aspires to the condition of a lover but hops always behind. The *Parlement* begins with his reflection upon love, of which he disclaims any personal experience ("I knowe nat Love in dede"), but which he praises and holds in awe. He reads about Love in books, wishing ardently to learn "a certeyn thing" and believing that he must, indeed, find it there, for "newe science" comes from old books like new corn from old fields. There have been various critical conjectures about what the "certeyn thing" must be: the nature of Love, the "true self and its happiness," a "satisfying doctrine of the future life," the relationship between true and false felicity, or the best way of making a literary "thyng."[52] I do not think that Chaucer meant the "thing" to be a puzzle, but in order to understand what this narrator might want to know, we must interpret aright the clues we are given about his character. First of all, he is an unsuccessful lover who nevertheless worships the God of Love and believes that his dream was inspired by Venus (the one with the "fyrbrond," and therefore not some sort of Venus *in bono*). Love has considerable power over him: when he thinks of it, he hardly knows "wher that I flete or synke" (7, 141–54), and his reaction when confronted with the conflicting inscriptions over the gate to Love's garden is one of extreme anxiety. Once in the garden, he is enthralled (like Amans in the *Roman de la Rose*) by its beauty, and he calls Cupid "oure lord" (171–210, 212). The leering tone of his description of Venus's scanty attire (she was 'wel kevered to my pay' [271]) identifies this aspiring lover as distinctly unphilosophic. He believes, too, that the maidens who served Diana were wasting their time, and that the speeches of the tercel eagles, with their pledges to die or serve forever without reward, are the noblest he has ever heard (283, 484–86). His point of view, in short, is that of a servant of Cupid.

52. Exponents of the views listed are, respectively, Dorothy Everett, "The *Parlement of Foules,*" in *Critics on Chaucer,* ed. Sheila Sullivan (Coral Gables, Fla., 1970): 48–56; Robertson and Huppé, *Fruyt and Chaf* 102; J. A. W. Bennett, "Some Second Thoughts on the *Parlement of Foules,*" in *Chaucerian Problems and Perspectives,* ed. Edward Vasta and Zacharias P. Thundy (Notre Dame, Ind. 1979): 132–46; F. H. Whitman, "Exegesis and Chaucer's Dream Visions," *ChauR* 3 (1969): 229–38; and R. C. Goffin, "Heaven and Earth."

The "thing" that he wishes to learn, therefore, is how to succeed in love. He cannot, of course, learn it from Macrobius; he does not learn it from the activities of the birds; and so he ends the poem as frustrated as he began, still reading and hoping to "mete some thyng for to fare / The bet" (in love). It is well to remember that the *Parlement* is a light, occasional poem, the least "preachy" poem imaginable. Its real purpose is to amuse. The source of its humor is the assumption, shared by Chaucer and his audience, that service to Cupid is foolish, but it would be wrong to characterize that as the "moral" of the *Parlement,* which is not a didactic poem. Everything in it is funny. It is funny that the narrator, an ineffectual, bookish fellow, wants to serve Love at all; it is even funnier that he thinks he can learn from books how to succeed in an enterprise in which success is by definition impossible. It is funny that he finds nothing in the *Somnium* that might apply to his own condition, that the august Scipio is reduced to shoving him into the garden of earthly love in a last-ditch attempt to teach him something, and that he learns nothing even from his experiences there. And the funniest thing of all is that, having been treated to a comprehensive survey of love in all its manifestations, what he wants is still to "fare the bet" in love: to cut a figure with the ladies. He is a hopeless fool, but a charming one: Love's fool, the figure most appropriate to the celebration of St. Valentine's Day.

The movement of the *Parlement,* then, is based upon an elimination of alternatives in the narrator's search for the secret of amatory success. The wisdom of Macrobius—that the earth is as nothing "at regard of the hevenes quantite," that "oure present worldes lyves space / Nis but a maner deth," and that one "ne shulde hym in the world delyte" (53–54, 66)—is not what he seeks. As a servant of Cupid, he does not know how to "werche and wysse / To commune profit," and he has not the imagination to learn it from the *Somnium.* Therefore he goes to bed in a condition of frustration: "For bothe I hadde thyng which that I nolde, / And ek I nadde that thyng that I wolde" (90–91). Chaucer uses the same formulation in the *Complaint unto Pity* and the *Complaint unto his Lady;* in both poems, that which the lover has but does not want is sorrow, and that which he wants but has not is the lady's favor. This is, of course, the situation of the narrator in the *Parlement,* whose reading of the *Somnium* fails to relieve his frustration in love. The formulation comes ultimately from the *De Consolatione* of Boethius, where

Philosophy uses it as an illustration of the inability of worldly things to confer happiness, precisely the philosophical point most relevant to the predicament of Chaucer's narrator.[53] Since Scipio fails to teach him anything about celestial love, the next stop is the garden of earthly love, which has two divisions: the temple of Venus and the "launde" of Nature, which is itself somewhat infected by Venerean attitudes. The double inscription over the garden gate has, I think, something to do with these two divisions, but I shall recur to that in a moment.

The "error" written in the face of the narrator as he enters the garden is—as Scipio explains (155–58)—that he hopes for success in love. The line is a humorous echo of *Paradiso* IV, 10–11, in which the pilgrim Dante similarly faces the dilemma of Buridan's ass as he contemplates the opposing concepts of free will and the compulsion exerted by natural disposition. The allusion is both amusing and ultimately relevant to the *Parlement,* in which the narrator might at any point escape from his error through the exercise of free will. But he never does, and so we see him at the mercy of the sense impressions he receives in the garden; like Amans in the *Rose,* he approves of all he sees. In fact, however, the narrator's uncritical description of the garden becomes more and more disquieting. Beginning with bright trees, angelic birdsong, frolicking animals and eternal sunshine, it moves to Cupid, filing his arrows—"some for to sle, and some to wounde and kerve" (217)—beside a well, which the narrator seems not to recognize as the dangerous fountain of Narcissus. Cupid is accompanied by Will, a significant personage even if she does originate in a mistranslation of Boccaccio,[54] for evidently the conjunction made sense to Chaucer. She may

53. (Philosophy speaks):

"First, then, since you were recently very rich, let me ask whether or not you were ever worried in spite of your abundant wealth."

"Yes," I answered, "I cannot recall a time when my mind was entirely free from worry."

"And wasn't it because you wanted something you did not have, or had something you did not want?"

"That is true," I answered. . . .

"Then wealth cannot give a man everything and make him entirely self-sufficient, even though this is what money seems to promise."

(III, Pr. 3, 4–7, trans. Green)

54. There exists an entire spectrum of opinion as to the origin of this line. Robert A. Pratt, "Chaucer's Use of the *Teseida,*" *PMLA* 67 (1947): 598–621, p. 607, believes that Chaucer's translation of Boccaccio's "voluttà,' (usually = "pleasure") was a

represent either the appetitive faculty by which men desire or the will by which they choose to serve Love. Chaucer makes the remaining personified attributes less attractive than they appear in the *Teseida,* and concludes with three so baneful (or so lewd) that he refuses even to name them.

From the heavenly garden, we descend—within only 35 lines—to the temple of Venus, a dark, hellish place whose fires are stoked by hot sighs, burning desire, and consuming jealousy. We have seen that the narrator nevertheless reveals leering admiration of Venus herself, in a line added by Chaucer to Boccaccio's text.[55] Chaucer adds, too, the detail of the two young suppliants to Venus (whose posture, at least, suggests indifference to them) and the narrator's comment that the servants of Diana, whose broken bows decorate the wall, were wasting their time (278–79, 283). The lovers portrayed in the frescoes—Callisto, Atalanta, Semiramis, Candace, Hercules, Byblis, Dido, Pyramus and Thisbe, Tristram, Isolde, Paris, Achilles, Helen, Cleopatra, Troilus, Scylla, Rhea Silvia (286–92)—are for the most part those we have seen repeatedly in warnings against love; as George Kane has remarked, they show that love brings unhappiness.[56] The last word in this description of Venus's temple associates these lovers with the idea of death: "Alle these were peynted on that other syde, / And al here love, and in what plyt they dyde" (293–94). This, then, is the Citherea to whom the narrator had hopefully addressed his invocation as he began to describe his dream; clearly, he had better look elsewhere for help "to fare the bet."

Without commenting further upon what he has seen, he does. Leaving the temple, he emerges again into the paradisal landscape, where he sees the "noble goddesse Nature" presiding "in a launde, upon an hil of floures" (302–3) over a great gathering of birds. Nature appears, we are specifically told, "right as Aleyn, in the

---

mistake attributable to haste; J. A. W. Bennett (*Parlement* 85) speculates that Chaucer deliberately "replaced the figure of Pleasure *(Voluttà)* by that of 'Wil'—Will in the sense of 'impulse' or 'desire,' a sense exemplified in the frequent medieval antithesis of Will to the rational faculty of Wit"; and David Chamberlain, "The Music of the Spheres and the *Parlement of Foules," ChauR* 5 (1970): 32–56, p. 40, maintains that Chaucer's translation of "Voluttà" is correct: " . . . Chaucer's 'wil' suggests the carnal desire of *voluptas* or *cupiditas.*"

55. Line 271: "The remenaunt was wel kevered to my pay."

56. Kane, *Chaucer* 59: "In the words of the 'old tattered book' of Scipio which the dreamer read so assiduously, they instance 'those who have surrendered to the pleasures of the body and have become, so to speak, its slaves, who in response to sensual passion have flouted the laws of gods and men.' "

Pleynt of Kynde, / Devyseth"; she is therefore to be interpreted not as an elemental life-force, but as the vicar of God and the servant of Reason. Her task is to preside over the birds as they "benygnely . . . chese" their mates, but as in the *De Planctu* she finds her work obstructed by the disobedience of her noblest creation. It is certainly true, as James Winny maintains,[57] that Nature admires the noble birds—the formel eagle, after all, is her most perfect creation—but there is no evidence that she shares the narrator's admiration of their windy and artificial love-pleading. Her wish, finally, is "to delyvere, and fro this noyse unbynde" (523) the birds, so that they may choose their mates expeditiously and go forth; this is not a "materialistic" attitude, however crudely it may be expressed by the lower fowl,[58] but a rational one in accord with God's plan. The tercels do not want mates, but "sovereign ladies"; in the fashion of courtly "lovers," they speak more of pain, "wo," servitude, betrayal, death, hanging, the carving of veins and the rending of limbs than of love. They are the most accomplished pleaders *par amours* that the narrator has ever heard, and they are finally—quite deservedly—frustrated. Nature's advice to the formel—"If I were Resoun, certes, thanne wolde I / Conseyle yow the royal tercel take" (632–33)—is not an attempt at humor, but an attempt to save the situation; this is not the Nature of Jean de Meun, who takes no account of Reason, but that of Alanus, who upholds it as the principle by which men should govern themselves. If they will not, however, she has no power to compel obedience.

Here, then, are two crushing defeats for the love represented by Venus and Cupid, to whom the narrator has declared allegiance: the classical lovers die ignominiously, and the passionate eagles meet with rejection. Only the common birds, who seek mates in the common fashion, emerge fully and joyfully requited. As the inscription over the garden gate suggested, earthly love offers two possibilities, the "mortal strokes" of love *par amours* and the "good aventure" of natural love. The lesson of the vision is plain: if the narrator really wishes "to fare the bet," he will transfer his allegiance to celestial love or, if his inclination is earthly, to natural love and the

57. *Dream-Poems* 129.

58. Winny writes (*Dream-Poems* 142), ". . . the matter-of-fact outlook of the more realistic birds is tried against a system of values which regards their materialistic arguments as ignoble."

founding of a family. But he refuses to accept or even acknowledge the evidence of his dream, and determines instead to "rede alwey" until he finds what he is seeking: the key to success in love *par amours*. That he is doomed never to find it is the final joke on this infatuated alter ego of Chaucer, reader of a poem in honor of St. Valentine's Day.

The poem of Chaucer in which the classical lovers figure most prominently is, of course, the *Legend of Good Women*. Like the other dream-visions, it is divided into segments, but in the *Legend* the relationship between the two divisions—the dream of Cupid and Alceste and the tales themselves—is clear enough: the tales are a penitential exercise of the poet, who has offended against Cupid in his other writings. There has never been any agreement, however, upon Chaucer's intention in telling these tales. They present several difficulties: most are brief, only bare outlines of the classical tales, and possess little interest in themselves; they vary in tone, with some appearing as near-parodies of the original and others as genuinely pathetic; and, whatever their prevailing tone, it is generally disrupted by the addition of a moral which is the same in every case: women are always good, while men are treacherous villains. Chaucer cannot really have meant to convey such a moral; clearly, it is the poet's device to placate the God of Love. But what ideas did he mean to convey with this odd collection of tales? The question becomes even more puzzling when we consider that the narrator of the *Legend of Good Women* (whom I will call "the poet") is more closely identified with Chaucer himself than any other narrator he created: he is not a lover (except of the daisy, whatever that means), and Alceste attributes to him the works of Chaucer. In order to understand what Chaucer has attempted in the *Legend of Good Women*, it will be necessary to examine briefly the sources of his allusions in this very allusive poem. I shall limit my discussion of the Prologue to the revised version, called "Text G."

Like the *Parlement of Foules* and the *Book of the Duchess*, the *Legend* begins with an appeal to the authority of "olde bokes." This defense of the wisdom of the ancients differs from the others, however, in insisting upon the value of written history as a guide to things so rare, or so far outside the scope of everyday experience, that they may be verified only by recourse to authority: "Goddes forbode, but men shulde leve / Wel more thyng than men han seyn with ye!" (10–11) Howard R. Patch noticed nearly fifty years ago that, in its context as introduction to a collection of tales about "good" women, this statement could only be intended to suggest the ecclesiastical commonplace that there are no good women.[59] The emphases of the Prologue, however, are confusing, and it is difficult to see how that suggestion might accord with the praise of the daisy immediately following. The poet leaves his books, he says, only in May, when the daisies bloom, for he admires the daisy above all flowers. John Lowes has shown that Chaucer took his material on daisy worship from some half a dozen French "marguerite" poems, in which praise of the daisy serves as a compliment to ladies named Marguerite. Despite extensive scholarly conjecture on Chaucer's possible intention of praising Queen Anne, the only thing we can be certain of concerning his praise of the daisy is that it is addressed to Alceste, whose death to save her husband Admetus is told by Hyginus and Boccaccio. Before being identified with Alceste, however, the daisy is surrounded by Christian imagery: Chaucer associates it with the sun, traditionally a symbol of Christ; describes it as "of alle floures flour, / Fulfyld of vertu and of alle honour," thus suggesting the Virgin; and insists upon its everlasting life ("as wel in wynter as in somer newe") (55–56, 58). He then inserts a passage praising the French poets from whom he borrows, but at the same time making it clear that his intention is not the same as theirs; he alludes as well to the "olde bokes" that are the source of the legends, but this time with the implication that they are not, actually, to be believed ("leveth hem if yow leste!").[60] Finally, he goes to sleep in his "lytel herber" and dreams of the meeting with Cupid and Alceste in the daisy-filled meadow.

The prologue has not thus far displayed much conceptual coherence, and in fact the appearance of Cupid and Alceste only makes matters worse. The initial praise of "olde bokes" suggested that we might be in the domain of an ironic treatment of love, but the Christian imagery surrounding the daisy seemed to make that unlikely. With the appearance of Alceste, not a figure of the *dits amoureux* and not one ordinarily associated with Cupid, the poem seems to be taking a new direction altogether. Cupid's accusation of the poet suggests that it will become a love-judgment, like the

59. *On Rereading Chaucer* (Cambridge, Mass., 1939), 131.

60. Line 88. Chaucer asserts (ll. 61–80) that, although his Prologue is obviously indebted to the poems of the flower-and-leaf tradition of debate, he is about something completely different: "That nys nothyng the entent of my labour." The warning (l. 88) against believing the stories he will tell in praise of women is, of course, a humorous allusion to the biased recounting and perverse interpretation he will offer.

Navarre; and indeed the *Legend* has more in common with the *Navarre* than has yet been noted. But the association of Alceste with the daisy, which connects the dream with the poet's daisy worship, muddies the water hopelessly. How can she serve as the Queen of Love, consort of Cupid—as silly a fellow in the *Legend* as he is elsewhere—and at the same time as the Queen of Daisies, symbol of Christian virtue? (One cannot here associate daisy worship with love-service, as in the French tradition, not only because of the Christian imagery that defines Chaucer's daisy but because the poet is not a lover.) It must be, then, as many critics have concluded, that Chaucer takes the legends themselves seriously, as demonstrations of the real, if pagan, virtue of faithfulness in love, which somehow foreshadows and anticipates the love of Christ. But then why does he so persistently "spoil" the legends with bathetic melodrama, sarcastic or flippant asides, and that tiresome insistence upon the faithlessness of men?

No one, so far as I know, has asked another question relevant to this very popular interpretation of the *Legend:* what is the purpose of Chaucer's depiction of the character of Alceste? Because she is explicitly identified with the daisy, because the poet praises her so highly, and because her story so clearly prefigures that of Christ—sacrifice of life for another's sake, descent into hell, and resurrection—few students of the *Legend* have noted that she speaks and behaves with perfect consistency as the consort of Cupid. And, despite McCall's assertion that this Cupid represents "the best in natural love,"[61] there is really nothing in the poem (except his association with Alceste) to distinguish him from the Cupid of the *dits amoureux,* lord and persecutor of lovers *par amours.* He holds "firy dartes," is accompanied by the classical lovers, and accuses the poet in unequivocal terms: "(Thou) thinkest in thy wit, that is ful col, / That he nys but a verray propre fol / That loveth paramours, to harde and hote" (258–59). The poet has offended by translating the *Roman de la Rose,* which makes wise men withdraw from Cupid; by writing the *Troilus,* which causes men to repose less trust in women; and by neglecting the many stories of good women that he might have read in "Valerye, Titus, or Claudyan," or "Jerome agayns Jovynyan" (255–81). The difficulty here is that these good women (cited as exceptions to the rule by the same writers whose misogyny enrages the Wife of Bath) were quite different from most of the

61. *Chaucer Among the Gods* 119.

women of the *Legend;* they were women like Penelope, Lucretia, Portia, the Sabines, the seven maidens of Milesia, and the wives of Niceratus, Scipio, and Lentulus, who "keped . . . here maydenhede, / Or elles wedlok, or here widewehede" (294–95), and who suffered for their virtue rather than for their misplaced faith in treacherous men. We have seen that the women of the *Heroides,* also cited by Cupid as a book about "trewe wyves and of here labour," were not, with the single exception of Penelope, regarded in the Middle Ages as good. Cupid's speech shows that he himself, not the poet he accuses, has garnered only "the draf of storyes, and forgete the corn"; evidently he has misread all the texts he cites.

Alceste does not point this out, nor does she make the argument later made by the poet that works such as the *Roman de la Rose* and the *Troilus,* when read correctly, tend "to forthere trouthe in love and it cheryce" (462). Instead, she makes a speech in which she (comically, and apparently inadvertently) insults first Cupid and then the poet by suggesting that the God of Love may have accused him based upon the false reports of "losengeours" and "totelere accusours"; that the poet, a silly fellow, takes no heed of what material he translates, and may not have noticed that it was offensive to Love; that Cupid ought to disregard the offenses of creatures as low as this poet in the order of creation; that the poet served Cupid well in youth; and that he will swear never to offend Cupid again, and will make amends by composing a poem about good women (326–431). Even granting that Alceste, a classical figure, might not espouse Christian wisdom despite her association with the daisy, this speech is not even what we might expect of a pagan spokesperson for Reason. Alceste is here presented as a servant of the God of Love who seeks to placate him at any cost and to bring the behavior of the poet into conformity to his law. When the poet tries to talk sense to the couple, protesting that his intention was always to further loyalty in love, she silences him abruptly with the most unreasoning statement of all: "Love ne wol nat counterpletyd be / In ryght ne wrong"—and condemns him to write a martyrology of love, "a glorious legende / Of goode women, maydenes and wyves, / That were trewe in lovynge al here lyves; / And telle of false men that hem betrayen" (446–67, 473–76). It will not do to lose sight of the fact that the absurd and illogical emphasis of the *Legend* upon the faithlessness of men derives from the command of Alceste herself. In her speeches and actions, her perspective is that of a servant of Cupid. It is all the more confusing, then, that Cupid proceeds directly to identify her to the poet in terms that recall the Christian shape of her history—"She that for her husbonde ches to dye, / And ek to gon to helle rather than he, / And Ercules rescued hire, parde, / And broughte hyre out of helle ageyn to blys" (501–4)—and then instructs the poet to tell her tale, "whan thow hast othere smale made byfore": "At Cleopatre I wol that thow begynne"!

The only clue we have to the meaning of this prologue, with its apparently conflicting emphases, is the collection of tales that follows. It has long been known that the women of the *Legend* are mainly figures from the *Heroides* not ordinarily considered virtuous; that in the tales Chaucer accentuates the pathetic elements and edits out details damaging to the characters of the women; and that he nevertheless supplies irreverent remarks upon the tales that damage the effects he seems to be trying to achieve. The only thing that all the legends have in common is that they are told to enforce a moral that runs counter to that traditionally assigned to the classical tales of love. The moral assigned to the tales by the poet in his attempt to placate Cupid is, of course, the familiar "lover's morality" given to them by the Old Whore in the *Roman de la Rose:* that all women are good and generous and that they are always betrayed by men. He takes this moral from the remarks of Alceste, a truly virtuous woman who, in the Prologue, speaks out of character as a servant of love. She is not, however, alone in the *Legend;* Lucrece, who is usually paired with Penelope as a virtuous wife, also appears in illustration of the *trouthe* of women and the treachery of men. We have seen that the tales of the *Heroides* are often wilfully misinterpreted in this way by lovers, whose perverse glosses on Ovid reveal their folly; women traditionally considered virtuous are not, however, usually included, presumably because they are not servants of Cupid and demonstration of their virtue cannot further his cause. Chaucer's innovation in the *Legend of Good Women,* then, is to include the truly good women Alceste and Lucrece with the Ovidian servants of Cupid in a demonstration of the "lover's morality" that all women are true in love and all men are false. Where might Chaucer have found the suggestion for this, and why would he have done it?

The suggestion, I think, came from the *Navarre,* where the theological virtues Foy and Charité and the conventionally wise figure Raison uncharacteristically argue on the same side as the love-virtues Largesse, Noblesse, Doubtance de meffaire, and others in the love-council of the lady Bonneürté. As we have seen, the members of the council use the classical *exempla* of love in an attempt to prove that women are more faithful lovers than men, and thus that the poet erred in the judgment of the *Behaingne*. The example of Dido is cited by Pais, a virtue which (as we may see in the *Parlement of Foules*[62] may appear associated either with Christ or with Cupid. This particular tale, violent as it is, is an odd choice for a gentle soul such as Pais, and that fact—along with her perverse gloss on Dido's tragic death—comically illustrates the distance between Christian peace and the love-virtue of the same name. Franchise cites Ariadne's and Medea's forgetfulness of friends, parents, and country as evidence of their loyalty (in love, of course); Doubtance sees an illustration of "perfect love" in the death of Thisbe for Pyramus (like the poet of the *Legend*, she says nothing of his death for her); and Souffissance—the lover's *summum bonum*, a virtue so great that she is "hors . . . des mains de Fortune"—cites the *exemplum* of Hero and Leander, to which the poet, never quick of apprehension, tardily objects that it tends equally to prove the faithfulness of men.[63] The theological virtue Charity mocks the nature proper to her by suggesting that the marriage of one of the lovers is no reason to abandon a love affair; and Foy comically demonstrates a total lack of faith in the tale told by the poet, protesting that the letters announcing the lady's marriage were false and demanding that he produce proofs.[64] Aside from their humorous irrelevance to the question at hand, these speeches, like that of Pais, demonstrate that the virtues of Christianity become perverted—indeed, inverted—when they are transferred to the domain of Love. The role of Raison is strikingly similar to that of Alceste in the *Legend:* just as Alceste defends the power of Cupid and pronounces sentence upon the erring poet, Raison explains the nature of Bonneürté, sovereign lady of love, and prepares Guillaume to receive the sentence of the judge. Both Raison and Alceste, of course, are comically ill-suited to such a role.

It is notable that no one in the *Navarre* ever preaches Christian morality; like the other *dits*—and like the Chaucerian love-visions—it is a sophisticated diversion, indirect in method and urbane

62. Line 240, where she sits before the temple of Venus "with a curtyn in hire hond." Hoyt Duggan reminds me that Peace is allegorically ambivalent in *Piers Plowman* as well, representing both the virtue and cowardice.

63. Lines 2077–2206, 2699–2822, 3171–3212, and 3213–3354.

64. Lines 2520–25, 2315–76.

in tone. Machaut's underlying assumption that love-service is against reason and religion is conveyed through the manifest absurdity of the doctrine derived by converting the classical *exempla* and the Christian virtues to the service of love. These elements appear in the poem both for the sake of the delightful comedy to be got from turning them on their heads and for the sake of their proper associations; that is, they remind the reader of the traditional Christian perspective on such matters. I believe that the *Legend,* which makes use of a similar situation and similar materials, shares the same intent. The poet of the *Legend* misuses the tales of Cleopatra, Thisbe, Dido, Hypsipyle, Medea, Ariadne, Philomela, Phyllis, and Hypermnestra by deriving a "lover's morality" from them, but he misuses the tale of Lucrece—and, finally, that of Alceste—even more pointedly. I think that we can conclude from the example of Lucrece, and from the character given to Alceste in the Prologue, that the tale of Alceste would have followed precisely the pattern set by the others. The poet would have told her story and concluded from it that women are ever so much more faithful and courageous than men; and thus, without further comment, the *Legend* would have ended. To sermonize upon the pecularities of Alceste's story, particularly upon the Christian symbolism of her rescue by Hercules, would violate not only the tone of the whole (about which I will have more to say in a moment) but the agreement with Cupid and his queen Alceste that the *Legend* should be a martyrology of love that praises women and blames men. In other words, the Alceste of the tale would have been the Alceste of the Prologue, with no indication except the bare outline of her story itself that any other meaning might be intended. Chaucer would have re-created Alceste as the servant of Love, just as he re-created Lucrece. It will be easier to understand why he would have wished to do this if we first look briefly at the nature and purpose of the *Legend* as a whole.

It may seem redundant to state—but it will not do to forget—that the *Legend of Good Women* is legendary, dominated by the idea of martyrdom. Students of the poem who have sought to show that it is "ironic" in tone have been troubled by the fact that some of the tales are more easily read in this way than others. Cleopatra is notorious, Hypsipyle and Medea conniving, Thisbe merely pitiable. However, because Chaucer was working out of a tradition in which all these women—as well as Dido, Ariadne, Philomela, Phyllis, and Hypermnestra—often appeared moralized together, whether in traditional fashion or in the almost equally well-established "lover's" fashion of the *Legend,* that did not matter to him. To him—and to Machaut, Froissart, Boccaccio, Dante, and the other learned poets of the High Middle Ages—these women were, first of all, Love's martyrs. Regardless of their characters, their sacrifices were considered foolish, but favorable notice of them ought to please Cupid, which is the task assigned to the poet in the *Legend.* The fact that, in most respects, the *Legend* is a conventional work made it easier to read in the Middle Ages than it is now. A poet attempting to placate Cupid would naturally give to the tales the "lover's morality" on them that we have seen again and again from the *Roman de la Rose* to the *dits* of Machaut and Froissart to Chaucer's own treatment of Dido in the *Hous of Fame.* Medieval readers recognized this conventional sort of perverse moralization of the tales; they did not stop to analyze the character of Thisbe or Philomela or to wonder why the poet would "spoil" the beauty of a pathetic tale with a flippant conclusion. Flippancy—and sarcasm, and noisy melodrama—were justified by the nature of the undertaking, which was to please the foolish god Cupid with an exercise in a familiar sort of perverse mythography. Most of the *Legend* is an old joke.

Like Machaut in the *Navarre,* however, Chaucer would not tell an old joke without a new twist. The *Legend* is not, fundamentally, a serious work, but the idea of martrydom, which reached its perfection in the sacrifice of Christ, was a serious idea to medieval Christians. The presence in the Prologue of Alceste—who does not belong with the ladies of the *Heroides*—constitutes a preliminary advertisement that the poem is not entirely as it seems. So does the tale of Lucrece. Whereas the moralizations of the other tales are conventionally wrong, a similar moralization applied to the tale of Lucrece is unconventionally wrong; it is a red flag. Medieval tradition did not support any way of thinking about Lucrece as a servant of Cupid whose sacrifice demonstrated the perfidy of men in love. Lucrece did not die for love, but for virtue. She is traditionally placed alongside Penelope, as an example "of wifhod the lyvynge"; properly, that is, she represents the same sort of "fyn lovynge" as Alceste. Her tale suggests the higher potential of the idea of martyrdom, a potential that must remain undeveloped in the *Legend* because of the constraints comically placed upon the poet. Chaucer reminds us of this with a reference to Christ in the conclusion to the tale of Lucrece. He begins and ends with the absurd moral about "the stable herte, sadde and kynde, / That in these wymmen men may alday fynde" (1876–77) and the "tirannye" of men: "The trewest ys ful brotel for to triste" (1885). In between, though, he inserts the information that "Crist himselve telleth / That in Israel, as wyd as is the lond, / That so gret feyth in al that he ne fond / As in a woman; and this is no lye" (1879–82). In accordance with the convention of the *Legend,* it is, of course, a lie; the allusion is apparently to the centurion in the eighth chapter of Matthew, who was not a woman but a man. The reference to Christ, however, functions as a reminder that the tale of Lucrece was traditionally a tale about martyrdom for virtue, not for Cupid. Although Augustine concluded that Lucrece's sacrifice was unnecessary—she did not herself sin because her body was used by another in a sinful act without the consent of her will—no one in the Middle Ages seems to have considered it foolish. It was an example of virtue, never moralized in any other way. In the *Legend,* however, Chaucer treats it in exactly the same way as the other tales, and supplies the same foolish moral on it, with no notice to Cupid—or to the reader—that anything is amiss.

He would, I am sure, have done the same with the concluding legend of Alceste, which like that of Lucrece was traditionally moralized in only one way, as an example of virtue. Alceste's virtue, though, was higher than that of Lucrece, for like Christ she died that another might live. V. A. Kolve has well demonstrated the connection in medieval iconography between the sacrifice of Alceste and that of Christ.[65] Her tale is not a common one in medieval literature, and it never appears in the love poems, for it was rightly seen to have nothing to do with love *par amours.* To include it in the *Legend* would have been Chaucer's way of emphasizing—without violating the conditions imposed upon the poem by the "Alceste" of the Prologue—that true love, and true martyrdom, have nothing to do with love *par amours.* There remains the question why Chaucer created the "Alceste" of the Prologue, and why he associated her in such a confusing way both with the daisy, symbol of resurrection, and with the foolish lord Cupid. Alceste and the daisy, I think, work in similar ways as symbols within the poem. The associations of the daisy were secular; in the French *dits,* it had traditionally stood for the admired lady, or the love-virtues of the lady. The associations of

65. "From Cleopatra to Alceste: An Iconographical Study of *The Legend of Good Women,*" in *Signs and Symbols in Chaucer's Poetry,* ed. John P. Hermann and John J. Burke, Jr. (University, Ala. 1981): 130–78.

Alceste, on the other hand, were religious, for her sacrifice and her "resurrection" by Hercules were seen as resembling events in the life of Christ. Chaucer turns both these symbols on their heads, associating the daisy with Christ and the Virgin and Alceste with Cupid. He thereby prepares the reader for his perversion, in the service of Cupid, of the tale of Alceste, at the same time hinting from the beginning at the higher meaning properly assigned to it; somehow, we know, Alceste and the daisy belong together. If Alceste had not appeared at all in the Prologue, readers would simply have been puzzled by the inclusion of her tale, so out of place among the tales of martyrs to Cupid; whereas, if she had appeared in her proper character, the poem would have become a debate between Charity and Cupidity. As it is, however, the poet outwits Cupid even as he gives the appearance of obeying his command. He does it in the same way that Machaut undermines the conclusions of the love-council of Bonneürté, by exposing the absurdity of the doctrine that results when Christian virtue is converted to the service of love *par amours*.

Throughout this discussion of the use of the classical heroines by medieval poets, I have tried to suggest that the ways in which they might be used were not infinite in number, but circumscribed and governed by convention. The conventions surrounding their use arose, I think out of the earliest response to the classical tales of love: simple moralization. From the time of the Fathers to that of the *Roman de la Rose,* we find the tales moralized in Christian terms by such writers as Marbod, Hildebert de Lavardin, Petrus Pictor, Bernard of Cluny, Jean de Hauteville, Alanus, Walter Map, and of course the mythographers and writers of *accessus*. This tradition does not disappear in the High Middle Ages—Dante, Petrarch, Boccaccio, Deschamps, Froissart, and even Gower still moralize the ancient heroes and heroines of love in precisely the same way—but there are added to it two other possible literary treatments of them:

1. They may be used symbolically, without explicit moralization, to characterize foolish lovers by association. Dante does this in the twenty-seventh canto of the *Purgatorio,* when he associates his still unperfected desire for Beatrice with that of Pyramus for Thisbe; the Fiammetta of the *Elegia* does it by persistently comparing herself to the tragic lovers of antiquity; and so, as we have seen, do the lovers of the *Roman de la Rose,* the *Espinette,* the *Ameto,* the *Filocolo,* the *Voir Dit,* the *Paradis d'Amour,* and numerous lyrics.

This is the convention Chaucer uses in the *Book of the Duchess,* when his narrator compares the knight's despair to that of Medea, Phyllis, Dido, and Echo, and in the *Parlement of Foules,* when he shows the narrator admiring Venus and her ornate temple with its paintings of the classical lovers. The centuries-long tradition of moralization against *fol'amors* that lay behind these allusions guaranteed that they would not be misread.

2. They may be misinterpreted by foolish lovers, again as a device for characterization; such "lovers' mythography" may be placed within the context of a debate, in which a lover defends the classical heroines while a wise counselor glosses them in traditional fashion, or it may occur in the absence of any explicit alternative. In the debates of the *Filocolo* and the *Echecs Amoureux* the arguments of Fiammetta and Diana, respectively, serve as a corrective to the lovers' misinterpretations of the classical tales; in many other poems, however, the poet depends upon the literary culture of his reader as a corrective. The foolish characters of the *Roman de la Rose* repeatedly misgloss the classical tales, but no one within the poem corrects them, though Reason suggests in general terms that the Lover has forgotten his *integumenta.* The same technique is used in the *Navarre,* the *Prison Amoureuse,* the *Trésor Amoureux,* the *Hous of Fame,* and the *Legend of Good Women.*[66]

The centuries that lie between us and these medieval works—centuries during which the classical tales of love have been first romanticized, then largely forgotten—have obscured the conventions that govern their allusions to the classical lovers. The result has been that the allusions, and to varying degrees the works in which they appear, have been misunderstood. As a survey of modern Chaucerian criticism reveals, we have forgotten why the classical heroines occur together in the first place (Cleopatra and Thisbe do not, after all, seem to us to have much in common), we are apt to regard the traditional moralizations of them as benighted (and to assume that Chaucer did, too), and when we find a speaker clearly approving of them we have no difficulty finding good reasons why he might have done so. While such responses are historically under-

66. Fleming (*Roman* 155) makes in passing the remark that the Lover of the *Rose* is the descendant of "a stock figure in Latin comedy who can be expected to represent a certain stock point of view." I have dedicated much of this book to demonstrating that the same is true of the lover/narrators of later French (and Italian, and English) poetry.

standable—it is not difficult to trace the process by which they have arisen—they have so far prevented us from reading medieval poetry as the poets meant it to be read. The conventions governing the use of the classical lovers by medieval poets are among the clearest and most circumscribed in all of literature. The poems are often difficult in other respects, but not in this one. The poets of the Middle Ages did not envision an audience who would have to struggle to define the literary associations of the classical lovers, and so they used them freely in environments in which those associations are critical to the meaning of the poems themselves. They used them, in other words, allusively. If we labor to recover the meaning of their allusions, we will be rewarded with a clearer understanding of Chaucer, and a new appreciation of certain French and Italian "monuments of dullness."[67]

67. The quotation is from Estrich (*"Navarre"* 29), who describes the *Trésor Amoureux* as a "monument of complicated philosophizing dullness."

Index